REVISITING MOR...

Edited by Viviene E. Cr...
and Mark S...

P

First published in Great Britain in 2016 by

Policy Press
University of Bristol
1-9 Old Park Hill
Bristol
BS2 8BB
UK
t: +44 (0)117 954 5940
pp-info@bristol.ac.uk
www.policypress.co.uk

North America office:
Policy Press
c/o The University of Chicago Press
1427 East 60th Street
Chicago, IL 60637, USA
t: +1 773 702 7700
f: +1 773-702-9756
sales@press.uchicago.edu
www.press.uchicago.edu

British Library Cataloguing in Publication Data
A catalogue record for this book is available from the British Library

Library of Congress Cataloging-in-Publication Data
A catalog record for this book has been requested

ISBN 978-1-4473-2186-6 paperback

Cover design by Liam Roberts
Front cover image: istock
Printed and bound in Great Britain by CMP, Poole
Policy Press uses environmentally responsible print partners

Contents

Contents

Contributors

Liz Beddoe is an Associate Professor in the School of Counselling, Human Services and Social Work at the University of Auckland in New Zealand. Publications include *Social work practice for promoting health and well-being: Critical issues* (2014), edited with Jane Maidment.

Michaela Benson is a Senior Lecturer in Sociology at Goldsmiths, University of London. She has written extensively on lifestyle migration and has research interests in migration, social class and the sociology of place and space. Her recent book is *Understanding lifestyle migration: Theoretical approaches to migration and the quest for a better way of life* (2014), edited with Nick Osbaldiston.

Sally Brown is a medical sociologist at the School of Medicine, Pharmacy and Health, Durham University. She is interested in qualitative health research methods as well as teenage well-being, men's health, and the sociology of screening, diagnosis and risk. A recent paper is: 'They think it's all up to the girls: gender, risk and responsibility for contraception', *Culture, Health and Sexuality*, published online: 1 October 2014.

Ian Butler is Dean of the Faculty of Humanities and Social Sciences at the University of Bath; he has written extensively on child welfare policy and social work practice. He is a Fellow of the Academy of Social Sciences and an Honorary Member of the Council of the NSPCC. He is the author along with Mark Drakeford of *Social work on trial: The Colwell Inquiry and the state of welfare* (2011).

Katharine Charsley is a Senior Lecturer in the School for Sociology Politics and International Studies at the University of Bristol. Recent publications include an edited collection *Transnational marriage* (2012) and an ethnographic monograph: *Transnational Pakistani connections: Marrying 'back home'* (2013).

Gary Clapton is a Senior Lecturer in Social Work at the University of Edinburgh. He specialises in adoption and fostering, child welfare and protection and fathers. His work includes *Social work with fathers: Positive practice* (2013) and a number of papers directed to changing current policies and practices in Scotland.

Colin Clark is Professor of Sociology and Social Policy at the University of the West of Scotland. His teaching and research interests are mainly located within the broad field of ethnic and racial studies, including issues of mobility, identity, citizenship and language. A recent paper is 'Glasgow's Ellis Island? The integration and stigmatisation of Govanhill's Roma population' (2014), *People, Place and Policy*, vol 8, no 1, pp 34–50.

Viviene E. Cree is Professor of Social Work Studies at the University of Edinburgh. She is a qualified youth and community and social worker. She has carried out extensive research into social work history, the profession and children's services and has published widely. A recent book is *Becoming a social worker: Global narratives* (2013).

William Fear is a chartered psychologist with a specialist interest in discourse analysis in organisational settings. He trained at Cardiff University School of Psychology and is particularly interested in the role of narrative in the construction of institutions and the use of language-based artefacts such as texts and stories.

Frank Furedi is a sociologist, commentator and author. He is currently working on the sociological history of the relation between morality and the performance of fear. He published *Moral crusades in an age of mistrust: The Jimmy Savile Scandal* in 2013.

Jim Greer is Principal Lecturer in Social Work at Teesside University. He is a registered social worker, a project manager and a member of the British Psychological Society. His interests are mental health, management and service improvement, use of new technologies in social care, and free speech and personal liberty.

David Grumett is Chancellor's Fellow in Christian Ethics and Practical Theology at the University of Edinburgh. His publications include *Theology on the menu: Asceticism, meat and Christian diet* (2010).

Mark Hardy works as a social worker for a local authority children and families practice team in central Scotland. He has previous experience of residential childcare and youth work and has written about recording policy and practice within residential childcare.

Neil Hume is a social worker in a local authority children and families' team in the North-East of Scotland. Previously he worked for several years in various criminal justice settings in Edinburgh.

Steve Kirkwood is a Lecturer in Social Work at the University of Edinburgh, with a focus on criminal justice, asylum seekers and research methods. His research involves a range of topics broadly related to justice and identity; he is originally from Wellington, New Zealand. A recent publication, *Researching celebrity historic sexual abuse allegations* (2014), is jointly authored with Mark Smith, Clare Llewellyn and Ros Burnett.

Elias Le Grand teaches social theory at the Department of Sociology, Stockholm University. A cultural sociologist, his research interests are in consumer culture, identity formation, socio-spatial divisions and youths. A recent publication is 'Class, community and belonging in a "chav town"', in *Mobilities and neighbourhood belonging in cities and suburbs* (2014), edited by Paul Watt and Peer Smets.

Heather Lynch was working as a social worker within a criminal justice service for women in central Scotland when she contributed to this volume. She is now undertaking a PhD in Social Work at Glasgow Caledonian University, where her interests include subjectivity and difference.

Dawn Mannay is a Lecturer in Social Science (Psychology) at Cardiff University. Her research interests revolve around class, education, gender, generation, national identity, violence and inequality. A recent paper is 'Who should do the dishes now? Exploring gender and housework in contemporary urban South Wales', in *Contemporary Wales*, vol 27, no 1, pp 21–39.

David McKendrick is a Lecturer in Social Work at Glasgow Caledonian University. He is interested in fear and its impact on social work practice.

Maggie Mellon, MSc, CQSW and Dip Child Protection, is a registered social worker with many years' experience, now working as an independent consultant. She writes regularly on social work issues for national and professional media and is currently Vice Chair of the British Association of Social Workers.

Anneke Meyer is a Senior Lecturer in Sociology at Manchester Metropolitan University. She has researched and written in the areas of child sexual abuse and paedophilia, gender and popular culture, childhood and parenting. Her publications include *The child at risk: Paedophiles, media responses and public opinion* (2007) and *Gender and popular culture* (2011), co-authored with Katie Milestone.

Malcolm Payne is a writer on social work and end-of-life care, and Honorary Professor at Kingston University, London and Emeritus Professor at Manchester Metropolitan University. His most recent book is *Modern social work theory* (2014).

Ethel Quayle is a Senior Lecturer in Clinical Psychology at the University of Edinburgh. She has conducted research for many years in technology-mediated crimes, collaborating internationally with government and non-government agencies in the context of research, policy and practice. A recent book, *Internet child pornography: Understanding and preventing on-line child abuse* (2012), is edited with Kurt Ribisl.

Mark Smith is a Senior Lecturer and current Head of Social Work at the University of Edinburgh. He has an interest in abuse allegations made against care staff and is currently working on an ESRC-funded project centred on allegations against the former BBC disc jockey, Jimmy Savile. One of his recent books is *Residential child care in practice: Making a difference* (2013), written with Leon Fulcher and Peter Doran.

Morena Tartari is a Lecturer in Sociology at the University of Padua, Italy. Her research interests include media, moral panic and regulation, deviance and social problems. Her latest publication is 'Moral panic and paedophilia: where's the risk?', in *Moral panics in the contemporary world* (2013), edited by Julian Petley, Charles Critcher and Jason Hughes.

E. Kay M. Tisdall is Professor of Childhood Policy and Co-Director of the Centre for Research on Families and Relationships, at the University of Edinburgh. Her academic and policy interests centre on children's rights and childhood studies. Recent papers include 'The transformation of participation? Exploring the potential of "transformative participation" for theory and practice around children and young people's participation', in *Global Studies of Childhood*, vol 3, no 2, pp 183–93.

Stuart Waiton is Senior Lecturer in Sociology and Criminology at Abertay University and author of *Scared of the kids: Curfews, crime and the regulation of young people* (2008) and *The politics of antisocial behaviour: Amoral panics* (2007). His latest book is entitled *Snobs law: Criminalising football fans in an age of intolerance* (2012).

Joanne Westwood has recently moved from the University of Central Lancashire to an appointment as a Senior Lecturer in the School of Applied Social Science at the University of Stirling. Her research interests are child welfare and children and young people's participation. Her latest publication is 'Childhood in different cultures', in *An introduction to early childhood studies* (2013), edited by Trisha Maynard and Nigel Thomas.

Preface

Viviene E. Cree, Gary Clapton and Mark Smith

This volume begins and ends with a question: how useful are ideas of moral panic to the social issues and anxieties that confront us today? Forty years on from the publication of Stan Cohen's seminal study *Folk Devils and Moral Panics*, does this remain a helpful way of thinking about social concerns, or should the concept be consigned to the sociological history books as an amusing, but ultimately flawed, theoretical device? 'Moral panic' is, after all, one of the foremost sociological terms that has crossed over from academic to public discourse; in doing so, it has lost a great deal of its rigour and, arguably, its value. All the contributors to the volume are, in their own ways, engaging critically with the relevance of moral panic ideas for their own understandings of some of the most pressing personal, professional and political concerns of the day. They do not all come up with the same conclusions, but they do agree that moral panics – no matter how we think of them – focus on the social issues that worry us most.

The volume takes forward findings from an Economic and Social Research Council (ESRC) sponsored research seminar series that ran between 2012 and 2014 at events across the UK. The seminar series was designed to mark the 40th anniversary of *Folk Devils and Moral Panics*; and to bring together international and UK academics, researchers and practitioners from a range of disciplines to debate and discuss moral panics in the 21st century. The three main organisers had, independently of one another, written about events and happenings that had caused great anxiety within social work and within society as a whole: satanic abuse (Clapton, 1993); sex trafficking (Cree, 2008); abuse in residential childcare (Smith, 2008 and 2010). In each case, we had challenged accepted accounts of the issues and asked questions about the real-life (often negative) consequences of holding particular conceptualisations of these difficult topics. We had not, at that time, used the concept of moral panic as the foremost tool for analysis, but we had all been interested in the ideas of discourse, labelling, deviancy amplification and social control, all of which connect with ideas of moral panic. With the 40th anniversary imminent, we saw this as offering an opportunity to revisit this, asking: what relevance does the idea of moral panic have for an examination of 21st-century social issues and anxieties?

The seminar series produced a number of outcomes: articles, blogs and this collection of papers. However, the collection is broader than the seminar series in two key ways: firstly, some chapters were especially commissioned because it was felt that there was a gap in the collection or because the writer had a particularly interesting approach to the issues; secondly, each section of the book ends with an afterword written by a social work practitioner who has been invited to reflect on the contributions from the perspective of practice. This demonstrates not only our commitment to knowledge exchange more generally, but also our belief that moral panic ideas have special relevance for social work.

Moral panics and social work

Although 'moral panic' is a sociological idea that has widespread intellectual interest, it has, as Cohen (1998) acknowledges, special relevance for social work. Social work as an academic discipline and a profession plays a central role in the process of defining social issues and then trying to do something about them – that is our job! So we have to be particularly alert to the part we play within this. We are, in moral panic parlance, 'moral entrepreneurs' and 'claims makers': we tell society (government, policy makers, other practitioners, members of the public) what the social problems are, how they should be understood and how they should be addressed. We do so, in 21st-century terms, through secular, professional and academic discourse, but at heart, what we are expressing is a set of ideas about how we should live and what it is to be human. In other words, we remain a 'moral' and, at times, moralising profession.

The concept of moral panic reminds us that our deeply held attitudes and values have origins and consequences in the real world, both positive and negative. And sometimes they are not the origins or consequences we expect them to be. Hence the lens of moral panic highlights the ways in which social issues that begin with real concerns may lead to the labelling and stigmatising of certain behaviours and individuals; they may precipitate harsh and disproportionate legislation; they may make people more fearful and society a less safe place. Focusing on some social issues may distract attention away from other, underlying concerns; so a focus on trafficking may, for example, ignore the realities of repressive, racist immigration policies, just as a focus on internet pornography may lead to legislation that undermines individual freedom, and a focus on child protection may inhibit our capacity to support families, as Featherstone et al (2014) have identified.

These are not issues about which we, as editors and contributors to this volume, have answers – but we do have questions. And it is our firm belief that social work must engage with these questions if we are to practise in ways that are truly emancipatory and in line with the social work profession's social justice principles.

A particular moment in the history of moral panics?

The years 2013 and 2014 have proved to be a very particular time in the history of moral panics for two, very different, reasons. The first reason is that a number of key protagonists from the early theoretical writing on deviance, moral panics and the state died in 2013 and early 2014.

- Stan Cohen, sociologist and author of *Folk Devils and Moral Panics* (1972), *Visions of Social Control* (1985), *States of Denial* (2001) and numerous other publications, died in January 2013.
- Geoffrey Pearson, social work professor and author of *The Deviant Imagination* (1975) and *Hooligan: A History of Respectable Fears* (1983), died in April 2013.
- Jock Young, criminologist and author of *The Drugtakers* (1971) and many other studies including, most recently, *The Criminological Imagination* (2011), died in November 2013.
- Stuart Hall, critical theorist, founding editor of *New Left Review* and author with Charles Critcher and others of *Policing the Crisis* (1978), died in February 2014.

We wished to mark the contribution of these great thinkers, and so we have included a commentary on each of them within this volume. This is not to suggest that they are the only people who have written about contemporary social issues in this way; in fact, Geoffrey Pearson was more concerned with the persistent nature of what he called 'respectable discontents' than about the sporadic eruptions of moral panics. But, as the collection will demonstrate, theorists from a wide range of academic disciplines have continued to engage with the concept of moral panics over the 40-plus years since 1972, sometimes arguing for its continuing value (for example, Goode and Ben-Yehuda, 1994) and at other times favouring alternative explanations, such as those around risk (for example, Beck, 1992, 1999) and moral regulation (for example, Hunt, 1999). More recently, scholars have attempted to move 'beyond the heuristic', to develop a way of thinking about moral panic that both informs, and continues 'to be informed by, movements and developments in social theory' (Rohloff and Wright, 2010, p 419).

The second reason why this has been a special time is because of what has been called the 'Jimmy Savile effect' in numerous press and media reports. It is difficult to discuss the scandal around Jimmy Savile, TV presenter and prolific sex offender, who died in October 2011, in a dispassionate way. In September and October 2012, almost a year after his death, claims emerged that Savile had committed sexual abuse over many years, with his victims ranging from girls and boys to adults. By October 2012, allegations had been made to 13 British police forces, and a series of inquiries followed. The revelations around the Jimmy Savile affair encouraged others to come forward and claim that they had been abused by celebrities: Stuart Hall (TV presenter, not critical theorist), Rolf Harris, Max Clifford and many others have been investigated and prosecuted. These events have encouraged us to ask wider questions in articles and blogs about physical and sexual abuse, and about potentially negative fall-out from the furore around historic abuse. This has not been easy: how do we get across the reality that we are not minimising the damage that abuse can cause, while at the same time calling for a more questioning approach to victimisation and social control? These questions remain challenging as we move forward.

The book

This book introduces a collection of papers that engage with a social issue through the lens of moral panic. It will be evident from the chapters that, as editors, we have not imposed a 'moral panic straightjacket' on the contributors; nor do we hold to the notion that there is one 'Moral Panic Theory' with a capital T. Instead, contributors have been invited to consider moral panic ideas very broadly, focusing on their capacity to add to a deeper understanding of the social problem under discussion. Because of this, the collection offers a number of opportunities for those who are already familiar with the concept of moral panic and for those who are not. For those who have been thinking about moral panic ideas for years, the papers will serve as a new 'take' on some of the puzzling aspects of moral panic theories. For those who are coming across the notion of moral panic for the first time, or have only everyday knowledge of it, the case-study examples of particular social issues and anxieties contained in each chapter will serve as an introduction not only to moral panic as a theoretical concept, but also to what, we hope, might become a new avenue of critical inquiry for readers in the future.

The book is divided into four parts: Gender and the family; Young people, children and childhood; The state, government and citizens;

and Moral crusades, moral regulation and morality. Each part contains an introduction, which includes a short retrospective on one of the four early theorists whom we have already identified. Five chapters follow, each exploring the case study of one social issue, asking how useful a moral panic lens is (or is not) to understanding this social problem. Each part ends of with an afterword written by a social work practitioner. The four parts are also available separately as a series of four books ('bytes'), with the aim of reaching as wide an audience as possible.

This collection should be read as an opening conversation. We are not seeking either consensus or closure in publishing this series; quite the opposite, our aim is to ask questions – of social problems, of professional practice and of ourselves. In doing so, we pay homage to Cohen's (1998, p 112) challenge to 'stay unfinished'; instead of seeking to resolve the contradictions and complexities that plague theory and practice, we must, he argues, be able to live with ambiguity. The series may help us and others to do just that, and, in doing so, may contribute towards the building of a more tolerant, open social work practice and a more tolerant, open society.

Acknowledgement
With thanks to the ESRC for funding the seminar series 'Revisiting Moral Panics: A Critical Examination of 21st Century Social Issues and Anxieties' (ES/J021725/1) between October 2012 and October 2014.

References

Beck, U. (1992) *Risk society: Towards a new modernity*, London: Sage.

Beck, U. (1999) *World risk society*, Cambridge: Polity Press.

Clapton, G. (1993) *Satanic abuse controversy: Social workers and the social work press*, London: University of North London Press.

Cohen, S. (1972) *Folk devils and moral panics: The creation of the mods and rockers*, London: MacGibbon and Kee Ltd.

Cohen, S. (1985) *Visions of social control: Crime, punishment and classification*, Cambridge: Polity Press.

Cohen, S. (1998) *Against criminology*, London: Transaction Publishers.

Cohen, S. (2001) *States of denial knowing about atrocities and suffering*, Cambridge: Polity Press.

Cree, V.E. (2008) 'Confronting sex-trafficking: lessons from history', *International Social Work*, vol 51, no 6, pp 763–76.

Featherstone, B., White, S. and Morris, K. (2014) *Re-imagining child protection: Towards humane social work with families*, Bristol: Policy Press.

Goode, E. and Ben-Yehuda, N. (1994) *Moral panics: The Social construction of deviance*, Oxford: Blackwell.

Hall, S., Critcher, C., Jefferson, T., Clarke, J. and Roberts, B. (1978) *Policing the crisis: Mugging, the state and law and order*, London: Macmillan.

Hunt, A. (1999) *Governing morals: A social history of moral regulation*, Cambridge University Press, New York.

Pearson, G. (1975) *The deviant imagination: Psychiatry, social work and social change*, London: Macmillan.

Pearson, G. (1983) *Hooligan: A history of respectable fears,* London: Macmillan.

Rohloff, A. and Wright, S. (2010) 'Moral panic and social theory: beyond the heuristic', *Current Sociology*, vol 58, no 3, pp 403–19.

Smith, M. (2008) 'Historical abuse in residential child care: an alternative view', *Practice: Social Work in Action*, vol 20, no 1, pp 29 – 41.

Smith, M. (2010) 'Victim Narratives of historical abuse in residential child care: do we really know what we think we know?', *Qualitative Social Work*, vol 9, no 3, pp 303–20.

Young, J. (1971) *The drugtakers: The social meaning of drug use*, London: Paladin.

Young, J. (2011) *The criminological imagination*, Cambridge: Polity Press.

Commentary: moral panics yesterday, today and tomorrow[1]

Charles Critcher

Introduction: mapping the field

This commentary offers a map of moral panic analysis. Like any map of a county or a country, it will contain some features that the user will find instantly recognisable and may even have visited. Other places will seem familiar, if only at second hand. Parts of the landscape will be wilder than others, with unusual names and forbidding prospects. But, with a bit of patience, it should prove an adequate guide for seasoned traveller and first-time visitor alike.

However, unlike for real maps, the moral panic cartographer is free to construct their own version of which places and routes to prioritise. Many anthologies of moral panic studies – and there are now a good number of them – have introductions that review moral panic analysis. Hier (2011a) divides analysts into three camps: the conventional, the sceptical and the revisionist. Krinsky (2013) perceives two waves of moral panic development, early and late. Rohloff et al (2013) outline fundamental conceptual issues and contemporary debates. Among the many careful evaluations, Garland's (2008) stands out. Each of these has its own utility.

My map starts with the two basic models of moral panic, explaining each before comparing the two. Next I attempt to summarise what accumulated studies have told us about five topic clusters and delivered to us as generalisations about moral panics as a whole. I then review briefly the many and varied criticisms of the concept. Finally, I consider the range of new directions that moral panic analysis may follow. I have made my own views clear but have not, I hope, skewed the arguments or evidence in their favour. A brief review cannot include everything that has ever been written about moral panics. The bibliography would then be longer than the text. So I have had to be selective. Apologies to those whose work is unjustly neglected in this account. To begin, then, at the beginning.

Cohen's processual model

Stanley Cohen published *Folk Devils and Moral Panics* in 1972. Based on his PhD, it analysed how British society reacted to seaside confrontations between members of two youth subcultures, Mods and Rockers, in the early 1960s. Cohen was less interested in the causes of deviance than in the process and consequences of labelling deviance. Labelling could amplify deviance, damaging the identities of the labelled and inviting them to embrace deviant identities and behaviour. Cohen set out to test these ideas on Mods and Rockers but ended up in a rather different place. Picking up on Jock Young's earlier reference in his study of drug takers (1971), he discovered a pattern of construction and reaction with wider purchase than Mods and Rockers: the moral panic.

> Societies appear to be subject, every now and then, to periods of moral panic. (1) A condition, episode, person or group of persons emerges to become defined as a threat to societal values and interests; (2) its nature is presented in a stylised and stereotypical fashion by the mass media; (3) the moral barricades are manned by editors, bishops, politicians and other right-thinking people; (4) socially accredited experts pronounce their diagnoses and solutions; (5) ways of coping are evolved or (more often) resorted to; (6) the condition then disappears, submerges or deteriorates and becomes more visible. Sometimes the object of the panic is quite novel and at other times it is something which has been in existence long enough, but suddenly appears in the limelight. Sometimes the panic passes over and is forgotten, except in folk-lore and collective memory; at other times it has more serious and long-lasting repercussions and might produce such changes as those in legal and social policy or even in the way the society conceives itself. (Cohen, 1973, p 9, numbers added)

Cohen stressed that these stages overlap. Progression through them can be thwarted or diverted. That is why I felt justified in calling it *a processual model of moral panics*.

Cohen's model is often mistakenly thought to be based on, and mainly concerned with, the mass media. He cast his net wider. He identified in moral panics four key agents: the mass media, moral entrepreneurs, the control culture and the public. The media are particularly important in the early ('inventory') stage of social reaction, producing 'processed or coded images' of deviance and the deviants. Three processes are involved. First is *exaggeration* and *distortion*, of who did or said what; second is *prediction*, the dire consequences of failure to act; and the third is *symbolisation*, the words Mod or Rocker signifying threat. The media install Mods and Rockers as folk devils. In normal practices of news making, the media focus most on those events and people disrupting the social order. To interpret such events they employ 'inferential structures', implicit explanations of what the behaviour is like, who perpetrates it and why it happens (what Cohen calls orientations, images and causation). They are primed for panic.

The second group are 'moral entrepreneurs', individuals and groups who deplore and seek to eliminate deviant behaviour. Cohen spent time and effort understanding their world-views and actions. The third group, the 'societal control culture', comprises those with institutional power: the police and the courts, local and national politicians. They are made aware of – 'sensitised' to – the nature and extent of the problem. Concern is passed up the chain of command to the national level, where draconian control measures ('innovation') are instituted.

The fourth group, the public who witness all this, have to decide who and what to believe. Cohen discussed the Mods and Rockers problem with individuals and groups, finding that they initially mistrusted media messages yet ultimately believed them.

The complex interplay between these four groups defined the problem, its remedies and the proposed solution, normally a change in the law or its enforcement. Mods and Rockers provoked a strengthening of one law, about drugs, and the introduction of a new one, about criminal damage. But, especially as the threat was largely mythical, such laws were more ritualistic than effective.

Laws confirm a primary function of moral panics: the reaffirmation of society's moral boundaries. Cohen argued that the 'affluent society' of the 1960s disconcerted traditionalists, fearful that the young were rejecting adult ideals: 'the response was as much to what they stood for as what they did' (Cohen, 1973, p 197). Future moral panics seemed inevitable. The pace of social change and the persistence of social inequality generate tensions that find an outlet in the identification and vilification of new kinds of deviant behaviour. Cohen's work was predictive. Seven years after his work, the authors of *Policing the Crisis* (Hall et al, 1978) demonstrated how the moral panic about 'mugging', now more heavily theorised, bore out many of Cohen's predictions. Fifteen years after that, there appeared a distinctively American take on moral panics.

Goode and Ben-Yehuda's attributional model

In 1994 Erich Goode and Nachman Ben-Yehuda published *Moral Panics: The Social Construction of Deviance*, with a second edition in 2009. American sociology had become focused on how and by whom social problems come to be defined. This approach, 'social constructionism', challenged the basic assumption that sociology could define, measure, explain and ameliorate social problems. On such issues as crime, mental retardation and homosexuality, definition and measurement foundered, and traditional sociology was unable to adequately explain the way that anxieties emerged and whether or not some campaigns and concerns gained traction and others did not. Social constructionism provided the tools to examine the way that claims for public attention were articulated.

Reviewing empirical studies in the constructionist tradition, Goode and Ben-Yehuda arrived at five defining 'elements or criteria' (Goode and Ben-Yehuda, 2009, p 37) of a moral panic.

Concern

Any moral panic involves a 'heightened level of concern over the behaviour of a certain group or category' (Goode and Ben-Yehuda, 2009, p 37) and its consequences. Indices of concern include opinion polls, media coverage and lobbying activity.

Hostility

Moral panics exhibit 'an increased level of *hostility*' towards the deviants, who are 'collectively designated as the enemy, or an enemy, of respectable society'. Their behaviour is seen as 'harmful or threatening' to the values and interests of society, 'or at least a sizeable segment' of it (Goode and Ben-Yehuda, 2009, p 38, original emphasis). Constructing such folk devils is integral to moral panics.

Consensus

In a moral panic 'there must be at least a certain minimal measure of consensus' across society as a whole, or at least 'designated segments' of it , that 'the threat is real, serious and caused by the wrongdoing group members and their behaviour' (Goode and Ben-Yehuda, 2009, p 38). Consensus can be challenged by organised opposition – 'counter claimsmakers'.

Disproportionality

Fundamentally, 'the concept of moral panic *rests* on disproportion' (Goode and Ben-Yehuda, 2009, p 41, original emphasis). It is evident where 'public concern is in excess of what is appropriate if concern were directly proportional to objective harm' (Goode and Ben-Yehuda, 2009, p 40). Statistics are exaggerated or fabricated. The existence of other equally or more harmful activities is denied.

Volatility

Panics are by their nature fleeting, subsiding as quickly as they erupt. The same issue may reoccur but individual panics cannot be sustained for long.

This I called an *attributional model of moral panics* because attributes are the defining characteristics. Central to this model is claims making about the problem: who makes claims, how and why. Such claims are frequently made by 'social movements', who perceive and seek remedies for problematic behaviour. Movements protest and demonstrate, appeal to public opinion and gain access to the media. They are susceptible in moral panics to irresponsible behaviour: prone to exaggerating the threat, polarising opinion and vilifying opponents. Apparently more scrupulous interests also play a questionable role: religious groups, professional associations and the police. The media are sometimes active in moral panics but more often are passive vehicles for others' claims making.

Goode and Ben-Yehuda assess three competing explanations of moral panics. First, the *grass-roots model* sees the sources of panics in widespread anxieties about real or imagined threats. In the second explanation, the *elite-engineered model*, an elite group manipulates a panic over an issue they know to be exaggerated, in order to divert attention away from their own inability or unwillingness to solve social problems. Third, *interest group theory* argues that 'the middle rungs of power and status' are where moral issues are most acutely felt. Goode and Ben-Yehuda suggest elites are marginal. The combined forces of grass-roots feeling and middle-class agitation lie behind the most effective panics. The wider explanation lies in the nature of collective behaviour.

The missing-child controversy of the 1980s is an oft-cited American example of moral panic. Although Best has since expressed severe reservations about the concept of moral panic (Best, 2013), he examined claims made about missing children and discovered that while the public (and politicians) had understood 'missing' to mean abducted by strangers, the category covered many forms of child absence, including having been removed by a non-resident parent (Best, 1990). Best was thus able to show that the claims making on behalf of various child welfare lobby groups and charities had led to something of a moral panic over child abduction and endangerment.

Comparing the two models

Comparing the processual model of Cohen with the attributional model of Goode and Ben-Yehuda reveals three basic similarities and three significant differences. The first similarity is their shared view that moral panics are an extreme form of more general processes by which social problems are constructed in public arenas. The second similarity is their observation that moral panics are recurrent features of modern society that have identifiable consequences on the law and state institutions. The third similarity is the perceived sociological function of moral panics as reaffirming the core values of society.

The first difference is how they assess the role of the media. In the processual version the media are strategic in the formation of moral panics. They may be the prime movers or offer endorsement to others already campaigning but they are always actively involved. In the attributional model, despite their greater prominence in Goode and Ben-Yehuda's second edition, the media's role is much more passive. They provide an arena where different versions can compete.

The second difference is specifying the most important agents in moral panics. In the processual model, state agencies, politicians and legislators do not merely react to moral panics but are frequently complicit in their construction. The attributional model places much more emphasis on the strategies adopted by claims makers. Their success or otherwise in persuading public opinion of their case is seen as the key to the eventual outcome.

The third difference is about how to conceptualise the language of moral panics. In the attributional model, the emphasis is on 'claims-making rhetoric', how campaigners adopt particular styles of argument. The processual model emphasises moral panics as activating ideological discourses, such as that around law and order.

Using either model, sometimes both and occasionally neither, moral panics have been studied extensively over the last 40 years. The accumulated findings will be reviewed for five clusters of topics: child abuse, drugs and alcohol, immigration, media violence and street crime. For a slightly different list of seven clusters see Cohen (2002, p xv).

Accumulated knowledge on five topic clusters

For each of these clusters we know quite a lot about how moral panics operate and the impact they have. There are multiple studies but these are only indicative, and mainly British ones can be cited.

Child abuse

We know that exceptional cases of physical or sexual abuse become drivers of child protection policy, regardless of their typicality or alternative evidence from social work agencies. The original construction of the paedophile as the dangerous stranger was subsequently modified by revelations about paedophiles in the priesthood and among celebrities. But his presence in and around the family is rarely acknowledged. Organisations apparently dedicated to saving children have their own self-serving agendas, while the media and public are highly susceptible to images of innocent children being damaged or corrupted (Jenkins, 1992; Kitzinger, 2004).

Drugs and alcohol

We know that consciousness-changing substances used for pleasure are a constant target for legal action because they jeopardise either order on the streets or the health of those who enjoy them. Laws governing the sale, possession or consumption of such substances are tightened continuously but can be enforced only selectively, to avoid criminalising swathes of young people. A huge and permanent disjunction exists between the policies and prognostications of police, politicians and the media and the views and practices of young people as a whole. Drug-advice agencies find their expertise consistently undervalued (Parker, Aldridge and Measham, 1998; Jenkins, 1999).

Immigration

We know that this is a serial moral panic, recurrent wherever people migrate to live alongside the indigenous population, especially if they are of a different colour. Accusations against the newcomers are invariably that they bring alien cultures, so refuse to integrate; that they make excessive demands on systems of welfare, education and housing; and that they are excessively involved in crime. In the UK these accusations have been made against migrants for the last century or more: Commonwealth immigrants in the 1960s and 1970s;

asylum seekers early in the 21st century; and currently migrants from Eastern Europe. Hostility to strangers is not difficult to mobilise and not confined to racist political parties. It is routinely reproduced by the popular press, confirmed by politicians of all shades and has reinvigorated the extreme Right in Europe (Finney and Simpson, 2009; Philo, Briant and Donald, 2013).

Media violence

We know that the advent of any new medium of communication, especially if electronically based, produces disquiet among guardians of childhood and culture. They fear that it will encourage children to seek pleasure in narratives of little intrinsic merit that proffer dangerous role models of violent and/or antisocial behaviour. Children enter a fantasy (or virtual) world where they can act out roles and emotions that in real life would be impossible or attract censure. Such fears are often based on ignorance about the medium's actual capacities or usage. The policies advocated – a mix of parental guidance and censorship of content – seem ill designed for the internet and social media. Professional moralists of all kinds, especially evangelical Christians in disguise, commonly advocate censorship, which the industry resists, while parents remain concerned but lack coherent control strategies (Barker and Petley, 1997; Livingstone, 2002).

Street crime

We know that interpersonal crime has always been a central concern of modern mass media. News depends on routine reporting of crime, which expands dramatically if new types or patterns of crime emerge, especially involving increased violence or use of weapons. This sustains the belief that levels of crime are increasing, even when they are not. Fear of being randomly attacked on the street by violent young men is prevalent in modern cosmopolitan societies, especially among those least likely to become victims. This pattern has prevailed for such 'new' crimes as mugging, knife or gun crime. Social causes, in the deprived structural position and limited cultural options of inner-city youth, are occasionally recognised but the solutions are repressive: more vigorous policing and longer sentences for the actual or a potential use of violence (Reiner, 2002; Jewkes, 2004).

These five groupings are by no means exhaustive. Others could easily be added. Panics about welfare scroungers exist but may be better analysed as an ideologically motivated and increasingly successful attack upon the basis of the modern welfare state. Terrorism is in a league of its own, an international confrontation way beyond the confines of the nation-state, indivisible from the western view of, and actions towards, the Muslim world. My initial view was that the moral panic concept seems ill equipped to deal with its global nature, but a recent collection has argued that it can be applied effectively (Morgan and Poynting, 2012). Reactions to occasional riots in the UK could be seen as moral panic, but may simply represent what the state has always done when confronted with insurrection: come down immediately with the full force of the law, without preamble or apology.

Looking across these five clusters, we can derive three general lessons for moral panic analysis. First is the status of the folk devil. Three of the five have a clear folk devil, in their purest forms paedophile, asylum seeker and mugger. But in the two others the problem is an object, such as an ecstasy pill or a computer game. Moral panics do not require a clear-cut folk devil, although they may be more effective when they do have one.

Second is the variable influence of pressure groups as claims makers. They are very active in relation to child abuse and violent media (think NSPCC and Internet Watch, respectively). In Britain one single organisation, MigrationWatch UK, has managed to set the national agenda from a website. But authoritative sources matter too. The police monitor and comment on drugs and alcohol or street crime. In all cases the media remain central to the moral panic but the materials they have to work with – news sources, statistical estimates , indicators of public opinion – are different in kind and quality.

Third is the inevitability of what Cohen called the 'measures resorted to'. Across all five clusters, the final solution is change in the law or its enforcement. Moral panics typically effect changes in the legal system. Their secondary effect is discursive. They establish, or seek to, a way of talking about a problem that brooks no argument. Child abuse, immigration or street crime become closed subjects: the problem is known; it remains only to find a (simple) solution. This does not work in quite the same way for drugs and media violence. A good number of primarily young people find these activities pleasurable and pursue them regularly, regardless of, and resistant to, campaigns against them. Laws may still be passed to regulate their use but are disregarded in practice. Those promoting moral panics do not always get their own way.

Moral panics in time and space

There are other empirical generalisations to be derived from an ever-expanding range of empirical studies (see Critcher, 2008). Increasingly important are the expanding geography and history of moral panic studies. They originally emanated from Anglophone countries: the US and Canada, Australia and New Zealand, as well as the UK, with supplements from Scandinavia. This is now changing. Moral panic analysis has gained a foothold in Central and Eastern Europe, in South America and the Far East. Krinsky (2013), for example, includes contributions from Brazil, Argentina, Poland and Japan. A scholar of Japan notes that 'though most of the relevant literature focuses on Europe and North America, non-western societies with modern media apparatuses are similarly susceptible to episodes of moral panic' (Toivonen, 2013, p 265).

There is an established argument about the 'export' of social problems and their associated moral panics from western societies, especially the US (Best and Furedi, 2001). We can now recognise national variations in sociological characteristics crucial to moral panics. Systems of politics, media, religion and law enforcement may appear similar in principle but differ in practice. It remains true that moral panics everywhere emerge from the interactions of the five Ps: press, politics, pressure groups, police and public. But exactly how the drama is played out will depend in part upon the patterns of interaction established by national tradition.

As the geographical perspective on moral panics widens, so does the historical one. It may seem as if moral panics started with Mods and Rockers, but of course they didn't. Hostility to those who are or behave differently or deviantly goes back a long way, as the histories of Jewish or Romany people show. The greatest moral panic of all time, the pursuit of witches, occurred principally in Europe in the Middle Ages. Its late appearance among the earliest settlers in the US prompted a sociological study influential on moral panic theory (Erikson, 1966). British examples exploring the history of moral panics without using the terminology include those on hooliganism over 150 years (Pearson, 1983) and 'dope girls' in the 1920s (Kohn, 2001). We are now getting a much clearer picture of moral panics in specific periods, such as the 18th and 19th centuries (Lemmings and Walker, 2009), or for particular issues over long periods, such as alcohol (Yeomans, 2014).

Such studies indicate that, with the important exception of witch-hunts, moral panics are a product of modernity. Preconditions for moral panics include a formally free press, a government willing to respond to popular pressure, campaigners able and willing to organise for legal change and a more general sense that social stability depends upon the maintenance of a secular moral order. These conditions did not exist in the UK before the late 18th century and in many societies do not exist today. That is why moral panics do not occur in closed societies. An impervious political system may create its own scapegoats but will not permit, nor respond to, independent agitation against moral evils. Thus, when societies move from closed to open social systems, as in Eastern Europe, we may expect to see moral panics where before there were none. They are, paradoxically, a product of culturally open societies.

Some progress, then, is being made in establishing what Cohen called 'a comparative sociology of moral panic that makes comparisons within one society and also between societies' (Cohen, 2002, p xxii). Appreciating the geographical breadth and historical depth of moral panic analysis assumes that the enterprise remains worthwhile. This is, however, a far from universal assumption. Its assumptions and practices continue to be challenged.

Criticisms of moral panic analysis

Reservations about moral panic analysis are wide-ranging and frequently expressed. The most oft-cited critique is McRobbie and Thornton (1995). Thoughtful reviews are Jewkes (2004) and David et al (2011). Best (2013) is particularly hostile. The following account summarises the basic critique and counterarguments for six areas of dispute: terminology, disproportionality, datedness, rigidity, politics and public credulousness.

Terminology

Critique. Some question the basic terms. 'Moral' tends to prevent links to apparently similar issues, such as health or food scares. Defining which are 'moral' issues is bound to be subjective and arbitrary. 'Panic' raises the objection that it imputes irrationality to people who may be genuinely and logically concerned. It pits the rational analyst against the irrational participants.

Counterargument. The term 'moral' is justified because there are some issues that are perceived to pose a threat to the moral order of society that are different in kind from those that do not, such as food or health scares. 'Panic' may not be wholly satisfactory but it is the nearest descriptor of a situation where collective emotion has taken over from rational discussion – as happens at the height of a moral panic.

Disproportionality

Critique. The logical basis of moral panic analysis is questioned. Goode and Ben-Yehuda claim that moral panic analysis rests on the ability to demonstrate that a response to a perceived social evil is disproportionate. This implies that we can assess what a proportionate response would be. For that, we need to have detailed knowledge about the 'real' dimensions of the problem. Critics say that often such data are unreliable or unknowable. Even if known, who is to say what is a 'proportionate 'response to, say, the rape and murder of a single child? Disproportionality does not work, but without it there are no grounds to decide what is a moral panic and what is not.

Counterargument. For most though not all social problems, it is clearly possible to establish what the basic facts are. It is therefore legitimate to assess whether the social reaction accords with the dimensions of the actual problem. Of course questions of interpretation arise, since facts do not always speak for themselves. And the symbolic pull of an event or issue has to be taken into account. But if we can never say whether the definition and proposed remedy of a social problem are appropriate, there seems little point in analysing the construction of social problems at all, other than to play intellectual games.

Datedness

Critique. A third set of criticisms emphasises the datedness of Cohen's model. Produced more than 40 years ago, it reflected the political system, cultural assumptions and media structure of that time. Each of these has become much more fluid. The advent of new and social media in particular has changed the locus of definitional power, so that many more voices are heard than was previously the case. Those in power can no longer be confident that their definitions of issues will prevail.

Counterargument. A model of the political and cultural systems of power constructed in the 1970s is clearly in need of updating to take account of the new 'mediascape'. Pressure groups may have become more sophisticated and governments more guarded than in the past but we cannot be sure. Yet the capacity of some sections of the press to construct or support a moral panic seems undiminished by the existence of social media. That should remain fundamental to a revised account.

Rigidity

Critique. The model is alleged to be mechanistic. The prescribed script robs those involved of any agency and the issue itself of any specificity. The model does not permit variations in processes or outcomes. If cases depart from the anticipated sequence, the model flounders and cannot explain such deviations. It is thus a self-fulfilling prophecy. Only those events that approximate to the model are recognised as moral panics.

Counterargument. This can be true only of careless use of the model. The originals are more flexible. They allow for strategic interventions altering the course of a moral panic, for panics that make a start but never gather momentum and for reasons why things turn out as they do. Testing the model against positive and negative cases is inherent in the approach.

Politics

Critique. For some, moral panic too readily becomes a term of political abuse. It is a way of discrediting conservative claims makers. Liberal or radical campaigns on social issues are not accused of mounting moral panics. This sleight of hand disguises essentially political judgements as intellectual ones.

Counterargument. This is a genuine temptation, though not for Goode and Ben-Yehuda, who explicitly deride some feminists for attempting to create moral panics around pornography. 'Progressive' forces should not be automatically exonerated, especially where claims are controversial. Sex trafficking may be such an instance. Still, since moral panics invariably defend the existing moral order, they will be favoured by conservatives and viewed sceptically by liberals.

Public credulousness

Critique. The approach is alleged to assume that people necessarily believe what is transmitted by the media, lack the critical abilities to decipher media representations and have no alternative sources of information.

Counterargument. Poorer moral panic studies do too often succumb to the temptation to assume that audiences consume media messages uncritically. However, it is clear that the media do have the capacity to set the agenda on social problems, if only because politicians believe that they represent public opinion. Audiences are media dependent on issues where they lack personal experience.

These are complex arguments that have had to be simplified here. There is no substitute for examining a range of case studies and issues to assess the validity of particular criticisms. My own view, if you haven't already guessed, is that it makes no sense to abandon a model that continues to prove so illuminating, always provided that we recognise its inherent limitations.

This is not to imply that the model has no need of extension or reform. It has. One line of development has been to fuse the 'processual' and 'attributional' models into a step-by-step approach to moral panic that has the virtue of clarity and usefulness (Klocke and Muschert 2010). Despite all the arguments and revisions, 'the future of moral panic analyses has never looked brighter' (DeYoung, 2011, p 131). It also, perhaps, looks a little unclear. The idea will run and run, but in which direction?

New directions

Risk

Ten years ago, writing the conclusion to my book on moral panics and the media (Critcher, 2003), I suggested how the concept of moral panic might be developed. I was particularly interested in connecting to innovations in sociological and cultural theory. One connection, obvious then and now, was to risk theory. This body of work associated with Beck and Giddens – to which Lupton (2013) remains an essential guide – argued that modern western societies had become extremely risk conscious. This applied as much to everyday, personal life as to the bigger issues of politics and public life. They formulated elaborate explanations of this development and explored its many ramifications.

At a very basic level, moral panics seem to embody a sense of risk. Most obvious is the case of children 'at risk' of abuse. But in other areas the sense of risk was palpable: risks of becoming a victim of crime; risks posed to the indigenous way of life by the presence of immigrants; risks to personal health and public order from alcohol or drug abuse; risks to the well-being of children and young people from their immersion in new media. These are, to be sure, different types and degrees of risk. But they share a sense of vulnerability and invite demands for protective strategies. 'The global scope of the risk society, its self-reflective quality and its pervasiveness create a new backdrop for standard moral panics' (Cohen, 2002, p xxv). In the work of Ungar (2001), risk theory has been used to discredit moral panic analysis, when the two seem highly compatible.

Discourse

Rethinking moral panics as specific forms of risk had considerable potential. But there was a second possibility. Both the processual and attributional models of moral panic paid close attention to the role of language in the construction of social problems. New labels are coined or old ones dusted off to encapsulate a moral panic: muggers, paedophiles, asylum seekers. But more than labels are required to succeed. It is also necessary to establish only one way of defining, explaining and remedying the problem. Moral panics become irresistible when they monopolise both the grounds and the terms of the argument. The concept best able to dissect such linguistic hegemony is discourse. This is an intellectual minefield that Mills (2004) has always helped me to pick my way across. Here, thankfully, we do not have to encounter the various schools of discourse analysis or their alarmingly complex terminology. It is enough to grasp their ability to explore moral panics as (to use one of their characteristic terms) a 'discursive construct'.

Having recognised the relevance of the two concepts of risk and discourse, it was a blindingly obvious step to put them together and produce the suggestion that moral panics could and should be viewed as extreme forms of risk discourse. Disappointingly, this idea has only rarely been taken up since (an exception being Cavanagh, 2007).

Moral regulation

At the beginning of the 2000s, risk and discourse seemed to be the most fruitful lines of development for moral panic analysis. But since then has emerged a third possibility, the concept of moral regulation. The idea is a simple one: that in any open society there is a continuous dialogue about the boundaries of morally acceptable behaviour and how to regulate what is regarded as unacceptable. In principle, this can mean that activities once regarded as unacceptable are legitimated, such as homosexual relationships. In practice, the boundaries are continuously redrawn to cope with new kinds of moral impropriety. The on-going debate about regulating the internet is an example.

Historian Alan Hunt (1999) analysed 19th-century movements for moral regulation in the UK and the US. Unsurprisingly, he found that moral regulation was aimed at such traditionally immoral activities as sex, drink and gambling. He argued that in each case there were organised advocates of regulation, usually middle class and often female, who adopted similar strategies. They identified and defined an immoral activity, specified who was involved in it, developed propaganda tactics and demanded legislative action. These are essentially the same ploys of claims makers in use today, despite huge changes in the social, economic and political context.

Moral regulation is now more complex since traditional religious teachings can no longer provide a list of inherently immoral activities. Arguments have to be made instead about the damage they inflict upon individuals or society as a whole. Hunt (1999, 2011) uses the concept of moral regulation to demonstrate the deficiencies of moral panic and ultimately prefers Foucault's concept of governance. Sean Hier (2002, 2008) wants to hold on to a version of moral panic, but against the much broader context of moral regulation, where there is a constant struggle over the process of 'moralisation': who or what should be made morally accountable. This takes us away from the normal territory of moral panics, into and way beyond issues such as health (the moralisation of smoking). In both these versions, moral panics assume an increasingly peripheral status. My own view is that there is still a distinctive set of issues that are inherently moral because they threaten the moral order (which is not true of smoking). Thus moral panics and moral regulation serve us better if they are confined to those types of issues. The debate continues (Critcher, 2009; Hier, 2011b; Hunt, 2011). Whatever version is adopted, the concept of moral regulation enables us to see that moral panics are sudden eruptions of concern about topics that are almost permanently the subject of moral regulation debates.

Psychological factors

A fourth possibility exists. There is, like a polo mint, a hole at the centre of moral panic analysis. The absence is any substantial explanation of the psychological mechanisms on which moral panics depend. At their most powerful they exert a psychological pull on all the crucial agents: campaigners, journalists, politicians, senior police officers and, sometimes, the general public. These become convinced that the threat is real, imminent and dire. The discourse becomes emotionally charged, the need to act overwhelming. Something seems to be going on above and beyond the immediate issue. As Young expressed it, 'the formation of a moral panic is a thing of energy and emotion rather than a simple mistake in rationality and information' (Young, 2011, p 255).

This problem, equally evident in debates about fear of crime in criminology or the culture of fear in sociology, was recognised by the original models. For Goode and Ben-Yehuda, answers lay in the nature of collective behaviour. Cohen used an analogy with disaster research to chart the tides of emotion. Hall et al (1978) posited the existence of social anxiety, a sense of being dislocated by social and cultural change that finds a scapegoat for its frustrations. Hunt (2011) has re-emphasised its importance, while Young refined it as 'the mass psychology of *ressentiment* and othering' (Young, 2009, p 74). Pearce and Charman (2011) apply the social psychological models of social representations and social identity theory to media and focus-group discourse about asylum seekers. Walby and Spencer are critical of the often speculative nature of psychological assumptions in moral panic studies and advocate 'empirically investigating what emotions do, how emotions align certain communities against others, and how emotions move people towards certain (sometimes violent) actions against others whose actions pose alleged harms' (Walby and Spencer, 2011, p 104). As they go on to argue, the challenge to moral panic analysis is radical, for it requires serious commitment to fieldwork beyond media and documentary analysis.

Conclusion

Our map of moral panic analysis is now almost finished. Along the way we have encountered contested terrain, boundary disputes and deep rifts. We ended by staring across uncharted waters. Exactly how the contours of moral panic analysis will alter is difficult to predict. The one certainty is that there will be change:

> Work on moral panics will not stand still. The challenge for scholars in the field is to retain the concept's utility, elegance and grasp on a particular aspect of social reality, whilst simultaneously allowing for the concept's development, extension and revision in empirical and theoretical dialogue with a rapidly changing social and cultural landscape. Future researchers must seek to steer a course, between, on the one hand, developing unreflective, 'orthodox' accounts of moral panic which merely reproduce aspects of a concept that, accordingly risks becoming outmoded, and on the other, overextending or stretching the concept so much that it becomes, ultimately, a catch-all term which encapsulates everything and nothing about the inter-relationship between the media, social problems, social policy and

public opinion in the contemporary world. (Hughes et al, 2011, p 214)

That will do for now.

Note
[1] This is a revision and update of my previous article: (2008) 'Moral panic analysis: past, present and future', *Sociology Compass*, vol 2, no 4, pp 1127–44.

References

Barker, M. and Petley, J. (eds) (1997) *Ill effects: The media/violence debate*, Abingdon: Routledge.

Best, J. (1990) *Threatened children: Rhetoric and concern about child victims*, Chicago: University of Chicago Press.

Best, J. (2013) 'The problems with moral panic; the concept's limitations', in C. Krinsky (ed) *The Ashgate research companion to moral panics*, Farnham: Ashgate Publishing.

Best, J. and Furedi, F. (2001) *How claims spread: Cross-national diffusion of social problems*, New York: Aldine.

Cavanagh, A. (2007) 'Taxonomies of anxiety: risks, panics, paedophilia and the internet,' *Electronic Journal of Sociology*, ISSN: 11983655, www.sociology.org/content/2007/__cavanagh_taxonomies.pdf

Cohen, S. (1973; 2002, 3rd edn) *Folk devils and moral panics*, London: Routledge.

Critcher, C. (2003) *Moral panics and the media*, Milton Keynes: Open University Press.

Critcher, C. (2008) 'Moral panic analysis: past, present and future', *Sociology Compass*, vol 2, no 4, pp 1127–44.

Critcher, C. (2009) 'Widening the focus: moral panics as moral regulation', *British Journal of Criminology*, vol 49, no 1, pp 17–34, doi: 0.1093/bjc/azn040.

David, M., Rohloff, A., Petley, J. and Hughes, J. (2011) 'The idea of moral panic – ten dimensions of dispute', *Crime, Media Culture*, vol 7, no 3, pp 215–28.

DeYoung, M. (2011) 'Folk devils reconsidered', in S. Hier (ed) *Moral panic and the politics of anxiety*, Abingdon: Routledge.

Erikson, K.T. (1966) *Wayward puritans: A study in the sociology of deviance*, New York: John Wiley and Sons.

Finney, N. and Simpson, L. (2009) *'Sleepwalking to segregation?' Challenging myths about race and immigration*, Bristol: Policy Press.

Garland, D. (2008) 'On the concept of moral panic', *Crime, Media, Culture*, vol 4, no 9, pp 9–30.

Goode, E. and Ben-Yehuda, N. (2009 [1994]) *Moral panic: The social construction of deviance*, Oxford: Blackwell.

Hall, S., Critcher, C., Jefferson, T., Clarke, J. and Bryan, R. (1978) *Policing the crisis: Mugging, the state and law and order*, London: Macmillan [2nd edn 2013].

Hier, S. (2002) 'Conceptualizing moral panic through a moral economy of harm', *Critical Sociology*, vol 28, pp 311–34.

Hier, S. (2008) 'Thinking beyond moral panic: risk, responsibility, and the politics of moralization', *Theoretical Criminology*, vol 12, no 2, pp 171–88.

Hier, S. (2011a) 'Introduction', in S. Hier (ed) *Moral panic and the politics of anxiety*, Abingdon: Routledge.

Hier, S. (2011b) 'Tightening the focus: moral panic, moral regulation and liberal government', *British Journal of Sociology*, vol 62, no 3, pp 523–41.

Hughes, J., Rohloff, A., David, M. and Petley, J. (2011) 'Foreword: moral panics in the contemporary world', *Crime, Media, Culture*, vol 7, no 3, pp 211–14.

Hunt, A. (1999) *Governing morals: A social history of moral regulation*, Cambridge: Cambridge University Press.

Hunt, A. (2011) 'Fractious rivals? Moral panic and moral regulation', in S. Hier (ed) *Moral panic and the politics of anxiety*, Abingdon: Routledge.

Jenkins, P. (1992) *Intimate enemies: Moral panics in contemporary Great Britain*, New York: Aldine de Gruyter.

Jenkins, P. (1999) *Synthetic panic: The symbolic politics of designer drugs*, New York: New York University Press.

Jewkes, Y. (2004) *Media and crime*, London and Thousand Oaks: Sage.

Kitzinger, J. (2004) *Framing abuse*, London: Pluto Press.

Klocke, B.V. and Muschert, G.W. (2010) 'A hybrid model of moral panics: synthesizing the theory and practice of moral panic research', *Sociology Compass*, vol 4, no 5, pp 295–309, doi: 10.1111/j.1751-9020.2010.00281.x.

Kohn, M. (2001) *Dope girls: The birth of the British drug underground*, London: Granta.

Krinsky, C. (2013) 'Introduction', in C. Krinsky (ed) *The Ashgate research companion to moral panics*, Farnham: Ashgate Publishing.

Lemmings, D. and Walker, C. (eds) (2009) *Moral panics, the media and the law in early modern England*, Basingstoke: Palgrave.

Livingstone, S. (2002) *Young people and new media*, London and Thousand Oaks: Sage.

Lupton, D. (2013) *Risk*, 2nd edn, Abingdon: Routledge.

McRobbie, A. and Thornton, S.L. (1995) 'Re-thinking "moral panic" for multi-mediated social worlds', *British Journal of Sociology*, vol 46, pp 559–74.

Mills, S. (2004) *Discourse*, 2nd edn, Abingdon: Routledge.

Morgan, G. and Poynting, S. (eds) (2012) *Global Islamophobia: Muslims and moral panic in the west*, Farnham: Ashgate Publishing.

Parker, H., Aldridge, J. and Measham, F. (1998) *Illegal leisure: The normalization of adolescent recreational drug use*, Abingdon: Routledge.

Pearce, J.M. and Charman, E. (2011) 'A social psychological approach to understanding moral panic', *Crime, Media, Culture*, vol 7, no 3, pp 293–312.

Pearson, G. (1983) *Hooligan: A history of respectable fears*, Basingstoke: Macmillan.

Philo, G., Briant, E. and Donald, P. (2013) *Bad news for refugees*, London: Pluto Press.

Reiner, R. (2002) 'Media made criminality: the representation of crime in the mass media', in M. Maguire, R. Morgan and R. Reiner (eds) *The Oxford handbook of criminology*, Oxford: Oxford University Press.

Rohloff, A., Hughes, J., Petley, J. and Critcher, C. (2013) 'Moral panics in the contemporary world: enduring controversies and future directions', in C. Critcher, J. Hughes, J. Petley and A. Rohloff (eds) *Moral panics in the contemporary world*, London: Bloomsbury.

Toivonen, T. (2013) 'Moral panic versus youth problem debates: three conceptual insights from the study of Japanese youth', in C. Krinsky (ed) *The Ashgate research companion to moral panics*, Farnham: Ashgate Publishing.

Ungar, S. (2001) 'Moral panic versus risk society: the implications of the changing sites of social anxiety', *British Journal of Sociology*, vol 52, no 2, pp 271–91.

Walby, K. and Spencer, D. (2011) 'How emotions matter to moral panics', in S. Hier (ed) *Moral panic and the politics of anxiety*, Abingdon: Routledge.

Yeomans, H. (2014) *Alcohol and moral regulation*, Bristol: Policy Press.

Young, J. (1971) *The drugtakers: The social meaning of drug use*, London: Judson, McGibbon and Kee.

Young, J. (2009) 'Moral panic: its origins in resistance, *ressentiment* and the translation of fantasy into reality', *British Journal of Criminology*, vol 49, no 1, pp 4–16.

Young, J. (2011) 'Moral panics and the transgressive other', *Crime, Media, Culture*, vol 7, no 3, pp 245–58.

Part One
Gender and the family

Edited by Viviene E. Cree

Introduction

Viviene E. Cree

To open each part of the book, we introduce the work of a key theorist within the 'moral panic' genre. The work of Stanley Cohen has played a central part in the creation of ideas around moral panic and these, as will be shown, have developed over time. Many of Cohen's ideas are reflected in the chapters in this and other parts of the book, while others have been taken forward in other writing in the field.

Stanley Cohen

Stanley Cohen (Stan) was born on 23 February 1942 in Johannesburg, South Africa and studied Sociology and Social Work at the University of Witwatersrand. He moved to the UK in 1963 with his wife, Ruth, where he worked as a psychiatric social worker and PhD student at the London School of Economics (LSE), studying social reactions to vandalism. Cohen was appointed to his first academic position in 1967, at the University of Durham, and in 1968, with Jock Young and others, he set up the first National Deviancy Conference, an initiative that was to challenge conventional ideas about crime and criminology for years to come. He moved to Essex University in 1972, where he became a professor in 1974. Stan and Ruth relocated to Israel in 1980; Stan was professor at the Hebrew University of Jerusalem until 1994. He returned to the LSE in 1995, where, as Chair in Sociology, he helped to establish the Centre for the Study of Human Rights.

Stan Cohen is widely held to be one of the world's pre-eminent sociologists; that he began his career as a social worker makes absolute sense, given his lifelong concern for theory developed from practice, for making connections between the personal and the political, and his deep concern for human rights. Cohen's first book, *Folk Devils and Moral Panics* (1972) was the book of his PhD study on the 1960s battles between mods and rockers. Here Cohen argued that the social reaction to the minor skirmishes between young people on the beaches in Clacton accelerated their bad behaviour and led to a widespread moral panic centred on young people. This book marked the beginning of the translation of the idea of moral panics from academic to everyday usage and, unsurprisingly, to a great deal of misuse of the concept too, as Cohen was acutely aware. He went on to write *Psychological*

Survival (1972), with the sociologist Laurie Taylor, exploring the closed emotional world within the maximum security H-wing at Durham Prison. *Prison Secrets* (1976) followed. In this, he again focused on prison, this time introducing the idea of 'dispersal of control' to describe the ways in which the state ever extends its reach into everyday life. *Visions of Social Control* (1985) took this idea further, pointing out that even seemingly benign interventions in the name of 'community' can be subverted and become ever-stricter measures of social control. In 1988, he published a collection of essays entitled *Against Criminology*, in which he promoted a 'sceptical' sociology of crime, deviance and control, in opposition to the statistically oriented correctionalism that pervaded criminology at the time.

Cohen's last book, *States of Denial, Knowing about Atrocities and Suffering* (2001), is an astonishing book that brings together his personal experience (in South Africa and later in Israel) with his criminological knowledge and insights and his passionate belief in human rights. He begins the book in South Africa, in his childhood home. Here he asks: how was it that he, as a young child, knew and didn't know about the injustice experienced by the indigenous black people? He goes on to ask: how do we see and not see atrocities and suffering throughout the world? His call in the end is that we must not be bystanders – we must act. This is a powerful message for social work, a profession that is so thoroughly implicated in social control and yet one that has such potential to make a difference in the lives of those who are disadvantaged. It is also a powerful message for all humankind – that we each have responsibility to challenge oppression where we see it.

In a small way, this book series attempts to live up to the challenge set by Cohen. Each of the chapters that follows in this part engages critically with something that has been identified as a social problem, and tries to encourage new ways of thinking about it. Stan Cohen, in the last months of his life, was very interested in and supportive of our moral panic project. We can only hope that he would have welcomed the outcome.

Stanley Cohen died on 7 January 2013.

Content of Part One

The chapters in Part One all begin from the starting-point of an exploration of gender and the family, asking if and how the concept of moral panic has meaning for the ways in which we think about, and act towards, gender and the family today. This part, along with others in the volume, is an eclectic collection; people are writing from different disciplinary backgrounds and different countries, and they have different 'takes' on moral panic theory. We have not tried to reconcile these differences; instead, readers are invited to make up their own minds or, rather, to ask their own questions in response to the questions posed by the authors. Not only are the chapters in this part a varied collection, but the part itself is, in important ways, incomplete – it cannot pretend, in so few chapters, to say everything that might be said about gender and the family today. There is, for example, no chapter about either men or fathers; this absence is one that we intend to address as our work progresses in the future. In spite of these cautionary words, Part One offers an exciting, and at times provocative, group of chapters that explore the connections between ideas of gender, class, 'race', youth and 'the family', and highlights the importance of not taking things for granted and of questioning the very basis of our beliefs. The social issues identified here all have consequences, often negative ones, for individuals and for society; such is the power of power panics.

Chapter One, by Morena Tartari, tackles head on two social problems that have emerged in Italy in recent years (and, of course, are familiar throughout the world): child abuse and intimate-partner violence, or rather, 'femicide'. In her chapter, Tartari argues that while these are legitimate subjects of concern, the social and political reaction to them has been disproportionate, leading to the passing of extremely harsh legislation against those deemed to be 'perpetrators' such as 'paedophiles'. What concerns her more, however, is the impact that these moral panics and the resultant increased anxiety have had on women and children. She asserts that women and children have increasingly been presented as weak and in need of protection, allowing the state to intervene in ever-stronger ways.

The next three chapters explore the intersections between ideas of femininity, motherhood, social class and 'race' in three very different contexts: South Wales (Dawn Mannay, Chapter Two), New Zealand (Liz Beddoe, Chapter Three) and the North of England (Sally Brown, Chapter Four). Dawn Mannay's chapter explores 'respectable and acceptable femininities' as they are negotiated in a discourse of what she describes as a 'pervasive discourse of lack, stigma and classed moral panics'. Her chapter builds from her own study of mothers and daughters in one of the most deprived communities in South Wales, one that, she argues, is illustrative of a 'spatial folk devil' that stigmatises all who grow up there. Nevertheless, strategies of resistance are evident in the women's lives, as demonstrated in the stories of Melanie and her daughter, Adele.

Liz Beddoe's Chapter Three reflects similar themes, but this time examines them in the context of the media characterisation of 'feral families' in the UK and New Zealand. She begins with an account of the characterisation of poor families in the UK, seen in TV programmes such as *Benefits Street*, and government initiatives such as the Troubled Families Programme (discussed in Chapters Twelve and Fourteen). From here, she opens up the subject to consider the connections being made in this discourse of moral panic between poverty, welfare dependency, child abuse, family violence and Maori families in New Zealand. She argues that this moral panic is not accidental; it is, rather, part of a deliberate tactic to target the 'underclass'.

In Chapter Four Sally Brown brings us back to the UK, this time to teenage parenting in the North of England. Here she examines the reality that while teenage pregnancy and motherhood figures have fallen in the UK, so concern for teenage pregnancy and motherhood has grown. The underlying assumption, she argues, is that the 'wrong kind' of women are becoming pregnant and having babies; teenage mothers are presented as 'bad' mothers who lack the necessary experience and parenting skills. Sally's research disputes this, and she concludes that the panic about teenage pregnancy and parenting is closely aligned to the panic about welfare 'scroungers' and the need to reduce the role of the welfare state.

Part One ends with a provocative contribution from Stuart Waiton, already a well-known figure in the body of literature on moral panics. He begins with the suggestion that as moral discourses in society have declined, so the panic about the family that we are currently experiencing in the UK might best be described as an 'amoral panic'. He then picks up the idea of 'early intervention', much loved in social work and social policy circles, and argues that by increasingly intervening early, the state extends its role and its power in ways that we have not begun to imagine. While the focus might, in theory, seem to be on families in poverty, the panic about parenting is generalised or normalised – we all become targets of intervention, and the autonomous self is diminished. This is a challenging place to end Part One, and the idea is picked up in the subsequent parts of the book.

References

Cohen, S. (1972) *Folk devils and moral panics: The creation of the mods and rockers*, London: MacGibbon and Kee Ltd.

Cohen, S. (1985) *Visions of social control: Crime, punishment and classification*, Cambridge: Polity Press.

Cohen, S. (1988) *Against criminology*, London: Transaction Publishers.

Cohen, S. (2001) *States of denial: Knowing about atrocities and suffering*, Cambridge: Polity Press.

Cohen, S. and Taylor, L. (1972) *Psychological survival: Experience of long-term imprisonment*, London: Pelican Books Ltd.

Cohen, S. and Taylor, L. (1976) *Prison secrets*, London: Pluto Press.

ONE

Women and children first: contemporary Italian moral panics and the role of the state

Morena Tartari

Introduction

This chapter interrogates moral panic through examination of the treatment of child abuse and femicide in Italy in recent years. The discussion builds on my own research in this field. I will argue that child abuse and intimate partner violence are social problems that have both generated moral panics in contemporary Italy. These issues are real phenomena and they must not be neglected or denied, but their severity may have been over-emphasised and over-represented within the public and media arenas, giving rise to peaks of public concern and anxiety that, in turn, have provoked reactions that can be seen as moral panics. As we will see, waves of concern about child abuse were apparent in the years 2006 to 2009; then a new kind of phenomenon emerged in 2012: 'femicide'. This term and its menace spread through different arenas under the pressure of feminist movements, moral entrepreneurs and politicians, thus provoking widespread social alarm and calls for action.

The chapter discusses my research into the emergence of these concerns and panics, the role of moral entrepreneurs and the disproportionality of the reaction, as well as the consequent legislation and the role of the state in reinforcing the social concerns. In what follows, I first explain how we can understand these issues as moral panics and what makes them such; then I identify some of the key ingredients of these contemporary moral panics; lastly, I discuss how the state can be seen as a particular kind of definer with strong power and control over the legitimisation of social concerns. I begin, however, with a brief introduction to the methodological approach taken in my study.

The approach used in my study

The methodological approach of this study is based on a flexible form of grounded theory (Charmaz, 2006) and the use of sensitising concepts (Blumer, 1969), stemming from the seminal work of Cohen (1972), Hall et al (1978), Beck (1992), Jenkins (1992), Goode and Ben-Yehuda (1994), Beck and Beck-Gernsheim (1995), Critcher (2003 and 2009) and Hier (2011). The corpus of data is constituted by national newspaper articles (from 1992 to 2013), TV programmes (2007 for the child abuse moral panic and 2012–13 for the femicide moral panic), 60 in-depth interviews with social actors involved in the emergence of panics, ethnographies of conferences and public events about child abuse and femicide, and journalism essays about these issues.

Child abuse and femicide as moral panics

Waves of heightened public concern about children and child abuse emerged between the 1980s and the 1990s across the United States and Europe, leading to numerous judicial inquiries (as discussed in full by de Young, 2004 and Jenkins, 1998). In particular, the focus of concern was a new kind of sex crime, the ritual abuse of children; and the perpetrators (the 'folk devils' in moral panic language) were held to be day-care providers and others who had contact with the children at the day-care centres. Although a great many of those who were accused of sexual abuse at this time were later acquitted, there were calls for changes in the law, sometimes successful. The moral entrepreneurs who had played such a significant role in the UK and the US panics also became well known in Europe, where they disseminated their studies at staff training events for professionals. Furedi (2004) has described this as a vital element in enhancing what he has identified as 'therapy culture', in other words vulnerability has become a salient feature of people, and the therapeutic culture fuels a representation of people as powerless and ill. Hence the problems of everyday life must be read as emotional problems, and this exacerbates audiences' anxieties concerning 'risks' and 'emotional damage'. In Italy, some professionals organised themselves into associations that became pressure groups and interest groups, and entered media arenas. They led moral crusades, sensitising parents to the innumerable risks for children and the danger of emotional damage, thus producing anxieties for both parents and a wider public. In particular, therapy culture gained consensus in social services and among social workers, and this engendered child-abuse moral panics.

Concerns about femicide are more recent; the term first appeared in Italy in 2012. Previously, Lagarde, a Mexican academic anthropologist and politician, had coined the term to describe the social phenomenon of the women killed in her country. She campaigned for the Mexican government to acknowledge the crime of femicide by extending the meaning of the term to encompass all crimes of hate and violence against women. The pioneering work of the feminist criminologists Russell and Radford (1992) identified femicide as a criminological category and brought it to public attention. In the Italian media, the term was used in a broad sense to refer to different situations ranging from abuse to murder. The femicide moral panic, which began as a cultural operation of sensitisation, followed the protests of the left-wing and feminist movements against the sexual scandals of Prime Minister Berlusconi. Campaigners railed against the image of the 'woman as sexual object' that had been highlighted by these scandals and by the media that Berlusconi owned; they also bemoaned the general degeneration of behaviour, and the potential threat of Berlusconi's re-election. In the wake of the political controversy, the media concentrated its attention on this kind of crime.

It is my contention that campaigns centred on child abuse and femicide have all the fundamental ingredients of a moral panic; the process of their development and decline is similar to the processes described by the classic moral panic models, as will now be explored in more detail.

Key aspects of the child abuse and femicide moral panics in contemporary Italy

Analysis of national newspaper articles between 1992 and 2013 clearly demonstrates the course taken by the panic around child abuse in Italy, as seen in the disproportionality between real crime rates, on the one hand, and concerns and reactions in the media and public arenas on the other (Tartari, 2013 and 2014). The terms 'paedophilia' and 'child abuse' entered the media lexicon in the 1980s, but it was in the 1990s that their frequencies increased exponentially, with a similar trend for each of them. The term 'paedophilia' now predominates, while the term 'child abuse' has become less visible. 'The paedophile' has become unequivocally a 'folk devil'; his representation is influenced by the construction of childhood in Western societies (Zelizer, 1994; James, Jenks and Prout, 1998), where the risks and menaces towards all children are perceived to have increased (Beck and Beck-Gernsheim, 1995).

The two main Italian national newspapers give different coverage to the perceived problem of child abuse: the left-wing newspaper emphasises social issues like this to a much greater extent. The media reflect the increase of public concern, and expert opinions enter the public debate. Interest groups are effective in gaining consensus among the elites, and moral entrepreneurs are efficient in drawing public attention to paedophilia issues – making a strong contribution to the creation of local moral panics. The emotional and moral components are over-represented in the discourses of moral entrepreneurs, and their claims are taken up by the state and its key institutions.

Politicians have progressively involved themselves in the child-abuse moral panics. The discourses of right-wing politicians stress the value of the traditional and patriarchal family, shifting the attention to paedophilia in order to underline the extra-familial nature of child abuse. In parallel, they promote a policy of uncertainty based on the sensationalisation of crimes and insecurity (Maneri, 2013). Left-wing politicians meanwhile focus their attention on children as victims to be protected, as subjects 'at risk of suffering by the hands of adults' (Critcher, 2009). This clashes with a progressive representation of children as participative subjects with agency: autonomous and active.

The child-abuse moral panics in Italy produced changes in the law, with the introduction of harsher penalties for crimes related to child abuse. The state funded public and private centres for the prevention and treatment of child abuse; it promoted campaigns against paedophilia; it supported public events against the phenomenon; and, through ministers, it sometimes took direct action by issuing ad hoc decrees. The state was receptive to the child-abuse moral panic and legitimated the claims raised by interest groups. The media, interest groups, experts and moral entrepreneurs, and the state with its institutions, created spirals of signification that led to moral panic.

Analysis of newspaper articles shows that the problem of femicide is also over-represented in the press, specifically in one of the main national newspapers that supports the social protests of left-wing women. While in 2006 cases of violence against women in the crime news were predominantly presented as murders of women by immigrants (Giomi and Tonello, 2013), by 2012 the focus was on intimate-partner violence. The victims were women involved in intimate relationships, not 'women in general'; the offenders were their partners, husbands, ex-partners or ex-husbands – men with whom they had had a relationship. The folk devil, in this instance, was now the 'man as a man'. Headlines like 'We have become the country where the male has a licence to kill' became common. Crimes figures were either over-emphasised or ignored or misused (see, for example, data from ISTAT and EUROSTAT). The publishing industry became interested in the phenomenon, and during 2012–13 the number of critical essays and popular works on femicide rapidly increased.

It is important to note that the interest groups involved in this moral panic were politically close to the interest groups of the child-abuse panic. The feminist movement and its related associations sought to raise funds from government sources, the aim being to reactivate already-existing centres for the protection of women or to create new centres for the treatment of women 'at risk' of violence, or victims of it. The sensitisation concerned risks and dangers that might originate from male power, from male cultural dominance and from the imbalanced relationships between men and women. The woman was represented as a victim, weak, unable to protect herself, in need of emotional, psychological, social and financial support. Left-wing politicians were active in underlining the 'gender question', while right-wing politicians did not constitute an effective opposition. How could they stand against something that was presented as so appalling? The femicide moral panic gained consensus among the elites and, in response to their demands, new and harsher penalties were introduced by the state.

Helping the weak: the rhetoric of the state close to citizens

Since the early 1990s, profound changes have taken place in the Italian social and political setting. In 1992, at national level a series of judicial inquiries were conducted against politicians and other members of Italian institutions. They revealed a system of corruption and illegal party funding in the form of bribes, with a consequent strong increase in public distrust of the institutions.

From 1994 to 2011, Berlusconi was Prime Minister four times: so-called 'Berlusconism' arose as a social, moral and political phenomenon (Giachetti, 2010; Genovese, 2011). Berlusconism is considered an expression of the crisis of moral values in conjunction with the country's structural crisis (economic, financial, political and institutional). Berlusconi engaged in direct dialogue with the masses and belittled the value of the civil service, institutions and magistrates. His governments promoted large-scale campaigns on the fear of crime, where risks and social anxieties became useful instruments with which to foster insecurity and uncertainty. Hence the state, through its action to protect citizens, and law and safety enforcement, could become reconciled with citizens and also 'converse' with them, thereby providing a representation of the 'state close to citizens'. As Jenkins (1992) suggests, a social, political and economic crisis is a factor that can sometimes engender panics, and the exaggeration of threats is sometimes a strategy to divert attention from a political and economic crisis. Paradoxically, the representations by feminist movements of women and children as vulnerable and victims gave liberal and conservative governments opportunities to reinforce the consensus. Citizens' mistrust of institutions fostered the direct relationship between the charismatic leader (Berlusconi) and the mass, the government and citizens.

The problem of safety (Maneri, 2013) thus became a core issue. The focus on marginal groups, the idea of a society with a high crime rate, the certainty of punishment, harsher sentences and reassurance were strategies and rhetorical instruments with which to govern citizens' mistrust. Paedophilia and femicide were crimes that forcefully entered the discourses on safety. Sensationalism on these themes was easy because they linked with moral and sexual issues.

Berlusconi's scandals disrupted the dialogue and the ideal bond of trust between himself and citizens. The power and dominance of Berlusconi became synonymous with immorality. The sex theme, originated by feminist discourses, became a sensitive topic on which different projects of moralisation (Hunt, 1999) converged and clashed.

As Jenkins argues, social problems and panics are closely connected to each other: a panic is an 'interlinked complex'. 'The continuity of personnel in the claims-making process, the heightened awareness of generalised dangers in the aftermath of a successful panic and the cumulative nature of problem construction' (Jenkins, 1992, p 12) are possible causes of interdependence for the child-abuse moral panic. Otherwise, femicide moral panic seems to utilise a 'socially available knowledge' (Best, 1990): like Berlusconi, men can become (sexual) perverts – corrupt, obscene abusers. Berlusconi became the symbol of immorality and danger. Both the moral panic about child abuse and the moral panic about femicide had feminist roots: children and women were presented as easy victims of the male as predator. The spread of therapy culture in social work (often, again, with its roots in feminist ideas) also played a key part in the development of these moral panics.

Critcher (2003) has argued that moral panics may be seen as either processual or attributional: put simply, in the first model the panic develops through seven stages (emergence, media inventory, moral entrepreneurs, experts, coping and resolution, fade away, legacy), while in the second it needs certain factors to develop (concern, hostility, consensus, disproportionality, volatility, claims makers). My research

suggests that both models can be seen in these Ital
moral panics. Consensus and disproportionality are
Consensus appears 'among elites across pressure grou
politicians, initially outside then inside government
p 150). Consensus is often reached through distortio
both in disproportionality and in its causes and eff
abuse and femicide moral panics, the threat was ex
absence of objective measures. The causes and effects
were distorted. Because an organised opposition to th
lacking, and a sufficient level of concern was present,
able to spread.

These moral panics also highlight the issue of the de
suggests (2003, p 134) that the explanation offered by I
is too inflexible, because it considers news sources out
unable to gain credibility. According to Critcher and
media, claims makers and different actors can alternate
secondary definers. I argue that only this latter perspe
the dynamicity of the situation in which panics devel
the moral panics considered, the activism of moral entr
interest groups as claims makers should not be under-e
(1990) suggests that their role is very important in pro
definition of the problem. Then the media act to amplify
concerns, translating them into issues interesting to the
ensuring the latter's constant attention. Finally, the stat
these definitions through its responses (changes to the law
funds for centres and so on). The state, and not just the m
problems and concerns and legitimates those of them tha
reinforce the image of a state close to citizens and helpin
The state is thus a sort of powerful secondary definer
power and control over the legitimisation of social concer
contends with the media for second place.

Conclusion: the 'polite state' model

'Women and children first' is an expression that readily de
the symbolic use of weakness by the state. It is a formula tha
us of the etiquette – the code of behaviour – of civilise
The state thus becomes symbolically 'polite' to citizens w
are weak and threatened. This image is an icon of Berl
(Mariotti, 2011), and the child-abuse moral panic can be vi
useful instrument that was used to reinforce this image. The
moral panic was different, not least because it emerged follo

decay of the Berlusconi era. But the consequences of both are equally profound. A culture of suspicion has arisen in the intimate relationships between children and parents, partners and relatives. This is the culture of the intimate enemy, where distrust is no longer (or not only) in the institutions, but in intimate relationships. Cohen (2011, p 239) comments on such a process:

> The gradual but massive influence of feminism plus the general 'discovery' of the victim created more loops of denunciation, more rules and regulations, more deviance – 'emotional abuse', 'hate crime' and 'sexual harassment' are typical examples – and hence moral panics to be identified and studied.

Child abuse and femicide are two examples of contemporary moral panics that are connected in the Italian social context; the state's complex and controversial role in this is a matter that should not be neglected.

References

Beck, U. (1992) *Risk society: Towards a new modernity*, London and Thousand Oaks: Sage.

Beck, U. and Beck-Gernsheim, E. (1995) *The normal chaos of love*, Cambridge: Polity Press.

Best, J. (1990) *Threatened children: Rhetoric and concern about child victims*, Chicago: University of Chicago Press.

Blumer, H. (1969) *Symbolic interactionism: Perspective and method*, Englewood Cliffs, NJ: Prentice Hall.

Charmaz, K. (2006) *Constructing grounded theory: A practical guide through qualitative analysis*, London: Sage.

Cohen, S. (1972) *Folk devils and moral panics* (3rd edn), London: Routledge, 2002.

Cohen, S. (2011) 'Whose side we were on? The undeclared politics of moral theory', *Crime Media Culture*, vol 7, no 3, pp 237–43.

Critcher, C. (2003) *Moral panics and the media*, London: Open University Press.

Critcher, C. (2009) 'Widening the focus: moral panics as moral regulation', *British Journal of Criminology*, vol 49, no 1, pp 17–34.

de Young, M. (2004) *The day care ritual abuse moral panic,* Jefferson: McFarland.

Furedi, F. (2004) *Therapy culture*, London: Routledge.

Genovese, R. (2011) *Cos'è il berlusconismo: la democrazia deformata e il caso italiano*, Roma: Manifestolibri.

Giachetti, D. (2010) *Berlusconi e il berlusconismo*, Varese: Arterigere.

Giomi, E. and Tonello, F. (2013) 'Women and crime in 365 days of Italian evening news', *Sociologica. Italian Journal of Sociology online*, 3: 1–29, www.sociologica.mulino.it/journal/article/index/Article/Journal:ARTICLE:709/Item/Journal:ARTICLE:709

Goode, E. and Ben-Yehuda, N. (1994) *Moral panics: The social construction of deviance*, Oxford: Blackwell (2nd edn, 2009).

Hall, S., Critcher, C., Jefferson, T., Clarke, J. and Roberts, B. (1978) *Policing the crisis: Mugging, the state and law and order*, London: Macmillan.

Hier, S. (ed) (2011) *Moral panic and the politics of anxiety*, London: Routledge.

Hunt, A. (1999) *Governing morals: A social history of moral regulation*, Cambridge: Cambridge University Press.

James, A., Jenks, C. and Prout, A. (1998) *Theorizing childhood*, Cambridge: Polity Press.

Jenkins, P. (1992) *Intimate enemies: Moral panics in contemporary Great Britain*, New York: Aldine de Gruyter.

Jenkins, P. (1998) *Moral panic: Changing concepts of the child molester in modem America*, New Haven: Yale University Press.

Maneri, M. (2013) 'Si fa presto a dire sicurezza', *Etnografia e ricerca qualitativa*, vol 2, pp 283–309.

Mariotti, C. (2011) 'Berlusconism: some empirical research', *Bulletin of Italian Politics*, vol 3, no 1, pp 35–57.

Russell, D.E.H. and Radford, J. (1992) *Femicide: The politics of woman killing*, New York: Twayne Gale Group.

Tartari, M. (2013) 'Moral panic and ritual abuse. Where's the risk? Findings of an ethnographic research study', in C. Critcher, J. Hughes, J. Petley, and A. Rohloff (eds) *Moral panics in the contemporary world*, New York: Bloomsbury Academic, pp 193–213.

Tartari, M. (2014) 'The ambivalent child. Sexual abuse and representations of childhood inside media and social arenas', *Interdisciplinary Journal of Family Studies*, vol 19, no 1, pp 1–19

Zelizer, V.A. (1994) 'Introduction', in *Pricing the priceless child: The changing social value of children*, Princeton, NJ: Princeton University Press, pp 3–21.

TWO

Myths, monsters and legends: negotiating an acceptable working-class femininity in a marginalised and demonised Welsh locale

Dawn Mannay

Introduction

The distinctiveness of Wales in terms of its political life and culture has grown considerably since the early 2000s (Mackay, 2010). Nevertheless, beneath the imagery of the definitive nation, Wales remains a complex and divided land in which a marginalised and demonised working class has come to characterise areas of Wales dominated by poverty and social exclusion. Such polarisation has a spatial dimension that is illustrated in the creation of new ghettos of prosperity and poverty that now dominate the Welsh socioeconomic terrain, and this 'stigma of place' permeates the identities of residents. The chapter begins by considering how moral panics about particular places create 'spatial folk devils'. The creation of moral panics through political discourses and mediated forms is then explored in terms of contemporary representations. Drawing on research with mothers and their daughters in a marginalised Welsh locale, the chapter examines the ideology of unity alongside the divisions of everyday life, and the ways in which respectable and acceptable working-class femininities are negotiated against a pervasive discourse of lack, stigma and classed moral panics.

Moral panics and folk devils: contemporary representations

As Cohen (1980, p 9) contends, societies are subject to periods of moral panic in which 'a condition, episode, person or group of persons emerges to become defined as a threat to societal values'. Moral panics are often discussed in relation to group criminality, incivility and disorder. However, arguably, the emphasis on collective behaviour has shifted to that of the morality of deficient individuals who require discipline; and these deficiencies are seen as a product of personal choice, where individuals are authors of their own immorality (Burney, 2005). Moral panics are often associated with the sociology of deviance, focusing on 'delinquency, youth cultures, subcultures and style, vandalism, drugs and football hooliganism' (Cohen, 2011, p vi). Nevertheless, the concept of morality also relates to wider discourses about appropriate ways of being that move beyond criminal behaviour and acts of resistance, to encompass socially constructed ideologies that form part of the invisible social order.

The nineteenth century was characterised by moral panics about the ignorance, ineptness and filthiness of working-class women (Delamont, 1978; Aaron et al, 1994; Beddoe, 2000) who were 'defined as a threat to societal values' (Cohen, 1980, p 9). These cultural artefacts of lack remain pervasive in constructions of acceptable working-class femininities; and are remade in current gendered and classed representations of immorality (Mannay and Morgan, 2013; Mannay, 2014). For example, in contemporary moral panics the media have cast working-class mothers as folk devils, responsible for tearing apart the moral fabric of society, where tabloid headlines scream 'family breakdown', 'scroungers' and 'welfare benefit crisis' (Atkinson et al 1998). The figure of 'chav mum' now circulates within a wide range of print media, reality television, news media, films and websites (Tyler, 2008), 'in camouflaged versions of traditional well-known evils' (Cohen, 2011, p viii). Importantly, these representations are always spatialised (Haylett, 2003; Skeggs, 2004), and the narrow sets of discourses and visual tropes that are now drawn upon to portray 'deprived' communities' (Fink and Lomax, 2012) create 'spatial folk devils'. The following section examines how the stigma of place and the creation of 'spatial folk devils' impact on the lives of mothers and daughters who reside in these marginalised areas.

Spatial folk devils: place, space and stigma in urban South Wales

Wales is often presented as a country where locality, community and belonging are of particular importance, but the nation can also be viewed as 'existing in relations of a paradox or antagonism' (Massey, 1994, p 3). Prior to the 1980s, the strength of the Welsh trade union movement contributed to the 'affluent worker' thesis (Adamson, 2010), which has permeated contemporary discourses of ubiquitous classlessness, an idea of shared values and attitudes that allude to a nation where Welshness is inherently working class. However, since 1980 the gap between rich and poor has widened and classlessness has become an imagined concept in a country where the divisions of class are both powerful and pervasive (Evans, 2010). Examining this class divide through geographical distribution illustrates the creation of new ghettos of prosperity and poverty, termed the 'Los Angelization' of socioeconomic terrain (Morrison and Wilkinson, 1995).

This chapter draws on a study[1] that took place in Hystryd,[2] a predominantly white urban area that ranks as one of the most deprived communities in Wales (Welsh Assembly Government, 2008). Nine mothers and their daughters participated in the project and took photographs, drew maps and made collages depicting meaningful places, spaces and activities (see Mannay, 2010; 2013a) and then, drawing on the interpretative model of 'auteur theory' (Rose, 2001), discussed them in individual interviews to ensure that I understood what their visual productions intended to communicate. I have selected data produced with two participants: one mother, Melanie, a mother of two in her thirties, and one daughter, Adele, in her twenties.

These participants were selected as their connections beyond the boundaries of Hystryd act as a constant reminder of how their home is viewed by outsiders. Place is both a heuristic mechanism for placing ourselves and others and a 'social construct arising out of our interactions with others around us' (Scourfield et al, 2006, p 15), but examining the coordinates of mothers' and daughters' social worlds in this study complicates the idea of a single Hystryd. However, the participants are aware of how outsiders view Hystryd in stigmatising and homogenising discourses, and negotiate this ascription in qualitatively different ways.

Melanie's story

Melanie recognises the ways in which her local area is stigmatised and she charts a route to acceptable motherhood and social mobility through her children's education. Faith schools are often seen as vehicles for social mobility (Schagen et al, 2002), and Melanie's project involves attending the church associated with a faith school that is situated in an affluent area outside of Hystryd. Melanie compares attending the church to "going to have a tooth pulled in the dentist", and she describes how she feels in this space outside the boundaries of Hystryd.

"Women go in hats, and the men, like, go in leather gloves and clip-o-clopity shoes, and they all, you know, they're all perfect, they got their Sunday *best* on (laughs) and then there's me and (partner) in our jeans and (laughs) thinking *oh no argh* ... I mean we're respectable people, you know we're *hard working* and that ... But we're not, *ever* gonna be at a level where, I think some of them in there are.... And even though they're *nice enough*, you know you're never gonna be, *welcomed* as much as anyone else."

Melanie suggests that in the space of the church she becomes what Bauman (1998) refers to as a 'defective consumer', illustrated by the material choices of consumption. The outward differences of apparel are accompanied by an affective realisation of the depth of class division, for although the church constitutionally is open to all, it is as if there is an invisible 'No Entry' sign that mediates the classed nature of this spiritual, religious and social space. The church is situated in an affluent parish outside of Hystryd, and for Melanie this affluence is apparent in the parishioners; she feels that she does not fit in terms of residence or socioeconomic status.

The tension within the space is palpable and Melanie has to negotiate and retain a respectable sense of identity while acknowledging a level of rejection, while members of the congregation may come to feel ill at -ease as they draw from a 'vicarious imagination of the other' (Rock, 2007, p 29) who is entering their space from the 'spatial folk devil' of Hystryd. Melanie adopts strategies of resistance:

"Sometimes I'm quite hard, and I think *F you, it's for my kids*, I'll sit here and suffer ... Whether you want me here or not ... It's tough."

There is a moral justification for being in this middle-class space, for attending engenders a respectable form of motherhood. As long as Melanie is prepared to leave Hystryd, to enter this affluent parish, she is able to display a normative femininity characterised by her 'capacity to care' (Holloway, 2006). However, the term 'suffer' reinforces Melanie's assertion that she does not want to be in this place, and sufferance also affords a form of self-protection because rejection is more palatable if you can reject the other. Thus, as Bennett et al (2008) suggest, detachment is a better notion than exclusion, but, despite Melanie's bravado, entering and re-entering this space is emotionally wearing, with the pain of continual perceptions, assumptions and judgements that question the legitimacy of the family marked by their Hystryd postcode as defective (Rogaly and Taylor, 2009; Skeggs, 2009).

Adele's story

In common with many working-class students (Ball et al, 2002), Adele attends a local university so that she can commute from home, and this journey engenders a recognition of the stigmatised discourses that surround her home. As discussed elsewhere (Mannay, 2013b), as a 'non-traditional' student Adele is negotiating a hybrid identity as she moves constantly between two qualitatively different spaces, and, like Melanie, she makes distinctions between herself and her more affluent peers:

> "Because I live at home it was like I wasn't, didn't really get on, not get on with them but I wasn't part of them ... like their parents are paying for them to come to uni ... And like half of them haven't even got jobs."

'Working' is central to working-class respectability. Those who 'haven't even got jobs' may have financial superiority, but Adele still retains a moral high ground because such students can be seen as a type of 'benefit person', and Adele, who worked as soon as she was old enough, "wasn't part of them". The same moral justifications and distinctions can be seen in relation to cleanliness: "I'm not like, I couldn't live in a student, like in the mess ... I couldn't do it."

Dirt forms a symbolic nexus from which working-class women struggle to disassociate (Evans, 2006), and Adele employs these distinctions to explain why she is not like the other students and why she does not socialise with them outside of university. However, as mentioned in relation to Melanie's account, detachment is a better notion than exclusion (Bennett et al, 2008), and such separation may also be engendered to limit any opportunities for her peers to make judgements about Hystryd and, in turn, her marked identity. In a discussion about a university field-trip where they passed through a low-income area that was ridiculed by Adele's peers, I asked Adele if any of the students knew where she lived:

> "No they don't even know 'cause they're not from here ... I think they'd probably, if they drove through here I think they'd probably have a heart attack. (laughs) (both laugh)"

In this way, Adele acknowledges Hystryd as a 'spatialised folk devil' and, although there is laughter, her account also suggests an element of concealment engendered as a protective force against being fixed as the object of comedy (Tyler, 2008) or being wounded by lack of respect (Bennett et al, 2008).

Discussion

The notion that everyone who lives in a 'spatial folk devil' like Hystryd must be a dysfunctional disaster from some underclass has lodged deep in the local social mythology. Stigma of place impacts on everyday lives, perceptions of others and perceptions of self. It can close down projects of social mobility and engender divided communities and divided selves. This feeds into a process of social spatialisation where residents are subject to the over-simplification, stereotyping and labelling that equates home, and simultaneously them, as something to be judged as deficient and 'defined as a threat to societal values' (Cohen, 1980, p 9).

As Thrift (1997, p 160) contends, 'places form a reservoir of meanings which people can draw upon to tell stories about and therefore define themselves'; and both Melanie and Adele are acutely aware of how they are stigmatised. The readings of families relate to who they are in regard to their postcode, so that they are never allowed to forget where they live; and conceptions of place are guided by moral panics around sink estates, where locals become coded by their residence in the 'next-door yet foreign place where the other neighbours live' (Toynbee, 2003, p 19). Accordingly, particular housing areas like Hystryd become 'spatial folk devils' and residents are ascribed with this marked identity that impacts on the practices and power relations that define their everyday lives

This does not mean that marginalised areas do not experience problems; as Blanford (2010) argues, parts of South Wales, still badly affected by deindustrialisation, are very difficult places to grow up in, as is demonstrated in the participants' accounts. However, central to all moral panics and their associated folk devils is that the issue's 'extent and significance has been exaggerated' (Cohen, 2011, p vii) in relation to either more reliable forms of evidence or other more serious social problems. Such exaggeration has altered the range of ways in which particular areas can be seen from both inside and outside, so that Melanie and Adele need to negotiate acceptable femininities against pervasive and vehement discourses of lack, disorder and the caricature of the 'chav mum' (Aaron, 1994; Tyler, 2008).

Conclusion

This chapter has reflected on the historical classed and gendered legacies that engender the creation of folk devils and has presented contemporary evidence to demonstrate the ways in which these folk devils are made, remade and circulated in the media. Drawing on the accounts of Melanie and Adele, the chapter has illustrated the affective impact of residing in a marginalised and stigmatised locale. Both Melanie and Adele employ strategies of resistance as they embark on educational projects of social mobility, but these journeys are undertaken with the recognition of stigma, the need to continually re-establish a moral sense of self, acts of necessary concealment and emotional costs; as Melanie says, "it's tough".

Acknowledgements

I would like to acknowledge the participants who made this article possible, and also Professor John Fitz, Professor Emma Renold and Dr Bella Dicks for supervising this research project. I am grateful to Professor Viviene Cree, Dr Gary Clapton and Dr Mark Smith for inviting me to contribute to this edited collection. Lastly, I would like to thank Dr Sara Delamont, whose anthropology module Myths, Monsters and Legends inspired the title of this chapter and who has been a continual source of support in my academic writing.

Notes

[1] The doctoral research project from which this paper is drawn was titled 'Mothers and daughters on the margins: gender, generation and education' and was funded by the Economic and Social Research Council.

[2] The name Hystryd is fictitious and was chosen to maintain the anonymity of the area.

References

Aaron, J. (1994) 'Finding a voice in two tongues: gender and colonization', in J. Aaron, T. Rees, S. Betts and M. Vincentelli (eds) *Our sisters' land: The changing identities of women in Wales*, Cardiff: University of Wales Press.

Aaron, J., Rees, T., Betts, S. and Vincentelli, M. (1994) *Our sisters' land: The changing identities of women in Wales*, Cardiff: University of Wales Press.

Adamson, D. (2010) 'Work', in H. Mackay (ed) *Understanding contemporary Wales*, Milton Keynes: The Open University and University of Wales Press, pp 59–90.

Atkinson, K., Oerton, S. and Burns, D. (1998) 'Happy families? Single mothers, the press and the politicians', *Capital & Class*, vol 22, no 1, pp 1–11.

Ball, S.J., Reay, D. and David, M. (2002) 'Ethnic choosing: minority ethnic students, social class and higher education choice', *Race, Ethnicity and Education*, vol 5, no 4, pp 333–57.

Bauman, Z. (1998) *Work, consumerism and the new poor*, Buckingham: Open University Press.

Beddoe, D. (2000) *Out of the shadows: A history of women in twentieth-century Wales*, Cardiff: University of Wales Press.

Bennett, T., Savage, M., Silva, E., Warde, A., Gayo-Cal, M. and Wright, D. (2008) *Culture, class, distinction*, Abingdon: Routledge.

Blanford, S. (2010) 'Cultural representation', in H. Mackay (ed) *Understanding contemporary Wales*, Milton Keynes: Open University and University of Wales Press.

Burney, E. (2005) *Making people behave*, Cullompton: Willan.

Cohen, S. (1980) *Folk devils and moral panics*, London: Routledge.

Cohen, S. (2011) *Folk devils and moral panics*, London: Routledge.

Delamont, S. (1978) 'The domestic ideology and women's education', in S. Delamont and L. Duffin (eds) *The nineteenth century woman*, London: Routledge, pp 134–63.

Evans, G. (2006) *Educational failure and working class white children in Britain*, London: Palgrave Macmillan.

Evans, N. (2010) 'Class', in H. Mackay (ed) *Understanding contemporary Wales*, Milton Keynes: The Open University and University of Wales Press, pp 125–58.

Fink, J. and Lomax, H. (2012) 'Inequalities, images and insights for policy and research', *Critical Social Policy*, vol 32, no 1, pp 3–10.

Haylett, C. (2003) 'Culture, class and urban policy: reconsidering equality', *Antipode*, vol 35, no 1, pp 33–55.

Holloway, W. (2006) *The capacity to care: Gender and ethical subjectivity*, London: Routledge.

Mackay, H. (2010) 'Rugby – an introduction to contemporary Wales', in H. Mackay (ed) *Understanding contemporary Wales*, Milton Keynes: The Open University.

Mannay, D. (2010) 'Making the familiar strange: can visual research methods render the familiar setting more perceptible?', *Qualitative Research*, vol 10, no 1, pp 91–111.

Mannay, D. (2013a) '"Who put that on there … why why why?" Power games and participatory techniques of visual data production', *Visual Studies*, vol 28, no 2, pp 136–46.

Mannay, D. (2013b) 'Keeping close and spoiling revisited: exploring the significance of "home" for family relationships and educational trajectories in a marginalised estate in urban south Wales', *Gender and Education*, vol 25, no 1, pp 91–107.

Mannay, D. (2014) 'Who should do the dishes now? Exploring gender binaries around housework in contemporary urban south Wales', *Contemporary Wales*, vol 27, no 1, pp 21–39.

Mannay, D. and Morgan, M. (2013) 'Anatomies of inequality: considering the emotional cost of aiming higher for marginalised, mature mothers re-entering education', *Journal of Adult and Continuing Education*, vol 19, no 1, pp 57–75.

Massey, D. (1994) *Space, place, and gender*, Minneapolis, MN: University of Minnesota Press.

Morrison, J. and Wilkinson, B. (1995) 'Poverty and prosperity in Wales: polarization and Los Angelization', *Contemporary Wales* vol 8, pp 29–45.

Rock, P. (2007) 'Symbolic interactionism and ethnography', in P. Atkinson, A. Coffey, S. Delamont, J. Lofland and L. Lofland (eds) *Handbook of ethnography*, London: Sage, pp 26–38.

Rogaly, B. and Taylor, B. (2009) *Moving histories of class and community*, London: Palgrave.

Rose, G. (2001) *Visual methodologies*, London: Sage.

Schagen, S., Davies, D., Rudd, P. and Schagen, I. (2002) *The impact of specialist and faith schools on performance*, LGA Research Report 28, Slough: National Foundation for Educational Research.

Scourfield, J., Dicks, B., Drakeford, M. and Davies, A. (2006) *Children, place and identity*, London: Routledge.

Skeggs, B. (2004) *Class, self and culture*, London: Routledge.

Skeggs, B. (2009) 'Haunted by the spectre of judgement: respectability, value and affect in class relations', in K.P. Sveinsson (ed) *Who cares about the white working class?* London: Runnymede Trust, pp 36–45.

Thrift, N. (1997) 'Us and them: reimagining places, reimagining identities', in H. Mackay (ed) *Consumption and everyday life*, London: Sage, pp 159–212.

Toynbee, P. (2003) *Hard work: Life in low pay Britain*, London: Bloomsbury.

Tyler, I. (2008) 'Chav mum chav scum', *Feminist Media Studies*, vol 8, no 1, pp 17–34.

Welsh Assembly Government (2008) *Welsh index of multiple deprivation 2008*, Cardiff: Welsh Assembly Government.

THREE

Making a moral panic: 'feral families', family violence and welfare reforms in New Zealand. Doing the work of the state?

Liz Beddoe

Introduction

New Zealand is in the midst of a campaign to cut welfare spending, aligned to the 'austerity' discourse preoccupying many countries. Over the period 2011–14, two significant government projects were developed side by side: a programme of welfare reforms (Welfare Working Group, 2011) and a new programme of interventions aimed at reducing the incidence of child abuse (Ministry of Social Development (MSD), 2012b). The two projects emanated from the same arm of government, the MSD, but they were not linked in their everyday activities. Both projects have generated significant public interest and are imbued with ideological content.

Negative framing of the poor – alongside amplified expressions of class disgust – amid the on-going programme of welfare reform has been noted elsewhere (Tyler, 2013). Links between child maltreatment and welfare claimants are also common (Warner, 2013). An analysis of the media discourse on welfare families in New Zealand has found significant linking of family violence to poverty and 'beneficiary' or claimant status, most noticeable in examination of the commentary on 'opinion pieces' or columns. A battle of words rages between advocacy groups (Wynd, 2013) that research poverty in New Zealand and those who would link the issue of 'welfare families' to child abuse and neglect.

This chapter explores the construction of a 'feral families' discourse in the New Zealand print media and considers whether this construction may constitute an example of the 'folk devil' so often manifest in a moral panic. Such families are characterised as being welfare dependent, prone to violence and predominantly Maori.

Framing of the poor

In all discussions of moral panics, the role of the media is germane. Iyengar (1990, p 19) argued that 'how people think about poverty is shown to be dependent on how the issue is framed'. Iyengar's influential paper on media framing associates the psychological conception of framing – ideas and terms employed to propose and consider choices – to the way mass media influence public opinion on the major social issues. In contemporary society 'media' is no longer a monolithic category. While the press and broadcast media may maintain significant influence on the framing of social problems, they are also subject to immediate challenge. A good recent example is the tranche of opinions of citizens, politicians and journalists that followed the screening of the television programme *Benefits Street* (Channel Four, 2014). The highly controversial documentary about the residents of a street in England elicited instant reactions in social media, followed up by stories, blogs and further television coverage. At one end of the spectrum of comments, residents were subjected to abuse and threats; at the other, there was nuanced discussion of how the programme framed the poor, essentially illustrating polarised opinions about the provision of welfare. This example demonstrates that although news and other media can fan the flames of moral panics, the audience is no longer passive, nor denied opportunities to stake a claim in the debates.

Gamson's (1992) constructionist approach to framing is useful, as it underlines the importance of audience engagement in interpreting media discourses; indeed, 'media discourses and public opinion are conceived to be two interacting systems' (Sotirovic, 2000, p 273) and journalists must condense all the available information into essential ideas or frames. Thus, in the example given above, journalists and commentators took standpoints, positioning themselves either as defenders of the documentary or as advocates for those participants deemed to be defamed by the programme. Gamson (1992) suggested that the success of media framing is influenced by the strategies employed by audiences: those people who use a cultural strategy (received wisdom, 'common sense', stereotypes and so forth) may be more impacted on by framing, while those with 'personal or vicarious experiential knowledge' are more likely to discount or ignore frames (Sotirovic, p 274). Such is the power of the audience that the residents of *Benefits Street* were allowed the right of reply: a programme screened after the final episode (Plunkett, 2014). Media framing is still potent, for while technology mediates reception of the news, unsympathetic media hostile to particular groups can exploit stigma.

Public reactions to social problems addressed in mainstream media issues reflect deeply held ideologies, preferences and prior judgements; words or phrases may trigger ideological and emotional responses. An audience may be unwilling to allow framing to alter their views, once that emotional response is triggered. Language is significant, and Bullock, Fraser Wyche and Williams (2001, p 233) have argued that along with 'rhetorical devices such as metaphors, catch phrases and imagery, news-handlers use reasoning devices that draw on causal attributions ... These powerful (but typically unnoticed) mechanisms affect viewers' judgments of responsibility and causality.' As noted by Sotirovic (2000, p 272), in the 'quest for a catchy phrase, welfare mothers became "welfare queens" ... welfare recipients became "welfare freeloaders" hiding the reality of illiteracy, abuse, illnesses, and addictions'. Whatever the motivations of the *Benefits Street* documentary makers, the television channel set the tone with the title, summoning a discourse bound to attract a large audience in 'austerity Britain'. The public is invited into the lives of people to assess their deservedness.

It has been noted in the UK, as elsewhere, that in the 'age of austerity' a common element of the discourse is the labelling of 'feckless' parents 'as scapegoats for moral and economic decline' (Jensen and Tyler, 2012). In New Zealand, there is evidence of moral framing of Maori (indigenous people of New Zealand) families and welfare beneficiary status, as shown in the following media story, linking child-abuse statistics to the beneficiary status of teen parents:

> "So it's not just a Maori problem, it's a New Zealand problem, and they are not the only ones that abuse their children but they are disproportionately high" ... Teenage parents were the most vulnerable group, Minister Bennett [MSD] said. About 4500 babies were born every year to teenagers receiving a benefit and 45 per cent would have another child while still on a benefit, she said. (Stuff [online news website], 26 July 2011)

Maori comprised nearly 15% (598,602 people) of the population of New Zealand in the 2013 census (Statistics New Zealand, 2014). The Maori population is youthful, with the 2013 census reporting that (33.1%) of people of Maori descent were aged under 15 years (Statistics New Zealand, 2014), and as compared with other children in New Zealand Maori children are over-represented in rates of child maltreatment (Cooper and Wharewera-Mika, 2013). While this is acknowledged as a significant problem to be addressed, it must be recognised that by far the majority of Maori children are well cared for (Cooper and Wharewera-Mika, 2013).

Cooper and Wharewera-Mika note that numerous historical sources such as early settler accounts of Maori family life reported supportive and warm child-raising practices (Cooper and Wharewera-Mika, 2013, p 170). When seeking understanding of the over-representation of Maori children in family violence, the persistent theme concerns colonisation and the subsequent enduring inequalities. The process of colonisation caused significant loss of land, severe erosion of language and traditional cultural practices and the breakdown of indigenous systems of community norms and justice. These losses are widely acknowledged as having a negative effect on Maori culture, health and overall socioeconomic well-being (Durie, 2001; Kruger et al, 2004). Kruger et al (2004, p 29) state that 'epidemic whanau violence and systemic dysfunction' is an outcome of persistent oppression and inequality.

While child maltreatment is recognised as a major challenge, Maori people appear to be targeted for particular vilification and association with the discourses of underclass and 'feral families' (Laws, 2012a). The entrepreneur of such a discourse can and will attempt to silence other voices by undermining their credibility or accusing them of some form of neglect:

> Children's Commissioner Cindy Kiro will wring her hands and preach that 'we' must stop harming 'our' kids but the truth remains. Being born to an underclass family, especially if you are Maori, increases the risk of child abuse and child murder by an exponential degree.... Again we will hear excuses and blame-shifting from the liberal apologists ... (Laws, 2008)

In the local manifestation, 'welfare-dependent families' have also been labelled as 'feral' and an emerging highly racialised underclass discourse is revealed and repeatedly linked to family violence:

> The children of welfare are now legion, and they are destined for the same lifestyle as their, usually, solo parent. They smoke, drink, drug, crime, victim, bash like no other group in the country. And then they breed some more. (Laws, 2008)

The folk devil: the construct of 'feral Maori families'

The elements of Cohen's original definition of a moral panic are: a 'condition, episode, person or group of persons' emerges as a potential threat to society; the nature of the threat is presented as a stylised or stereotypical version of itself by the media (the 'folk devil'); moral entrepreneurs and 'experts' present this threat and possible solutions to the public and, lastly, the threat then disappears and is forgotten, or deteriorates and becomes more visible, often being institutionalised in some lasting way (Cohen, 2002, p 1). The 'folk devil' is generally depicted by the media in an easily recognised form (Thompson, 1998, p 8) and the threat is generally not to something trivial, but to something that is integral to the society in question (Thompson, 1998, p 8).

In the introduction to the third edition of *Folk Devils and Moral Panics*, Cohen considers that the objects of moral panics are both 'new' threats and manifestations of old threats (Cohen, 2002, p vii); they are damaging per se and also symptomatic of deeper problems (Cohen, 2002, p viii); and they are at once transparent and opaque, easily recognisable, but in need of explanation to the public by 'experts' (Cohen, 2002, p viii). Stories of family violence, in particular of child abuse, are often couched in terms of moral degeneration, what can be coded as 'a world gone mad', framed as phenomena symptomatic of the decline of modern society. This decline is often attributed to the stigmatised other – those who are poor, immigrants, members of ethnic and religious communities, welfare beneficiaries – and is the beloved target of the right-wing blogger, 'do-gooder liberals' and academics. The 'bleeding hearts' are seen by the powerful to coalesce around an unreasonable defence of those held responsible for the decline.

Moral panics ideas are useful in exploring the role of claims makers in the discourse of the 'feral' Maori family. It can be argued that the news media is playing a role in bolstering fear and social anxiety about the presence and impact of 'dangerous' welfare-dependent Maori families and communities. Does this suggest that we have a moral panic, where framing has created a unique folk-devil, tapping into the vein of racism that exists in New Zealand society? My answer is both yes and no. Yes, because the promotion of a racist discourse sits alongside the neoliberal state project of cutting benefits to many vulnerable people on quasi-moral grounds, and thus potentially giving support to those who sponsor the welfare-reform agenda. The framing of a racialised underclass discourse, with a 'bonus' link to child maltreatment, may bolster the New Zealand government's social policy direction by permeating the public consciousness with such a negative portrayal. No, because there is also some evidence that these views are at the extreme end of a continuum and not widely shared in New Zealand society. I also feel that the notion of 'feral Maori families' is a racist trope too offensive to attract the more socially acceptable moral entrepreneur who might be needed to justify this discourse as in itself constituting a moral panic.

It is useful to explore the manifestation of such a discourse here. In New Zealand, politician and columnist Michael Laws wrote a series of articles over 2008–12 in which he addressed 'feral families', more commonly just referring to his subjects as 'the ferals'. That the feral Maori family folk devil has some potency is evidenced in online comments. Abusive language and racist stereotypes abound, often always interwoven with gender and class labels. While Laws was not the only commentator drawing on racialised underclass discourse, he was perhaps the most prolific and vitriolic. In an article entitled 'The inevitable result of a boy born bad', reporting on a young male arrested for a serious sexual assault on a child, Laws wrote of

> that sub-species of humanity with which we co-exist
> – the ferals. These evolutionary antisocials have created
> their own nihilist culture and provide 90 per cent of this
> country's social problems. They have core characteristics
> that distinguish them: poor education, transience, a
> dependence upon drink and/or drugs, a criminal history,
> a welfare lifestyle and they are disproportionately Maori.
> (Laws, 2012a)

Later in 2012, Laws' column 'The Tragic Life of JJ Lawrence' referred to the death of a toddler, but he reserved his personal acrimony for the mother:

> All the usual ingredients are present: ethnicity, welfare
> dependence, drugs, previous violence and the feral
> boyfriend. But there is another ingredient that we often
> overlook – the feckless and useless mother who sets up her
> child for harm … simple messages can go out now – and
> especially to Maori mothers … If you can't handle the job,
> stop breeding. (Laws, 2012b)

Other newspaper columnists have attempted to invoke the 'troubled families' approach. For example, Dita De Boni writes, 'Where social services, the police and many others are involved with a family, it doesn't seem to prevent a big tragedy occurring – even when the family is known to be a wellspring of trouble.' In introducing the UK 'Troubled Families' scheme, she notes 'An ex-crime reporter once told me that police had told her that in any given community, there will be a handful of families that cause the majority of trouble – and cost to the taxpayer' (De Boni, 2011) . She then mentions five cases of child abuse, all involving Maori families. This New Zealand media framing has been analysed in detail by Provan (2012, p 202), who noted that 'murdered Maori children are more likely to be named in a "roll of dishonour", thus framing family violence as solely a Maori problem'. A further attack on Maori is then rendered palatable. Du Fresne (2010) criticises Maori leaders for preferring to spend their time reminding Pakeha (European New Zealanders) of the impact of colonisation rather 'than grappling with the ugly reality of Maori violence', and thus attempts to extinguish an accepted analysis of the historical trauma, the 'multiple and compounded layers of pain, grief and loss experienced by indigenous people since European contact' (Freeman, 2007, p 108).

Those presenting a more nuanced and sympathetic view of child poverty, for example Freeth (2013), who called on business people to contribute more, face a barrage of critical comments, including this:

> A quarter of all Kiwi children are raised in families ... where cigarettes, alcohol, gambling and drugs come first. Three generations of state sponsored dysfunction has made these families a costly blight on the working/middle class ... Is it time for a few draconian laws to clean the gutters and reduce the pests? (*New Zealand Herald*, Comment, 6 March 2013)

Such an invocation of eugenic arguments accompanies welfare reforms that have heralded greater surveillance and control of those claiming benefits. Such policy reflects the moral framing intrinsic to policy development. In New Zealand the Future Focus policy introduced in 2010 is an approach that requires sole parents on the Domestic Purposes Benefit (DPB) to be in part-time work once the youngest child turns six (Ministry of Social Development, 2010). Failure to conform incurs sanctions that are outlined in the Social Security (New Work Tests, Incentives, and Obligations) Amendment Act 2010. Further reforms in 2012 included requiring sole parents on the DPB who decide to have another child while on DPB to return to work after the child's first birthday. One policy that caused much critical comment was that mothers on DPB and their daughters will be offered free contraception to prevent pregnancies that may lead to their having to leave the work-force (Trevett, 2012). In addition, beneficiaries must enrol their pre-schoolers with a general practitioner and complete health checks. Children aged 3 must attend 15 hours a week of early childhood education. Failure to comply results in the sanction of a 50% benefit cut (Ministry of Social Development, 2012a).

Conclusions

Wacquant (2009, p 100) argued that in both the criminal and welfare systems 'public vilification racial accentuation and even inversion, and moral individuation work in tandem to make punitive programs the policy tool of choice and censorious condemnation the central public rationale' for the implementation of more punitive justice and welfare programmes. New Zealand is not alone in its examples of the framing of welfare-claimant folk devils alongside a political platform of stringent welfare reforms. While in New Zealand claims makers such as media commentators have clearly employed a central device of moral panic, identifying targets that are easily amplified as folk devils, this has not produced the 'screaming' headlines observed elsewhere. Is there hope, then, that the public might reject the most draconian reforms, despite the potent imagery of evil, feral, dysfunctional 'welfare families'? New Zealand has a history of investing in social development policies to develop community responses to intransigent problems such as child abuse and health inequality, and this has included specific policies to develop community capacity (see, for example, Humpage, 2005; Elizabeth and Larner, 2009). As such, the claim of a world over-run by dangerous 'welfare dependent' families must be examined critically against some evidence that New Zealanders resist an extreme form of welfare reform (Humpage, 2011), thus failing to produce the volatility of a classic moral panic.

References
Bullock, H.E., Fraser Wyche, K. and Williams, W.R. (2001) 'Media images of the poor', *Journal of Social Issues*, vol 57, no 2, pp 229–46.
Channel Four (2014) 'Benefits Street', www.channel4.com/ programmes/benefits-street (accessed 17 January 2014).
Cohen, S. (2002) *Folk devils and moral panics* (3rd edn), London: Routledge.

Cooper, E. and Wharewera-Mika, J. (2013) 'Healing: towards and understanding of Maori child mistreatment', in T. McIntosh and M. Mulholland (eds), *Maori and Social Issues*, vol 1, Wellington: Huia, pp 169–86.

De Boni, D. (2011) 'Our unruly families', *New Zealand Herald* (12 December).

Du Fresne, K. (2010) 'Reveal-all culture undermines bounds of bad behaviour', *Dominion Post* (12 October).

Durie, M. (2001) *Mauri ora: The dynamics of Maori health*, Auckland: Oxford University Press.

Elizabeth, V. and Larner, W. (2009) 'Racializing the "Social development" state: investing in children in Aotearoa/New Zealand, *Social Politics: International Studies in Gender, State & Society*, vol 16, no 1, pp 132–58.

Freeman, B. (2007) 'Indigenous pathways to anti-oppressive practice', in D. Baines (ed) *Doing anti-oppressive practice*, Halifax, NS: Fernwood, pp 95–110.

Freeth, A. (2013) 'The sad business of child poverty: businesses cannot sit on hands while children go hungry, uneducated, abused and neglected', *New Zealand Herald* (6 March).

Gamson, W.A. (1992) *Talking politics*, Cambridge, England: Cambridge University Press.

Humpage, L. (2005) 'Experimenting with a "whole of government" approach: indigenous capacity building in New Zealand and Australia', *Policy Studies*, vol 26, no 1, pp 47–66.

Humpage, L. (2011) 'What do New Zealanders think about welfare?' *Policy Quarterly*, vol 7, no 2, pp 8–13.

Iyengar, S. (1990) 'Framing responsibility for political issues: the case of poverty', *Political Behavior*, vol 12, no 1, pp 19–40.

Jensen, T. and Tyler, I. (2012) 'Austerity parenting: new economies of parent-citizenship', *Studies in the Maternal*, vol 4, no 2.

Kruger, T., Pitman, M., Grennell, D., McDonald, T., Mariu, D., Pomare, A., Mita, T., Maihi, M. and Lawson-Te Aho, K. (2004) *Transforming whanau violence: A conceptual framework*, Wellington: Te Puni Kokiri-Second Maori Taskforce on Whanau Violence.

Laws, M. (2008) 'Child abuse symptom of human race evolving into them and us', *Sunday Star Times* (27 December).

Laws, M. (2012a) 'The inevitable result of a boy born bad', *Christchurch Press* (4 March).

Laws, M. (2012b) 'The tragic life of JJ Lawrence', *Sunday Star Times* (18 November).

Ministry of Social Development (2010) *Future Focus changes to the welfare system*, Wellington: NZ Government.

Ministry of Social Development (2012a) *Welfare Reform Paper E: Social obligations for parents*, Wellington: NZ Government.

Ministry of Social Development (2012b) *White Paper on Vulnerable Children*, Wellington: NZ Government.

Plunkett, J. (2014) 'Benefits Street: residents to get the right of reply in live TV debate', *Guardian* (online) (16 January), www.theguardian.com/media/2014/jan/16/benefits-street-residents-live-broadcast

Provan, S. (2012) *The uncanny place of the bad mother and the innocent child at the heart of New Zealand's 'cultural identity'*, New Zealand: University of Canterbury Christchurch, http://hdl.handle.net/10092/7393.

Sotirovic, M. (2000) 'Effects of media use on audience framing and support for welfare', *Mass Communication and Society*, vol 3, nos 2–3, pp 269–96, doi: 10.1207/s15327825mcs0323_06.

Statistics New Zealand (2014) 2013 Census ethnic group profiles: Maori, www.stats.govt.nz/Census/2013-census/profile-and-summary-reports/ethnic-profiles.

Stuff.co.nz (2011) 'Maori child abuse disproportionately high: Minister' (26 July), www.stuff.co.nz/national/politics/5338700/Maori-child-abuse-disproportionately-high-Minister

Thompson, K. (1998) *Moral panics*, London: Routledge.

Trevett, C. (2012) 'Free birth control for beneficiaries', *The New Zealand Herald, Online* (8 May), www.nzherald.co.nz/nz/news/article.cfm?c_id=1&objectid=10804206

Tyler, I. (2013) *Revolting subjects: Social abjection and resistance in neoliberal Britain*, London: Zed Books.

Wacquant, L. (2009) *Punishing the poor: The neoliberal government of social insecurity*, Durham, NC: Duke University Press.

Warner, J. (2013) 'Social work, class politics and risk in the moral panic over Baby P', *Health, Risk & Society*, vol 15, no 3, pp 217–33.

Welfare Working Group (2011) *Reducing long-term benefit dependency: Recommendations,* Wellington: Institute of Policy Studies.

Wynd, D. (2013) *Child abuse: What role does poverty play?* Auckland: Child Poverty Action Group.

FOUR

The wrong type of mother: moral panic and teenage parenting

Sally Brown

Introduction

In many Western countries where teenage pregnancy rates are considered by policy makers and others to be too high, such as the UK, USA and Canada, governments have made concerted efforts to reduce teenage pregnancies (for example, Social Exclusion Unit, 1999), while a considerable body of research into the lived experiences of teenage parents has built up (for example, Kirkman et al, 2001; Geronimus, 2003; Whitley and Kirmayer, 2008). In earlier decades, becoming pregnant as a teenager was most likely to be seen as a moral problem due to the mother-to-be being unmarried, and that was often swiftly solved by marriage to the young father-to-be. In more recent years, the 'problem' has been relabelled as a social one, mainly as part of a discourse about social exclusion, and in health terms, as a discourse about risks to both mother and child.

However, despite this shift to regarding teenage pregnancy and parenting as social and health problems, the moral overtones have not gone away, and, it could be argued, have resurfaced in recent years. For example, when the Conservative leader David Cameron harangued the UK parliament at Prime Minister's Question Time in 2008 about the death of Peter Connelly, he did so on the (false) premise that Peter's mother was a teenage mother; this was, as he presented it, all the evidence that was needed of her guilt. Since then, a sense of moral panic about welfare benefit scroungers has been promulgated by the UK's Coalition government as part of its austerity agenda, and young parents have been positioned, implicitly and indeed explicitly, among the ranks of the scroungers. This link between pervasive stereotypes of teen parents dependent on benefits and the ideological assumption that early child-bearing stems from poor individual choices and lifestyles has a direct (and negative) impact on young parents' well-being.

This chapter will first outline the connections between the austerity agenda, young parents and moral panic, using the model of moral panics developed by Goode and Ben-Yehuda (1994) as a framework for analysis. It will then present findings from recent research in which young parents discussed the stigmatisation they experience, and their resulting self-surveillance as a response to their perceptions about constantly being judged by people around them. The chapter will conclude by discussing how young parents both acknowledge and resist the stigmatising discourse of moral panics around teenage pregnancy and parenting.

Teenage parenting as a moral panic

Goode and Ben-Yehuda (1994) argue that a moral panic exists when a substantial proportion of a population regard a particular subgroup as posing a threat to society and moral order as a result of their behaviour, and demand that something must be done – that something often being 'strengthening the social control apparatus of society' (Goode and Ben-Yehuda, 1994, p 31). They argue that there are five crucial criteria for a moral panic: concern, hostility, consensus, disproportionality and volatility. Turning to the issue of teenage pregnancy and parenthood, in this case-study example we can see evidence of *concern* in that anxiety is sparked by what is presented in the media as large numbers of teenagers having babies, particularly when compared to other European countries, and this is described as a threat to the fabric of the community and the institution of the family. Concern is also present in terms of the harms that are said to be caused, to both mothers and babies, by teenage pregnancy and parenting, and therefore 'something must be done' to stop babies being born into circumstances that, it is claimed, will lead to their growing up disadvantaged from the start. There is evidence of *hostility* to the teenagers, in terms of portraying them as 'folk devils' who want to get 'something for nothing', particularly in the context of a rhetoric about benefit 'scroungers', and also in terms of stories being told, for example, about teenagers getting pregnant in order to get a council flat ahead of other more 'deserving' cases. There is *consensus* about this being a problem, seen in the broad negative social reaction in speeches by politicians and stories in the popular press. The size of the problem is exaggerated, as demonstrated by the data discussed below, thus demonstrating *disproportionality*; and we can see *volatility* in the way the problem emerges suddenly, and may disappear just as quickly. One interesting aspect of teenage pregnancy as a moral panic is the way it emerges, disappears and then re-emerges, never quite going away completely, although the social and political context might be subtly different in each iteration. Garland (2008) reminds us that there is always a *moral dimension* to the social reaction, which can be seen in statements from politicians and the press relating to the family, particularly about 'Broken Britain' and on-going fears about the 'breakdown of the family'. That the 'deviant conduct' in question is seen as *symptomatic* of wider problems within society is demonstrated by, for example, Prime Minister David Cameron's linking of poor parenting to social unrest (Cabinet Office, 2011a), or using a single mother with a pregnant teenager as one of his examples justifying the introduction of the 'Troubled Families' initiative (Cabinet Office, 2011b).

As for the true scale of the problem, according to the Office for National Statistics (2011) the teenage birth rate has been falling steadily for 30 years, and in 2010 was at its lowest point since 1968. In addition, conception rates increased in all age groups excepting the under-20s; in other words, fewer teenagers are getting pregnant, and fewer of those who do get pregnant are carrying the baby to term. However, in order to have a moral panic, people must believe that there is something to panic about and, despite these figures, a survey conducted in 2013 in the UK found that people think teenage pregnancy is about 25 times higher than it actually is: the survey showed that people think 15% of under-16s get pregnant every year when official figures suggest it is about 0.6% (Ipsos-MORI, 2013). Lawlor and Shaw (2004) argue that:

> Health professionals and the general public should be wary of claims that the rate of teenage pregnancy in Britain is 'high' and increasing in an alarming way. International comparisons suggest that the rate is moderate and that the past six decades have seen a decline rather than a rise.... We believe that the selective reporting of international and time comparisons by policy makers results in a 'manufactured risk' and has more to do with moral panic than public health. (Lawlor and Shaw, 2004, p 123)

As far as welfare benefits are concerned, the Coalition government's welfare reforms will mean that parents under the age of 25 years will have their benefits reduced, and UK Prime Minister David Cameron has suggested that under-25s should have no rights to housing benefit at all, meaning that young parents would find it very difficult to live independently, as they are likely to be in low-paid work, and in need of housing benefit even if they are in work. The age range of the parents targeted by the reforms signals a widening scope of concern to include parents in the first half of their 20s, a broadening of the concept of 'young' that appears to reflect largely middle- and upper-class views about acceptable life-course transitions. This discourse is one where education and career are prioritised, with child-bearing being delayed until a career is established, as the preferred life course, and early motherhood is positioned as undesirable, if not irresponsible (Perrier, 2013; Wilson and Huntington, 2005).

Changes to the benefits system have been linked to the increasing stigmatisation of benefit claimants, including the use of increasingly harsh language to describe some groups (Garthwaite, 2011) and an assumption promoted by some sections of the media that to be a claimant automatically makes a person someone who 'scrounges' off 'the taxpayer'. A rise in rhetoric about 'strivers' versus 'skivers' brings to mind the distinction between 'deserving' and 'undeserving' poor, originally enshrined in the Elizabethan Poor Law of 1601 and reinforced by the Victorian Poor Law Reform Act of 1834. A frequently used example of the undeserving, and in this sense a classic folk devil, is the stereotypical teenage single mother who gets pregnant in order to get a council flat, at the expense of hard-working families. This example persists despite there being no evidence to support it, and despite the fact that over 90% of new housing-benefit claimants in the years 2010–12 were in work (Brown, 2012). However, it works as a useful stereotype because it encapsulates several moral panics in one – teenagers having sex, non-taxpayers getting something for nothing, lazy shirkers getting more than hard-working strivers, the wrong type of women having babies, the dangers of an 'underclass' out-breeding the middle class (Arai, 2009). The stereotype also performs the two functions as outlined by Garland (2008), in that it encompasses several moral dimensions to the panic, such as people getting things they are not entitled to at the expense of those who are entitled, and it is seen as symptomatic of wider problems, in particular, problems such as inter-generational dependence on benefits and cultures of worklessness, ideas that persist despite their being shown to be inaccurate (MacDonald et al, 2013).

There is often an unspoken assumption that to be a teenage mother is to be a bad mother who lacks experience and parenting skills, and a theme in much of the research literature highlights the efforts made by young mothers to prove themselves to be 'good' mothers (Kirkman et al, 2001; Romagnoli and Wall, 2012). In addition, poor parenting has been blamed for many social ills, including the UK riots of summer 2011, with David Cameron saying about the rioters, 'Perhaps they come from one of the neighbourhoods where it's standard for children to have a mum and not a dad' (Cabinet Office, 2011a). The policy response is individualised in terms of offering parenting-skills classes, rather than addressing wider social questions, with Sarah Teather, then Children's Minister, announcing pilot parenting lessons in three areas of the country, saying that 'it is the government's moral and social duty to make sure we support all parents at this critical time' (Teather, 2011).

Evidence from research

The consequences of the moral panic around teenage pregnancy and parenting can be seen in the day-to-day lives of young people, and this chapter will now present and discuss findings from a study exploring the experience of being a young parent. Interviews and focus groups were held with young parents and parents-to-be in a city in the North of England with a reputation as a 'hot spot' for high rates of teenage pregnancy. In all, 17 people took part in interviews (nine young people and eight older family members) and two focus groups (one with five participants and one with seven) were held. The participants frequently raised issues of being judged and feeling stigmatised as a young parent by, and those issues are focused on here. Names and some other minor details have been changed to ensure anonymity.

All but one of the pregnancies of those who took part in the study had been unplanned, and participants talked about being scared to tell their parents, and also fearing what other people would say about them:

> "It was the main fact that I was scared, scared about what people are thinking and everything." (Haley, age 16, mum of Riley, age 6 months)

Several participants talked about being called offensive names at school and on social media; some had overheard comments made in the street about them being "a bit young to have a baby", or had been on the receiving end of "mucky looks" on the bus or in the street. This made them feel very conscious that they were being watched all the time and therefore had to behave in ways that would not bring further criticism upon them.

Jamie: We can't just nip to the shops, just whack any clothes on and nip to the shops –

Naomi: – if we're on our own you can do that –

Jamie: – we've got to always be at our best.

Naomi: It's like teenagers do, but when you've got the baby with you, you have to think, you always have to think what would everyone else think about what I look like today or what I'm wearing, what I'm acting like, what I'm doing, so you've always got to be conscious, you've got to care what everyone else thinks. Which isn't nice.

(Jamie, age 18, and Naomi, age 17, parents of Jordan, age 8 months)

Naomi went on to say that on first becoming a parent she had felt that everyone was looking at her and judging her and reported comments that people had made to her, with the result that she stopped leaving the house.

It was suggested that stereotypes in the popular press about young parents led to these judgements, and also led to all teenage parents being seen as the same:

> "They always say 'kids having kids' and things like that. Yeah, alright, some people might not be able to cope when they are young but others can, they sort of tar you all with the same brush really and say you can't cope. I've proved a lot of people wrong." (Nikki, age 19, mum of Louise, age 3)

> "There's never anything good [in the papers] – I think that's what portrays us as bad people, bad parents." (Naomi, age 17)

It is interesting to note that Naomi says that teenagers are seen as bad people as well as bad parents, which fits in with the discourse that teenagers become parents because of flaws they have, whether those be poor life-style choices or lack of ambition. Also interesting is Nikki's comment that people use the phrase 'kids having kids', a phrase that has been used by politicians in both the UK and the USA when describing teenage parents, usually disparagingly.

Jenny, age 19, the mother of Ava, age 8 weeks, described the impact of feeling judged all the time:

> "When you are a young parent you feel like, personally I feel like I'm on edge all the time, thinking people are going to judge me. You hear about all these stories about young parents who get the kids taken off them and things like that, and a lot of the time people assume that you are not

going to be a very good parent because you are young, so I think it makes you feel like you have to prove yourself to everyone, like when health visitors come round you have to prove that you're a good parent."

Participants were also conscious of operating within a discourse about benefit scroungers, with the stereotype being one of someone who would be claiming benefits and perhaps even deliberately getting pregnant in order to obtain access to benefits:

"When I found out I was pregnant and told one of my friends, he went 'oh, you are only doing it to get the money' and I was like 'no, I didn't do it to get the money, it wasn't meant to happen', and he was like 'people only get pregnant for money, to get a house', and all this and I was like 'well, I'm staying at home so I'm not doing it to get a house. I'm staying at home where the baby is going to be happy.'" (Zara, age 19, mum of Ellie, age 4 months)

There was strong resistance to this rhetoric, with all the young participants expressing a keen desire to go back to college or find a job, and not to be dependent on benefits:

"I do want things in life and in order to get them I need to work hard for what I want and then my family will benefit from it. I don't want to be living off the state." (Becky, age 18, pregnant)

Becky's 19-year-old partner and father of her baby was working, and they were trying to find a house together. The young fathers who were not working all reported trying to find work; several of them had had jobs but had been made redundant, or were only able to pick up short-term, insecure work. For some young people, the baby was a turning point, making them determined to get back into education when they had not previously done well, and all the young people who discussed work and education expressed a strong commitment to supporting their family.

Conclusions

The current moral panic around teenage pregnancy and parenting is closely linked to rhetoric about scroungers and the need to reduce the role of the welfare state. This rolling back of the state is partly as a result of austerity policies and partly to reduce 'cultures of dependency' and to encourage people into work. Young parents are well aware of operating within this discourse; they acknowledge the existence of stereotypes and labels attached to young parents but refuse to accept them as applying to them. However, although they resist being stereotyped, the awareness that others around them are looking at them through that lens has a profound effect on their self-perception and, in some cases (for example, Naomi), on their day-to-day lives.

These findings suggest, for social work and social policy, that there is an opportunity to support young parents to achieve their wishes. They are determined to be good parents and to demonstrate this to the outside world; they are keen to work and not be dependent on the state. However, in a context of continuing high unemployment rates for young people, with many more trapped in a cycle of low-paid, insecure work, the prospects for young parents operating in this discourse of moral panic seem bleak.

References

Arai, L. (2009) *Teenage pregnancy: The making and unmaking of a problem*, Bristol: The Policy Press.

Brown, C. (2012) 'The majority of new housing benefit claimants are in work', *Inside Housing*, www.insidehousing.co.uk/tenancies/majority-of-new-housing-benefit-claimants-in-work/6521183.article (accessed 6 January 2014).

Cabinet Office (2011a) PM's speech on the fightback after the riots, www.gov.uk/government/speeches/pms-speech-on-the-fightback-after-the-riots (accessed 25 November 2013).

Cabinet Office (2011b) David Cameron's speech on plans to improve services for troubled families, www.gov.uk/government/speeches/troubled-families-speech (accessed 4 August 2014).

Garland, D. (2008) 'On the concept of moral panic', *Crime Media Culture*, vol 4, pp 9–30.

Garthwaite, K. (2011) 'The language of shirkers and scroungers? Talking about illness, disability and Coalition welfare reform', *Disability and Society*, vol 26, no 3, pp 369–72.

Geronimus, A.T. (2003) 'Damned if you do: culture, identity, privilege, and teenage childbearing in the United States', *Social Science and Medicine*, vol 57, pp 881–93.

Goode, E. and Ben-Yehuda, N. (1994) *Moral panic: The social construction of deviance*, Oxford: Blackwell.

Ipsos-MORI (2013) *Perils of perception*, Survey for Royal Statistical Society and King's College, London.

Kirkman, M., Harrison, M., Hillier, L. and Pyett, P. (2001) '"I know I'm doing a good job": canonical and autobiographical narratives of teenage mothers', *Culture, Health and Sexuality*, vol 3, no 3, pp 279–94.

Lawlor, D.A. and Shaw, M. (2004) 'Teenage pregnancy rates: high compared with where and when?' *Journal of the Royal Society of Medicine*, vol 97, no 3, pp 121–23.

MacDonald, R., Shildrick, T. and Furlong, A. (2013) 'In search of "intergenerational cultures of worklessness": hunting the Yeti and shooting zombies', *Critical Social Policy*, vol 34, no 2, pp 199–220, doi: 10.1177/0261018313501825.

Office for National Statistics (2011) *Frequently asked questions: Births and fertility, August 2011*, London: Stationery Office.

Perrier, M. (2013) 'No right time: the significance of reproductive timing for younger and older mothers' moralities', *The Sociological Review*, vol 61, no 1, pp 69–87.

Romagnoli, A. and Wall, G. (2012) '"I know I'm a good mom": Young, low income mothers' experiences with risk perception, intensive parenting ideology and parenting education programmes', *Health, Risk and Society*, vol 14, no 3, pp 273–89.

Social Exclusion Unit (1999) *Teenage pregnancy*, London: Stationery Office.

Teather, S. (2011) 'Free parenting classes to be offered to over 50,000 mothers and fathers', https://www.gov.uk/government/news/free-parenting-classes-to-be-offered-to-over-50000-mothers-and-fathers.

Whitley, R. and Kirmayer, L.J. (2008) 'Perceived stigmatisation of young mothers: an exploratory study of psychological and social experience', *Social Science and Medicine*, vol 66, pp 339–48.

Wilson, H. and Huntington, A. (2005) 'Deviant (m)others: the construction of teenage motherhood in contemporary discourse', *Journal of Social Policy*, vol 35, no 1, pp 59–76.

FIVE

Amoral panic: the fall of the autonomous family and the rise of 'early intervention'

Stuart Waiton

Introduction

In 2008, I suggested that the concept 'moral panic' was, in many respects, past its 'sell-by' date; the idea of amoral panic was offered as an alternative (Waiton, 2008). My analysis was based on the following observations:

- the use of morality is declining as a framework for panics
- the importance of amoral categories like 'risk' and 'safety' as central tenets of panics is growing
- individuals are engaged with as diminished subjects
- old 'moral' institutions are undermined rather than shored up by these panics
- 'panics' are normalised and institutionalised.

In this chapter, I will take this argument further by examining the transformation that has been taking place in 'The Family', an institution once central to moral panic theorising, associated with moral values and understood and defended as something that was 'at the heart of society' (Goode and Ben-Yehuda, 1994, p 8). I pose the question: to what extent is the 'future of the nuclear family' the basis for panics today (Cohen, 2011, p xxii)? In particular, I look at the way the idea of the 'autonomous family' has all but disappeared from government and policy discussions of the family, and conclude by suggesting that we need to understand the rise and rise of 'early intervention' policies and initiatives as an illustration of the amoral panic that has developed around the family in the 21st century.

The rise and rise of 'early intervention'

The opening sentence of the UK government's document *Next Steps for Early Learning and Child Care*, published in 2009, reads: 'Everyone agrees that the first few months and years are the most important in a child's life.' The document goes on to explain that it is a child's mother and father that bring up a child – not governments – but then adds: 'but parents need support' (Department for Children, Schools and Families, 2009, p 3). This is just one of a plethora of documents that have been produced in recent years exploring the issue of intervention, early intervention and 'support' for families.

This mass of documents is further supported by various reports looking specifically at the issue of early intervention, one of the most noticeable being *Early Intervention: Good Parents, Great Kids, Better Citizens* (2008), written jointly by the Labour MP Graham Allen and the Conservative MP Iain Duncan Smith. This report emphasises the importance of early intervention for many of the key social policy areas in the UK. It consequently proposes a significant increase in the need to fund early-intervention initiatives. Over the period 2003–13, billions of pounds have been spent on programmes connected with early intervention, most particularly on the development of Sure Start Centres (Stewart, 2013). Strongly influenced by claims about neuroscience and the development of the infant's brain, early intervention was a central social policy in the US in the 1990s, a decade that George H.W. Bush proclaimed was to be the 'decade of the brain' (Wastell and White, 2012, p 402). In the UK, as we moved into the new millennium the then Prime Minster, Tony Blair, stated that if he had an extra billion pounds to spend, he would spend them on the under-fives (Parton, 2006, p 97).

At the level of political rhetoric (and the lack of political dissent), government policy developments, funding of social policy initiatives and, arguably, also in terms of engagement and enthusiasm among childcare professionals, early intervention has become of major significance in the UK (as it has in the US).

The autonomous family

The idea expressed in *Next Steps for Early Learning and Child Care* that 'parents need support' has become increasingly expressed in government policy documents. For example, launching Every Parent Matters in 2007, the then Education Secretary, Alan Johnson, set out the 'vital role of parents in improving their child's life chances', but also noted, 'Traditionally, parenting has been a "no-go" area for governments. But now more than ever government needs to be supportive of parents who are themselves increasingly seeking help' (Directgov, 2007). Intervention in the family and to prop up the family is not new, of course (Donzelot, 1977; Cullen, 1996). However, for much of the last two centuries there was a greater hesitancy about intervening in a unit – or, indeed, an 'institution' – that was seen as being at the 'heart of society'. For the establishment, the family was understood as a conservative body, a moral rein upon degeneracy and against militancy (Phillips, 1988). It was also seen as an important unit for developing a sense of personal responsibility and 'self-government', a liberal, Millsian 'castle' (Mill, 1999). As such, the idea of intervening in the family was (until recently) seen as problematic.

Looking at the discussion about the family in the 19th century, one gets a profound sense of how important the ideal of the autonomous ('bourgeois') family was. At a time when classical liberalism flourished, the family was seen as both an ideal and an embodiment of the bourgeois value of independence. As Berger and Berger (1983, p 110) noted, this family was protestant in nature, based on the socialisation of highly autonomous individuals; rejecting tradition, it saw action and belief as being self-generating, constructed internally by the self-piloting individual and based upon a morality of hard work, diligence, attention to detail, frugality and the systematic development of will-power. The development of strength of character was essential. The question was: how can this character be formed? The answer was simple. To have strong characters, you needed strong families. And to have strong, independent individuals, you needed the independent, private family.

The ideal of moral independence faced constant difficulties in the Victorian period with regard to the poor, with the contradictory need to support those in desperate need while maintaining personal responsibility. There was also an elitist suspicion, held by some at least, that certain sections of society lacked the capacity to develop their moral independence. However, this remained a contested area, often reflecting the elite's own belief or disbelief in the liberal project of the time (Jordon, 1974, p 25). In the main, policies demonstrated a keen interest in preserving the autonomy of families. Even where charity was given to families, this was largely done only if it could be seen to be improving rather than undermining the moral independence of those involved. In contrast to family policy developments today, it was the development of the 'character' and 'self-reliance' of parents that was seen as key, rather than the development of parenting itself (Jordon 1974, p 26).

The end of autonomy

Discussing modern-day panics in Britain and America, Joel Best argued that 'by the turn of the millennium, it was hard to identify many successful social problems campaigns mounted in either country solely by conservative claimsmakers' (Best, 2008, p x). This change can be seen with reference to the family, or what are now much more likely to be presented and discussed as 'families'. As gay marriage becomes not only legalised but promoted by the Conservative Prime Minister and Mayor of London, it is clear that traditional morality is not the force it once was. In both politics and social policy, we find little sense of an 'institution' being defended, and talk of 'The Family' has largely been replaced by the concern about 'parenting'. However, as Furedi notes, the decline of traditional morality associated with the family has not meant a decline in moralising and anxiety about families. Indeed the reverse appears to have happened, with 'virtually every social problem' becoming associated with poor parenting. Added to this, the inflated importance given to parenting (or parental determinism) as the cause and solution of social problems has resulted in 'all parents' being seen as potential problems (Furedi, 2014, p ix).

This growing problematisation and professionalisation of parenting has come, Reece (2006) argues, with what Furedi (1997) and Heartfield (2002) have described as the diminishing of subjectivity. Reece defines the modern framework for legal developments within the family as 'post-liberal'. Here she notes that not only has the conservative moral framework surrounding the family declined, but so too has the liberal sense of autonomy, privacy and responsibility that was the founding essence of the ideal 'bourgeois' family.

In her various studies of the post-liberal subject, Reece goes on to explore the ways in which the liberal subject is now conceptualised and critiqued in key political and social theories. In *Divorcing Responsibly* (2003), for example, Reece explores a variety of influential thinkers who have challenged the idea of the liberal subject, from Anthony Giddens to Catherine McKinnon, Charles Taylor and Amitai Etzioni. Rather than there being such a thing as individuals with free will, subjectivity is understood within these theories to be socially constructed, not simply in terms of individuals being merely influenced by other people and events, but to our very core and sense of self we are, these theorists argue, the product of external forces and relationships.

Taken to its logical conclusion, this understanding of the subject means that the individual self or agent disappears, as does the idea that we can be responsible, as individuals, for anything. To resolve this extreme representation of the totally passive individual, Reece argues, the idea of the post-liberal subject has emerged. This post-liberal person is not a subject-less being, but nor is he or she an autonomous agent. Rather, this new subject is one that is constantly developing through continuous interactions and reflection – especially in the personal realm (Reece, 2003, pp 13–39). Rather than (conservative) morality and the liberal subject governing relationships in UK family policies, we now have the post-liberal approach, one that draws back from the idea that individuals are simply responsible for their own actions and instead understands that we are inter-subjects, subjects constantly constituted through our interactions with others, and, consequently, individuals who need to have conversations with one another. Crucially, though, these conversations are not simply between individuals but are to be encouraged, supported and facilitated by (often therapeutic) experts.

Reece illustrates the way in which the autonomous family was undermined in law from the early 1980s, when the idea of parental rights was downgraded and criticised as an 'outdated view of family life which has no part to play in a modern system of law' (Reece, 2006, p 463). Part of this downgrading of parental rights incorporated a view of a post-liberal parent – a parent who could not and should not be expected to deal with parenting matters on their own. Within this context, being a responsible parent no longer meant being autonomous, independent and self-governing, but rather the opposite. Now, the correct approach to responsible parenting was to ask for advice. 'Seeking advice', as the *Supporting Families* document explains, *is* responsible behaviour. In other words, the 'moral agent has become someone who accepts that he or she needs lessons in how to approach moral dilemmas' (Reece, 2003, p 154). Indeed a moral agent or unit (like the 'autonomous family') who believes that they do not need expert instruction has become problematic: a fiction, in the eyes of post-liberal thinkers, a delusion of grandeur that acts as a barrier to necessary support that professionals can bring.

Amoral anxiety

As the morally autonomous family declines as an ideal and as something that is expected or indeed desired, anxiety has grown about the need to support 'post-liberal' parents ever earlier in their parenting. Indeed, in Scotland new legislation has been passed giving every child a state 'named person' to oversee their interests from birth (Smith, 2014). Often framed within a 'liberal' desire to support parents, the early-intervention framework is predicated upon a diminished sense of parental capacity. Consequently, despite the focus in practice often remaining on poorer families, the trend is for the 'panic' or anxiety about parenting to be generalised – or normalised – and for state institutions to construct policy around this diminished, post-liberal subject.

Early-intervention policies and initiatives have also emerged within a context where concerns about 'risk' and 'risk focused prevention' have become influential (Farrington, 2002). Here anxieties about parents and families are expressed not through the language of morality but 'through the language of health, science and risk' (Furedi, 2011, p 96), or 'discourses of "risk" and "harm"' (Hunt, 2003, p 166). As Lee notes, unable to develop a coherent moral ideal or sense of purpose, the authorities have adopted an approach aimed at 'reducing and managing risk': the aim of moral improvement or the ideal of moral responsibility is here replaced by the ersatz value or norm of 'keeping us safe' from harm (Lee et al, 2014, p 14).

The 'scientific' basis for early intervention is provided by the use (and abuse) of neuroscience. Despite growing criticism of the illegitimate use of this science, early intervention as a core policy objective continues to grow in significance (Bruer, 1999; Wastell and White, 2012; Gillies, 2013). Where part and parcel of the Victorian moral movements, or indeed the liberal approach by individuals like John Stuart Mill, was to challenge and develop the beliefs of adults in society, today early interventionists are preoccupied merely with our behaviour; where concern used to be with the human mind, today our interventions are reduced to concerns about the biological brain (Tallis, 2012). Within this modern-day determinism, not a million miles away from the craniology of the 19th century, the understanding of humanity, of childhood, families, neighbourhoods and even society itself is reduced to an analysis of neurons.

Conclusion

The enthusiasm for early intervention can appear as a new form of dynamism in society, a new sense of purpose among professionals and a new framework for meaning and the development of grand projects. However, predicated upon the idea that if we do not intervene in a child's life before the age of three, then it is too late, early intervention is better understood as the outcome of a collapse of belief. Biological determinism was influential in the 19th century (Lombroso, 2009), but at the same time there were competing ideas and beliefs about how to transform individuals and society. Belief in religion, or the liberal individual, or indeed in the possibility of socialism all embodied a sense of human capacity, of moral or social advancement. Similarly, with the development of the state in the 20th century there were at different times a passion for education, for social and youth work, or even for prisons, as institutions that could uplift young people and even rehabilitate adults. Today, through the prism of early intervention and the 'myth' of the first three years (Bruer, 1999), all of these forms of political, moral, individual or collective improvement are lost.

The early years framework has serious implications for the understanding of individuals and their capacity to overcome difficulties. As well as reflecting a diminished sense of the capacity for institutions, elites and beliefs to have an impact on children over the age of three, it also suggests that individuals themselves lack the capacity to change and to develop as they grow. The diminished post-liberal self is discovered in the early years interventionists who are convinced, especially with the help of brain science, that after a 'bad' first few years of life the individual is doomed to a life of antisocial behaviour (Allen and Duncan Smith, 2008).

This panic about young children and their families, expressed through a scientific and risk-based framework of early intervention, in many respects is built upon an opposition to, or at least a sense of unease about, old-fashioned traditional family values: values that can be seen as extreme, dogmatic, rigid, authoritarian and, in terms of the therapeutic idea of 'well-being' (Scottish Government, nd), potentially abusive. It likewise reacts to the ideal of autonomy and the independence of the family – a problematic place and space that takes place 'behind closed doors' and away from the ever-growing importance of professional 'support' and intervention.

I would like to end by concluding that the family today is less an institution around which moral panics can be located, than a new site for amoral elite anxieties to be expressed and the diminished subject to be kept safe.

References

Allen, G. and Duncan Smith, I. (2008) *Early intervention: Good parents, great kids, better citizens*, London: Centre for Social Justice; Smith Institute.

Berger, B. and Berger, P. (1983) *The war over the family: Capturing the middle ground*, London: Hutchison.

Best, J. (2008) 'Foreword', in S. Waiton, *The politics of antisocial behaviour: Amoral panics*, London: Routledge.

Bruer, J. (1999) *The myth of the first three years: A new understanding of early brain development and lifelong learning*, New York: The Free Press.

Cohen, S. (2011) *Folk devils and moral panics* (3rd edn) London: Routledge.

Cullen, J. (1996) 'The return of the residuum', in L. Revell and J. Heartfield (eds) *A moral impasse: The end of capitalist triumphalism*, London: Junius.

Department for Children, Schools and Families (2009) 'Summary', in *Next steps for early learning and child care*, Nottingham: DCSF Publications.

Directgov (2007) 'Department for Education and Skills recognises "Every Parent Matters"', http://webarchive.nationalarchives.gov. uk/+/www.direct.gov.uk/en/nl1/newsroom/dg_066880 (accessed 5 February 2015).

Donzelot, J. (1977) *The policing of families*, London: John Hopkins University Press.

Farrington, D.P. (2002) 'Developmental criminology and risk-focused prevention', in M. Maquire, R. Morgan and R. Reiner (eds) *The Oxford handbook of criminology* (3rd edn), Oxford: Oxford University Press.

Furedi, F. (1997) *Culture of fear: Risk-taking and the morality of low expectations*, London: Cassell.

Furedi, F. (2011) 'The objectification of fear and the grammar of morality', in S.P. Hier (ed) *Moral panics and the politics of anxiety*, London: Routledge.

Furedi, F. (2014) 'Foreword', in E. Lee, J. Bristow, C. Faircloth and J. MacVarish, *Parenting cultures*, Basingstoke: Palgrave Macmillan.

Gillies, V. (2013) 'From baby brain to conduct disorder: the new determinism in the classroom', paper presented at *Gender and Education Association Conference*, 25 April, https://www.academia.edu/3549456/ From_Baby_Brain_to_Conduct_Disorder_The_New_Determinism_ in_the_Classroom (accessed 3 May 2014).

Goode, E. and Ben-Yehuda, N. (1994) *Moral panic: The social construction of deviance*, Oxford: Blackwell Publishing.

Heartfield, J. (2002) *The 'death of the subject' explained*, Sheffield: Sheffield Hallam University Press.

Hunt, A. (2003) 'Risk and moralisation in everyday life', in R.V. Erikson and A. Doyle (eds) *Risk and morality*, Toronto: University of Toronto Press.

Jordon, P. (1974) *Poor parents: Social policy and the 'cycle of deprivation'*, London: Routledge.

Lee, E., Bristow, J., Faircloth, C. and MacVarish, J. (2014) *Parenting cultures*, Basingstoke: Palgrave Macmillan.

Lombroso, C. (2009) '"Criminal craniums" from Criminal Man 1876', in N. Rafter (ed) *The origins of criminology: A reader*, London: Routledge.

Mill, J.S. (1999) *On liberty*, Oxford: Oxford University Press (first published 1856).

Parton, N. (2006) *Safeguarding children: Early intervention and surveillance in a late modern society*, London: Palgrave Macmillan.

Phillips, J. (1988) *Policing the family: Social control in Thatcher's Britain*, London: Junius.

Reece, H. (2003) *Divorcing responsibly*, Oxford: Hart Publishing.

Reece, H. (2006) 'From parental responsibility to parenting responsibly', in M. Freeman (ed) *Law and sociology: Current legal issues*, Oxford: Oxford University Press, pp 459–83.

Scottish Government (nd) 'Well-being: a guide to measuring meaningful outcomes', www.scotland.gov.uk/Topics/People/Young-People/gettingitright/background/wellbeing (accessed 24 June 2014).

Smith, E. (2014) 'Universal state guardian is a cuckoo in the nest', www.thinkscotland.org/thinkpolitics/articles.html?read_full=12373 (accessed 24 June 2014).

Stewart, K. (2013) 'Labour's record on the under fives: policy, spending and outcomes 1997–2010', LSE Social Policy Working Paper, http://sticerd.lse.ac.uk/dps/case/spcc/wp 04.pdf (accessed 13 June 2014).

Tallis, R. (2012) *Aping mankind: Neuromania, Darwinitis and the misrepresentation of mankind*, Durham: Acumen Publishing Ltd.

Waiton, S. (2008) *The politics of antisocial behaviour: Amoral panics*, London: Routledge.

Wastell, D. and White, S. (2012) 'Blinded by neuroscience: social policy, the family and the infant brain', *Families, Relationships and Societies*, vol 1, no 3, pp 397–414.

Afterword: when panic meets practice

Maggie Mellon

I am an independent social work practitioner and commentator with a particular interest in the interface between research, policy and practice. In 2014 I was appointed as Chair of the Policy, Ethics and Human Rights Committee of the British Association of Social Workers and look forward to contributing to the promotion of ethical practice and the continuing development of professional opinion and policy. Moral panics that influence social work and social workers are clearly well within the scope of this committee and the contributions on family and gender in this part are of great relevance to future discussion and work.

In this afterword, I have chosen to reflect particularly on the issues of widening definitions of abuse and harm, and grounds for interference and regulation of private and family life, which are raised particularly by the contributions by Tartari (Chapter One) and Waiton (Chapter Five). These chapters both describe the ways that moral panics have allowed the greater encroachment of government into private and intimate relationships. Family life has, they argue, been gripped by a succession of moral panics about everything from satanic or ritual abuse to rioting youth. Waiton goes as far as to assert that the family is 'a new site for amoral elite anxieties'. Gender relations are currently at the heart of a number of contemporary scandals, often played out as criminal trials of historical events. Tartari explores the ways in which child abuse and gender panics have the apparently paradoxical effect of over-emphasising the vulnerability of women and children and the villainy of men, to the advantage of opportunistic politicians. The contributions of Mannay (Chapter Two), Beddoe (Chapter Three) and Brown (Chapter Four) all provide additional insights into increasing government interest in, and attempts to control, family life and personal relations and the impact that this has on both individuals and families.

Suspicion of families (as 'hotbeds' of both gender and generational abuse and neglect) is now a generally accepted starting-point for social work contact with families. At a time when working and welfare poverty, malnutrition and homelessness are all increasing, so 'child protection' is now the main, if not the only, reason for social workers to be involved with families. Social work agencies seem to have prioritised protecting children from possible risk, rather than protecting families, to the extent that supporting families is not even seen as part of the role of social workers in safeguarding the welfare of children. The suspicion of fathers has become so great that depictions or descriptions of fathers in social work publications are invariably either as absent or as violent and abusive (Fatherhood Institute, 2014). Meanwhile, women have not escaped blame or the kind of stigma described by Mannay in Chapter Two; single mothers, particularly but not exclusively those on benefits, have been the object of panics and stigma under both Labour and Conservative Westminster governments. Blaming families for social problems is not, of course, a uniquely UK approach to policy, nor is blaming particular kinds of families. Beddoe's contribution in Chapter Three describes the ways in which New Zealand government policy on tackling 'problem families' demonised Maori families, thus demonstrating that 'blaming it on the family' can become blaming it on particular ethnicities, cultures or religions. Or, as Brown discusses in Chapter Four, teenage parents are held to be a bad thing not just for the young parent or their child, but also for society. But children are not only victims in a moral panic: they may also come under suspicion for the 'abuse' of other children; police in Scotland have recorded 'crimes' by children as young as three years old (*The Herald*, 2014). Waiton's family as 'a site for anxieties' thus makes the territory for social work a lot larger. Definitions of abuse and harm as grounds for social work and other official intervention in family life have stretched considerably to take in this larger ground.

Reviewing this from my own perspective of nearly 40 years' working in policy and practice in social work, it seems to me that whereas social work practice used to be concerned with working with families and individuals suffering some form of adversity, or posing risks to themselves or others, at some point in the later 20th century the family began to be understood as a risk. This does not mean that there was no oppression or injustice back then. But today, the right to private and family life seems to be increasingly seen, through official eyes at least, as a barrier to the protection of children, of women, of others described as 'vulnerable', from all sorts of risk and harm within their families and intimate relationships. Of course, no one would argue against the need for protection of children and others who cannot defend themselves from abuse. Social workers' role in this is necessary and is often done well. However, the chapters in this part point to ways that definitions and understandings of harm, abuse and neglect, and categories of villains and victims, have been steadily widened. During one panic, *all* women and *all* children are considered vulnerable, and *all* men are suspects. During another, *all* adults are suspect of posing risk of abuse to children. In the grip of yet another panic, *all* children are made suspects in the abuse of other children. Each panic is accompanied by a new and wider definition of the problem that acts to obscure the actual risk and scale of a real problem; the perverse consequence of widening the net makes protection more rather than less difficult.

The role of children's charities as claims makers and moral entrepreneurs in this net-widening process cannot be ignored. These charities' origins in the 19th century were as rescuers of children from parental cruelty and neglect. For example, the NSPCC (National Society for the Prevention of Cruelty to Children) began its existence advocating greater prosecution of parents whose children were injured or killed because of burning or 'overlying' (that is, for being poor and not having a fireguard or a separate bed for children). Today, wider definitions and lower thresholds for intervention in relation to alleged child neglect and greater use of prosecution has become a top campaign issue for those charities. For example, the NSPCC states:

> The current legal and policy framework across the UK views neglect as a persistent behaviour with serious effects. This focus on long-term behaviour discourages early intervention, but taking action at an early stage will significantly improve outcomes for the child. (NSPCC, 2012)

'Neglect' was defined as follows in a major report commissioned by Action for Children and the Scottish Government; this definition was subsequently used to claim a huge increase in cases of child neglect:

> Neglected children include those who experience **any or all** [emphasis added] of:
>
> • being left alone in the house or in the streets for long periods of time
> • lack of parental support for school attendance
> • being ignored when distressed, or even when excited or happy
> • lack of proper healthcare when required
> • having no opportunity to have fun with their parents or with other children. (Daniel et al, 2011)

The report goes on to warn that: 'Of all forms of maltreatment, neglect leads to some of the most profound negative and long term effects on brain and other physical development, behaviour, educational achievement and emotional well being' (Daniel et al, 2011).

Exposing a child to domestic violence is in itself now considered an act of neglect. The term 'domestic violence' is itself increasingly being used to describe non-criminal domestic arguments and skirmishes that do not involve any injury. The official definition of domestic violence was broadened in 2013 in England and Wales to include 16- and 17-year-olds and to include new forms of controlling and coercive behaviour. It states:

> Any incident or pattern of incidents of controlling, coercive or threatening behaviour, violence or abuse between those aged 16 or over who are or have been intimate partners or family members regardless of gender or sexuality.
>
> This can encompass, but is not limited to, the following types of abuse:
>
> * psychological
> * physical
> * sexual
> * financial
> * emotional. (Home Office and Browne, 2012)

I would argue that this definition prompts a number of critical questions. For example, can anyone over 16 years old who has not been raised by wolves in the wilderness claim never to have been both a 'perpetrator' and a 'victim' of domestic violence under this definition? If every family squabble or row can be described as domestic violence, if every sexist joke or clumsy 'pass' can be described as sexual assault, if risk becomes the determinant of everything in adult–child interaction, and all adults (and children?) are held to be dangerous unless proved otherwise, I believe that serious cases can hide in plain view.

Definitions of risk and harm have also been stretched in the case of the fervour that has been created around early years policies in Scotland and England. These have been based on claims originating in the US that pre-birth and the first three years of a child's life 'hard wire' the infant's brain and largely determine her or his future. Based on this theory, intervening early in the early years to prevent harm is essential and has become a cornerstone of government policy, north and south of the border. These assertions have been debunked in a number of academic publications (for example, Wastell and White, 2012; Featherstone et al, 2012, 2013 and 2014). *Guardian* journalist Zoe Williams (2014) has also written an accessible article that summarises the arguments. In Chapter Five, Waiton points to the lack of evidence for the claims of irretrievable brain damage and lifelong harm that are now routinely directed at poor parents, that is, parents in poverty rather than bad parents. But, unfortunately, such bad science is being routinely believed and acted upon in social work decisions about children. Pre-birth or pre-discharge child protection conferences are now regularly convened on the basis of 'risks' to the child's development and attachments that 'might' exist, rather than on any actual evidence that any child has or will come to harm. These conferences consider measures (including the removal of a child at birth) that might be necessary to prevent some future *possible* harm. The victims of these decisions are usually parents in poverty and adversity, but increasingly, it seems that families who are 'different' or who oppose professionals are the target of over-zealous action. Indeed, being oppositional and hostile to professionals can now in itself be taken as evidence of risk, but so also it is claimed can 'disguised compliance', which involves appearing to agree with professionals.

Claims about the early years and the long-term irreversible damage alleged to result from neglect, alongside wider definitions of abuse, neglect and harm are now associated with the policy of earlier decisions on adoption. Rather than being used as a last resort, as the law originally intended, 'forced' adoption against the wishes of parents is being promoted as a first resort of early intervention (Narey, 2011). Social workers are tasked to ensure that plans for the adoption of children are made and carried out within 26 weeks of the child of becoming 'looked after'. This is held to be the 'child's timeframe' (Brown and Ward, 2013); the so-called evidence for a child's time frame, the now well-known image apparently showing massive differences between the brain of a neglected child and that of a normal child, is given pride of place. Nevertheless, concern for children in families with no money, no fuel, shoddy and damp housing has not gone so far as making sure that families in difficulty are offered support, and help has been given no such urgency in official or professional guidance. Benefit sanctions that leave parents without money for food, fuel, rent, fares to school are not seen as germane to child protection. 'Getting it Right for Every Child' (Scottish Government, nd), the policy in Scotland that should have heralded a move to provide support to families, has become enshrined in Scottish law as effectively a charter for professionals and not for families (Mellon, 2013a and 2013b). The term 'family' does not appear once in the Children and Young People Act 2014 that is supposed to make 'getting it right' for children a legal duty.

This brings me to my final comment and my final question. Should we not be asking why some issues that *should* have us all reaching for the panic alarm go unremarked at the time? It is only decades later that what have been real injustices and abuses come back into public view again. When this happens, we are all expected to ask 'how on earth could that have been allowed to happen'? The internment of girls in Ireland's Magdalene laundries and the forced adoption of their children, the deportation of thousands of children to the British colonies in the 20th century have all been the subject of films, documentaries, inquiries. These historic injustices all happened well into the 20th century, within living memory. So too are the now well-known abuses of children in remand homes, young offenders institutes and children's homes within the living memory of social workers. No panic alarm seemed to be sounded about these at the time, by social workers or others. The authorities of the day facilitated and funded these forced removals, separations and adoptions. The children's charities and religious orders were congratulated for their work in rescuing children and giving them 'new lives', thus ending what was held to be the 'cycle' of deprivation and depravity. Will today's fervour for early intervention and forced adoption be the scandal of tomorrow? Will social workers currently initiating or cooperating with removal at birth, with the ending of contact between parents and their children, look back and wonder why they acted in this way? Will they find themselves in front of some parliamentary inquiry, or giving evidence in a criminal trial? I would rather that we did something about it now. Tomorrow's inquiries, inquests and reviews are always too late.

References

Brown, R. and Ward, H. (2013) *Decision-making within a child's timeframe: An overview of current research evidence for family justice professionals concerning child development and the impact of maltreatment*, Working Paper 16, 2nd edn, London: Childhood Wellbeing Research Centre.

Daniel, B., Burgess, C. and Scott, J. (2011) *Review of child neglect in Scotland*, Stirling: University of Stirling.

Fatherhood Institute (2014) 'Study shows Scottish dads airbrushed out of family services' publicity', *Fatherhood Institute*, www.fatherhoodinstitute.org/2014/study-shows-scottish-dads-airbrushed-out-of-family-services-publicity.

Featherstone, B., Broadhurst, K. and Holt, K. (2012) 'Thinking systemically – thinking politically: building strong partnerships with children and families in the context of rising inequality', *British Journal of Social Work*, vol 42, no 4, pp 618–33.

Featherstone, B., Morris, K. and White, S. (2013) 'A marriage made in hell: early intervention meets child protection', *British Journal of Social Work* (advance access), doi: 10.1093/bjsw/bct052.

Featherstone, B., White, S. and Morris, K. (2014) *Re-imagining child protection: towards humane social work with families*, Bristol: Policy Press.

Home Office and Browne, J. (2012) 'New definition of domestic violence and abuse to include 16 and 17 year olds', https://www.gov.uk/government/news/new-definition-of-domestic-violence-and-abuse-to-include-16-and-17-year-olds (accessed 5 February 2015)

Mellon, M. (2013a) 'Children and young people's bill is a missed opportunity', *The Herald* (24 May), www.heraldscotland.com/comment/columnists/children-and-young-people-bill-is-a-missed-opportunity.21163028.

Mellon, M. (2013b) 'Serviceland. The dark world of the named person', *Scottish Review* (18 December), www.scottishreview.net/MaggieMellon137.shtml.

Narey, M. (2011) 'The Narey Report. A blueprint for the nation's lost children', *The Times* (5 July), www.thetimes.co.uk/tto/life/families/article3083832.ece (or access the report at: www.mnarey.co.uk/adoption-advisor.php).

NSPCC (National Society for the Prevention of Cruelty to Children) (2012) *CORE-INFO: Emotional neglect and emotional abuse in pre-school children*, London: NSPCC.

Scottish Government (nd) 'Getting it right for every child', www.scotland.gov.uk/Topics/People/Young-People/gettingitright/background (accessed 5 February 2015).

The Herald (2014) 'The terrible three-year-olds: police record five toddlers committing offences' (29 May), www.heraldscotland.com/news/home-news/the-terrible-three-year-olds-police-record-five-toddlers-committing-offences.1401357096.

Wastell, D. and White, S. (2012) 'Blinded by neuroscience: social policy, the family and the infant brain', *Families, Relationships and Societies*, vol 1, no 3, pp 397–414.

Williams, Z. (2014) 'Is misused neuroscience defining early years and child protection policy?' *The Guardian* (26 April), www.theguardian.com/education/2014/apr/26/misused-neuroscience-defining-child-protection-policy.

Part Two
Moral panics in our time?
Childhood and youth

Edited by Gary Clapton

Introduction

Gary Clapton

In common with the other parts of this book, a key theorist within the 'moral panic' genre is now introduced. Although Geoffrey Pearson does not actually use the term 'moral panic' to outline the social reaction to issues and anxieties, his work has played a key part in the development of thinking around the issue of deviance, especially deviance associated with young people, a central theme within moral panic writings. For this reason, we have chosen to include him in this volume.

Geoffrey Pearson

Geoffrey (Geoff) Pearson was born on 26 March 1943 in Manchester, England and studied moral sciences (Philosophy and Psychology) at Cambridge University. He worked with people with disabilities in Sheffield before going to the London School of Economics to undertake training in psychiatric social work (interestingly, Stan Cohen was also a qualified psychiatric social worker). After qualifying, he returned to Sheffield to practise as a psychiatric social worker. Pearson went on to become a Lecturer in Social Work at Sheffield Polytechnic, and then took up a similar position at University College, Cardiff. It was here that he published his first major work, *The Deviant Imagination* (1975), which examined the ideological underpinnings of a wide range of theories of deviance. This book also established Pearson's critical perspective on many of the policies and attitudes towards young people that were popular at that time, especially those that were built on ideas of young people's dangerousness.

In 1976, Pearson moved to the University of Bradford. Here he wrote *Hooligan: A History of Respectable Fears* (1983), his most influential work; *Hooligan* was voted one of seven 'iconic' studies in British criminology in 2007. In *Hooligan*, Pearson traces the recurrence of explosions of concern about youth crime (we might call them 'moral panics', although he does not). He draws attention to the reality that these explosions of concern are always accompanied by a harping-back to a halcyon time in the past when (supposedly) life was better all round. He argues that there was never a 'golden age'; instead, there will always be 'respectable fears', whether they are centred on the behaviour of hooligans, garrotters, artful dodgers or whoever else is the current focus of fears. (Again, moral panic discourse would call these groups 'folk devils'.)

In 1985, Pearson became Professor of Social Work at Middlesex Polytechnic, and a member of the Central Council for Education and Training in Social Work. He worked on various projects at this time; one was a study of multi-agency policing, commissioned after the Scarman Report of 1981 (this report, into the Brixton riots in London, had emphasised that there were very poor relations between the police and the black community). Pearson went on to publish a study of drug users, entitled *The New Heroin Users* (1987), in which he highlighted that heroin users were often living in areas that were multiply disadvantaged – by poverty, unemployment and poor housing. Pearson moved to Goldsmiths University in 1989 as Professor of Social Work, and later as Professor of Criminology. He was editor of the *British Journal of Criminology* for eight years and a member of the Runciman Inquiry into drugs and the law, which was commissioned by the Police Foundation in 2000 to look at the workings of the UK's Misuse of Drugs Act 1971. He was also vice-chair of the Institute for the Study of Drug Dependency at this time, and continued to conduct empirical research into young people's drug use. Pearson retired in 2008, but went on to chair the Independent Commission on Social Services in Wales; this produced a very critical report in 2010.

This volume, concerned as it is with the current social issues and anxieties (the 'respectable fears') of the day, owes allegiance to Pearson's critical thinking and scepticism, as well as, we hope, to his passion. When Pearson was asked to comment on *Hooligan* in 2007, he said: 'I still think *Hooligan* is a stunningly funny book, and I wouldn't change a word of it, other than a few digs at ASBOS, chavs, parenting orders and neighbours from hell' (Berry, 2008: 832).

Geoff Pearson died on 5 April 2013.

Content of Part Two

The chapters in Part Two introduce some of the many issues and concerns surrounding young people, children and childhood; what links them is their use of a moral panic perspective (some more explicitly than others) to understand what is going on both in and behind the various anxieties that are discussed. Part Two, along with the other parts of the book, contains chapters that draw from the disciplines of sociology, social policy, psychology and social work. All the chapters in this part highlight the importance of not taking things for granted and of questioning the basis of our beliefs. The social issues identified here all have consequences, often negative ones, for individuals and for society; such is the power of panics.

Chapter Six, by Ian Butler, sets out the big picture facing social work and social workers. He outlines the propensity for panic that surrounds social work with children and families, especially when, as is inevitably the case, a tragedy occurs. Professor Butler makes the telling point that, while tragedies frequently happen, it takes a certain conjunction of political and economic conditions for one to become a 'cause célèbre' in which social workers are pilloried as the whipping boys (and girls) for societal consciences, as mediated through the opinion writers and editors of the press.

The remaining four chapters in this part explore how moral panic work might help us to grasp the essence of concerns relating to child trafficking, childhood, the internet and child sexual abuse and, one of the most recent manifestations of alarm, child sexual exploitation. Joanne Westwood's Chapter Seven looks at the contemporary concerns surrounding child trafficking. She draws on historical examples of panic surrounding child trafficking and identifies continuities in the ways that the issue was discussed in the 19th century and today, pointing out the sensationalist tones that work to mask the structural causes that underpin trafficking. In Chapter Eight Kay Tisdall takes a key aspect of moral panic work, claims making, and subjects a letter to the press to a thorough analysis of the various claims contained within it, the implicit moralising about childhood and good and bad parenting, and considers the various personal claims inherent in the list of signatories. In Chapter Nine, about child pornography, Ethel Quayle asks us to look at where our gaze is drawn to and, just as important, where it is drawn away from. Also pointed out is the disproportionate emphasis on the dangers of the internet, to the detriment of its benefits. Chapter Ten, by Anneke Meyer, analyses the various contentions, claims and concerns that have arisen in the aftermath of the publication of an inquiry into child sexual exploitation in one UK city.

The different contributions in the other parts of this volume have subject matter in common, in that material and discussion points about young people, children and childhood will also be found elsewhere, for instance Part One, on gender and the family, has a contribution about moral panics in Italy that include children. In Part Three, on the state, the issue of children and the internet is addressed. This is probably inevitable, in that panics about young people and children draw in adults, families and the state. In addition, such panics raise big questions about morals, moralising and those that moralise – the subject matter of Part Four, on moral crusades. Such unifying demonstrates the utility of a moral panic lens. While we do not expect total agreement, we hope that Part Two will not only help to illuminate the subject matter covered in other parts but also stimulate interest in adopting a greater scepticism when, as is inevitable, a fresh 'urgent' worry about children emerges and makes claims on us.

References

Berry, L. (2008) 'Review of *Hooligan: A History of Respectable Fears'*, *British Journal of Social Work*, vol 38, no 4, pp 830–2.

Pearson, G. (1975) *The deviant imagination*, New Jersey: Holmes & Meier Publishers.

Pearson, G. (1983) *Hooligan: A history of respectable fears*, Basingstoke: Macmillan.

Pearson, G. (1987) *The new heroin users*, Oxford: Basil Blackwell.

Scarman, Lord (1981) *The Brixton disorders, 10–12 April 1981*, London: HMSO.

SIX

Child protection and moral panic

Ian Butler

Introduction

> A condition, episode, person or group of persons emerges to
> become defined as a threat to societal values and interests; its
> nature is presented in a stylised and stereotypical fashion by
> the mass media; the moral barricades are manned by editors,
> bishops, politicians and other right-thinking people; socially
> accredited experts pronounce their diagnoses and solutions;
> ways of coping are evolved or (more often) resorted to.
> (Cohen, 1972, p 9)

As well as providing an enduring and invaluable analytical tool for
understanding the politics of control and the manufacture of social
order, in this definition of a moral panic Cohen also inadvertently
captured almost exactly how working in child protection has felt for the
last 30 years. The majority of the children's workforce would recognise
the sense of threat; the over-simplifications; the moral outrage; the
endless and seemingly futile attempts to 'never let this happen again'
and the many, many ways in which countless experts have pointed out
how the job might be better done.

This chapter will argue that by applying Cohen's analysis to the social
practice of child protection, particularly to those cases that achieve the
status of a national 'scandal', we can learn far more about the politics of
welfare and the state's relationship to troubled and troublesome families
than we can ever learn about how to look after vulnerable children.
In particular, it will explore how iconic child deaths can be used to
construct a 'condition, episode, person or group of persons ... defined
as a threat to societal values and interests' – the idea at the core of what
is implied by Cohen's formulation of a moral panic.

Learning from our mistakes

This is not to wholly set aside the improvements in child-protection practice that have derived from the innumerable public inquiry reports, Serious Case Reviews and Individual Management Reviews that have been published over the last 30 years. I would suggest, however, that the gains are increasingly marginal, except in so far as they promote compliance with existing protocols, as most such reports have become formulaic and repetitive.

One might even argue, particularly in relation to the more widely known cases, that they have had the opposite effect as far as protecting children is concerned. For example, the cumulative effect of reporting child abuse by reference only to its most notorious failures, often involving the death of a child, is to reinforce the view that child abuse is sporadic, dramatic and perpetrated only by monsters. We know, on the other hand, that much child abuse is systemic, incredibly ordinary in many ways and perpetrated across the whole social and psychological spectrum.

The consequence of this is that, for at least 30 years, public, political and professional focus has remained on the mechanisms of regulation rather than on the mechanisms of causation as far as child abuse is concerned. Public policy focuses much more on the training and management of the workforce than it does on the causes and correlates of child abuse; practitioners talk about 'safeguarding' but less about 'promoting welfare' (see section 17 of the Children Act 1989) and the popular imagination focuses on the failures of social workers much more frequently than on the failures of the political and social contexts in which they operate.

Where the study of such cases is more useful, perhaps, is in what they tell us about the contemporary state of social work as a form of social practice and about how certain individuals and families are understood and managed by the state. It is in this sense that they can be understood, as per Cohen's original definition, if not as a form, then as instruments of moral panic and, in that sense, part of the politics of control.

Scandals

I have described elsewhere (Butler and Drakeford, 2003; 2005) how scandals are not haphazard events that arise from specific, exceptional practice failures. Rather, they are very likely – if not inevitable – only in very particular circumstances, and they arise, build and subside in a consistent and predictable way.

They arise and fall at key points of transition in societal values and interests and at specific moments in the transition of public policy affecting certain groups of individuals and families; in short, at points of major upheaval in the nature, scope and operation of the welfare state. By the same token, where there is no fundamental tension in a particular policy field or in the societal attitudes and values in which it is embedded, there are no scandals – no matter how grievously young people may suffer. Where scandals do not occur is just as interesting as where they do. For example, broadly speaking, the youth justice 'arms race' since the mid-1990s, whereby successive governments have sought to be tougher on crime and criminals than their predecessors, has met with little opposition, and despite over 20 years of Chief Inspector of Prisons Reports that testify to the endemic bullying, atrocious living conditions and ill-treatment of children and young adults in custody there has been hardly a trace of scandal (Drakeford and Butler, 2007).

It is important therefore to distinguish between the underlying events that form the basis of a scandal and the scandal itself. Scandals do not happen because children die or are seriously harmed at the hands of their parents or those responsible for their care. These may be necessary conditions, but they are far from sufficient.

Children die at the hands of those who are supposed to be looking after them almost every week of the year, every year. These deaths are certainly tragedies, but they are not scandals. Almost all such child deaths remain known to only a small number of relatives and professionals. In that sense, by far the majority of child deaths remain within the relatively private domain. Scandals occur when such routine, almost domestic affairs, become public property in a way that excites sustained or intense interest and that calls for explanation.

Scandals are formed from highly selected cases. It is true that events that become scandalised will often share certain common characteristics; 'pantomime' heroes and villains; a degree of foreignness or the exotic; an element of the macabre; a contradiction between the scene of the scandal and the ostensible purpose of such places (for example, a child is not supposed to be injured by its parents, harmed by its doctor and so on), but even these are not necessary.

In any case, this is not a complete definition of a scandal. So far the events would amount to no more than 'news' and not every child death even makes it into the news. For what might amount to a no more than a news story to become a scandal, the underlying events somehow have to come to be regarded as symptomatic or emblematic of something far more widespread than the specific instance.

What is odd, though, is that what is newsworthy to a wider audience and potential material for a scandal might not appear in the least bit wrong or unusual to those on the 'inside'. In almost all of the welfare scandals since 1965, the events described are to many of those closest to them no more than simply business as usual. What happens is that the events that lie at the core of a scandal take on a significance and a set of meanings that were not obvious to those most closely associated with them. Many of these meanings derive from the underlying, subterranean policy pressures and the transformations that are underway; although they may also become the site across which a whole variety of political and moral hobby-horses are ridden. A number of these have been described in detail elsewhere – the death penalty in Colwell or latent racism in Climbié, for example (Butler and Drakeford, 2003; 2005; 2011).

In that sense, scandals don't just happen, and certainly they don't just happen because things 'go wrong' – things go wrong every day. Scandals are constructed. New meanings are applied to events that are quite different to those applied to the same events by those who inhabit the world in which the scandal originates – it is at this point that the connection between iconic child deaths and Cohen's fundamental account of a moral panic becomes more obvious.

Even when the underlying events are quite clearly outrages in any terms (such as murder or sexual abuse), in order to be scandalised, the events have to be transformed from the familiar and mundane into the public and symbolic, and for that, sustained interest from wider constituencies of interest is critical. That process of transformation begins with discovery. Someone becomes aware of certain events and wants something done about them. They might be a whistle-blower from within an institution, the relative of someone affected by the events at the core of the scandal or a complete outsider with an agenda of their own.

Discovery is not enough, however. The audience for the discovery needs to be widened. The public have to hear and have their interest engaged, and here the media have an important part to play in the construction of a scandal. This presupposes that there is an audience for the scandal. This goes to the heart of the scandalising process, especially when one considers that the events that lie at the heart of a scandal might have gone on for years.

'Why does this matter now?' is the most important question to answer in understanding any scandal. It is at this point that we begin to get a sense of what the fundamental issues are, of which the scandal is merely the outward representation.

One of the key players in the scandal process is the Public Inquiry. Inquiries should not be seen as neutral events. Almost all of them are set up apparently to 'establish the facts', but in doing so the Inquiry is itself an active player in the struggle to make sense of what has happened, adding its own voice to the construction of events. The reports that they produce, the most enduring record of the 'truth' of what happened, in their choice of language, tone and internal structure can add or change our understanding of what the 'facts' were.

Elsewhere and at greater length than this chapter will permit, Mark Drakeford and I have provided many examples of why certain scandals appear and disappear and try to locate them in their sociopolitical context (Butler and Drakeford, 2003; 2005). One of the threads that we have tried to follow in our work is what successive scandals tell us about the state of social work at a particular time. In the Colwell case (Butler and Drakeford, 2011), for example, it was precisely the arriviste and potentially dangerous profession of social work that was 'on trial'. More broadly, however, beyond the tragic circumstances of one child in a particular family, in the hands of Sir Keith Joseph and, later, David Owen, Barbara Castle, James Callaghan and Harold Wilson, the case became an opportunity by which a new set of relationships between the state and its more troubled and troubling families was debated and a site where the architecture of the welfare state was reconfigured in the face of the economic necessities of the 1970s, rather than the 1948 consensus on which it had been built.

While other tensions were debated, such as the death penalty or where the balance should fall in relation to 'tug-of-love' cases, the Colwell scandal was essentially about the difference between a 'problem family' and a 'family with problems' and how the state, and its social workers in particular, should respond in the post-Seebohm, oil-crisis, three-day-week world in which the Colwell case was constructed. It may be worth recalling that it was the Colwell case that paved the way for the first wave of virulent antisocial work media coverage that ran through the reporting of the inquiries into the deaths of Heidi Koseda, Kimberley Carlile and Tyra Henry that clustered after the Jasmine Beckford case and that continued, with occasional lulls, right through the 1980s to the Cleveland Inquiry – a period that saw what one commentator called the emergence of the 'peculiarly British sport of social worker baiting' (Greenland, 1986, p 164).

In terms of Cohen's initial formulation, in this wave of moral panic it was the practice and practitioners of social work as well as certain types of 'problem' family that were clearly identified as the 'condition, episode, person or group of persons' that had emerged 'to become defined as a threat to societal values and interests'.

Peter Connelly and the politics of neoliberalism

The most recent iconic case, that of Peter Connelly, speaks to another set of sociopolitical stresses: the identification of new 'threats' and a new set of moral barricades to erect. In this instance, the process of discovery and the generation of the scandal apparently owed more to the press than to an inquiry, a court judgment or a specific 'outsider' (but see Jones, 2014 for a compelling and disturbing account of the web of political and journalistic intrigue that surrounds this case). Space does not permit a detailed exploration of how the worst excesses of tabloid reporting woefully and reprehensibly wove a web of meaning around a child's tragic death, largely for immediate political purposes of their own. There was the familiar virulent misogyny aimed at the key protagonists; the implicit racism in the tabloid accounts that lingered over what was portrayed as the sinister and foreign-sounding consultant who had failed to diagnose Peter Connelly's severe spinal injuries; and there was much of the 'political correctness gone mad' theme that was perhaps best summed up in the *Sun*'s 14 November 2008 headline 'Incompetent, politically correct and anti-white'.

More importantly for our purposes, the Connelly case provided an important illustration of and an opportunity to justify a marked shift in societal attitudes towards the kinds of families that Peter Connelly's came to typify and to signal a decisive shift in the politics of welfare.

Even at the point where the Connelly case entered the media (through a heated exchange between the Prime Minister, Gordon Brown and David Cameron, the Leader of the Opposition, on 12 November 2008 as part of Prime Minister's Questions in the UK Parliament), the symbolic nature of the case took precedence over the mere facts and even over the child himself:

> Let's be clear. This is a story [sic] about a 17 year old girl who had no idea how to bring up a child. It is about a boyfriend who could not read but could beat a child, and it's about a social services department that gets £100M per year and cannot look after children. (*Hansard*, 2008)

The potential of the Connelly case to provide the embodiment of the 'Broken Britain' narrative that Cameron hints at here and that was to become important in the Conservative Party's 2010 general election campaign was eloquently captured in an article in the *Observer* in August 2009 (Anthony, 2009). Here, the 'bland and unremarkable ... shabby pre-war slice of suburbia' that was Connelly's home is revealed to contain

> all the potent symbols and sordid realities of the feckless, desensitised version of contemporary life.
> Hardcore pornography, internet chat sites, vodka bottles, attack dogs, animal faeces, fleas, lice, Nazi paraphernalia, knives and replica guns formed the harsh backdrop to Peter's truncated life and brutal death.

The two families at the heart of Anthony's narrative:

> were always unlikely to heal each other's brutalised psyches and self-inflicted wounds. When they came together, they instead turned a grim domestic drama into a social tragedy that reverberated far beyond the squalid confines of their semi-detached Tottenham home.

Part of Anthony's message is the same as Cameron's: that this is not so much a failure by the welfare state, in the person of the hapless social worker, but a failure of the welfare state in that it was the welfare state that created families such as that in which Peter Connelly lived and died:

> it is also a function of a welfare system that allocates subsidies and material security to those with children. The noble intention is to arrest economic deprivation at birth, yet too often it helps foster the very conditions it seeks to combat. The more the state intervenes, the more it is required to intervene and therefore the more chance that its intervention will, as in the case of Baby P, not be enough....
> There is no easy solution to the societal malaise this case highlights, but the fact remains, as many social workers will testify, there is a growing class of state dependants who have gained few if any life skills other than an ability to work the system.

To a limited degree, social work is again a focus for opprobrium but, in reality, it is not a major casualty — at least as a profession. While social workers were busying themselves over which College not to join and sorting out their HCPC from their SWRB application forms, the profession had already moved to the political margins. The real focus of the Connelly scandal, those around whom a panic was being engendered, to return to the specific theme of this chapter, are the individuals and families that social work once sought to help, to empower and on whose behalf the profession once advocated.

After the general election of May 2010, the rhetoric, used both in the media and politically to invoke such families became much more shrill and unpleasant and perhaps reached its peak around the introduction, in December 2011, of the 'Troubled Families' project (TFP) (see Butler, 2014 for a more detailed account). The TFP was seen by Prime Minister Cameron as part of the 'social recovery' that he believed Britain needed as much as any economic 'recovery'. According to Cameron, 'while the government's immediate duty is to deal with the budget deficit my mission in politics – the thing I am really passionate about – is fixing the responsibility deficit' (Cabinet Office, 2011).

The TFP was to be as much an exercise in remoralising as it was in welfare selectivity. Beyond that, it is also an exercise in reframing the general perception of those at the margins of society as somehow responsible for their own conditions and beyond the capacity or the willingness of the state to help, precisely as Anthony's article in the *Observer* had suggested and which the Connelly case seemed to exemplify.

It is not necessary to elaborate here the glee with which the right-wing press in the UK echoed and amplified these sentiments as it awaited the arrival of the 'crack teams' that would soon 'turn up at people's homes to get them out of bed for work, make sure their children go to school or ensure alcoholics or drug addicts go to rehab' (*Daily Mail*, 18 October 2011; see also Jensen, 2013).

Of course the proximate origins of the TFP lay in the riots of the summer of 2011. However, it is important to note the continuity in tone and language in the media representation of the TFP at its launch and subsequently. It is an extension of what Tyler (2013, para 3.1) tellingly calls the 'scum semiotics' that characterised political and media accounts of the 2011 riots.

The subterranean currents that flowed in and out of the 2011 riots and into the TFP run deep in the politics of neoliberalism and signal a decisive move away from Keynesian economics, post-war collectivism and welfare universalism that has characterised much of the politics of the global North in the last 20 years. Indeed, curbing the 'social turmoil generated at the foot of the urban order by public policies of market deregulation and social welfare retrenchment' (Wacquant, 2010, p 210) is a significant structural innovation and a 'major transnational political project' (Wacquant, 2010, p 213) (see also Bauman, 2004; Harvey, 2005; Davies, 2011).

This is a great deal for one short life and brutal death to carry.

Conclusion

Scandals such as the Connelly case provide a biography; a photograph; an address; a real life story around which opinions and attitudes can crystallise to fuel or signal the development of a moral panic. Their lasting value is not in developing the capacity to protect children but to alert us to the interests, motives and agendas of those who express moral outrage and to the varied analyses of 'politicians and other right-thinking people' who will in turn 'pronounce their diagnoses and solutions'.

This is why there will always be welfare scandals; not because professional practice is infinitely perfectible but because the state continuously defines and redefines its relationship to certain of its citizens, particularly those who, arguably, need its protection most.

References

Anthony, A. (2009) 'The killers of Baby P came from decades of abuse and dysfunction', *Observer* (16 August).

Bauman, Z. (2004) *Wasted lives: Modernity and its outcasts*, Cambridge: Polity Press.

Butler, I. (2014) 'New families, new governance and old habits', *Journal of Social Welfare and Family Law*, vol 36, no 4, pp 415–25.

Butler, I. and Drakeford, M. (2003) *Social policy, social welfare and scandal: How British public policy is made*, London: Palgrave Macmillan.

Butler, I. and Drakeford, M. (2005) *Scandal, social policy and social welfare* (2nd rev. edn), Bristol: Policy Press/BASW.

Butler, I. and Drakeford, M. (2011) *Social work on trial: The Colwell Inquiry and the state of welfare*, Bristol: Policy Press.

Cabinet Office (2011) *Troubled Families Speech*, www.gov.uk/government/speeches/troubled-families-speech

Cohen, S. (1972) *Folk devils and moral panics*, London: MacGibbon and Kee.

Daily Mail (2011) 'Helping 100,000 troubled families has saved the taxpayer £1.2BILLION by cutting crime and benefits, says Eric Pickles', *Daily Mail* (18 October), www.dailymail.co.uk/news/article-2988128/Helping-100-000-troubled-families-saved-taxpayer-1-2BILLION-cutting-crime-benefits-says-Eric-Pickles

Davies, J.S. (2011) *Challenging governance theory: From networks to hegemony*, Bristol: Policy Press.

Drakeford, M. and Butler, I. (2007) 'Everyday tragedies: justice, scandal and young people in contemporary Britain', *Howard Journal of Criminal Justice*, vol 46, no 3, pp 219–325.

Greenland, C. (1986) 'Inquiries into child abuse and neglect (CAN) deaths in the United Kingdom', *British Journal of Criminology*, vol 26, no 2, pp 164–72.

Hansard (2008) House of Commons Debate (28 November), *Hansard*, vol 482, part 162, col 762.

Harvey, D. (2005) *A brief history of neoliberalism*, Oxford: Oxford University Press.

Jensen, T. (2013) 'Riots, restraint and the new cultural politics of wanting', *Sociological Research Online*, vol 18, no 4, www.socresonline.org.uk/18/4/7.html

Jones, R. (2014) *The story of Baby P: Setting the record straight*, Bristol: Policy Press.

Tyler, I. (2013) 'The riots of the underclass? Stigmatisation, mediation and the government of poverty and disadvantage in neoliberal Britain', *Sociological Research Online*, vol 18, no 4, p 6, www.socresonline.org.uk/18/4/6.html

Wacquant, L. (2010) 'Crafting the neoliberal state: Workfare, prisonfare and social insecurity' *Sociological Forum* vol 25, no 2, pp 197–220.

SEVEN

Unearthing melodrama: moral panic theory and the enduring characterisation of child trafficking

Joanne Westwood

Introduction

The issue of child trafficking came to prominence in the early part of the 21st century as international migrations of children became more visible in the UK, attracting the attention of non-governmental organisations (NGOs), politicians and the national news media. The trafficking of children is not a new phenomenon; in the late 19th century campaigners were successful in lobbying for an increase in the age of consent, partially as a result of the media exposé of the 'white slave trade' orchestrated by the newspaper editor William Stead (Bristow, 1978). The phenomenon of child trafficking has also been previously characterised as a moral panic (Goode and Ben-Yehuda, 1994; Cree et al, 2012). Moral panic writings go some way towards explaining the conditions that provide fertile ground for the amplification of risk that is embedded in media representations and policy discourses associated with child trafficking. This chapter will illustrate how the issue of child trafficking continues to be defined, drawing on a model developed from the literary genre of melodrama. The chapter discusses the features of a moral-panic perspective that are relevant to understanding the construction of child trafficking.

What makes this a moral panic?

Moral-panics thinking was originally used to explain the crisis in policing of young people (Cohen, 1972) and has been applied to many social issues in the intervening period (Goode and Ben-Yehuda, 1994; Critcher, 2003). Thompson (1998) identifies a number of common features of a moral panic: there is a campaign or a crusade over a period of time; the issues appeal to those who are concerned in some way about social breakdown; there is a lack of clarity in moral guidelines; politicians and the media are found to be at the head of public debates; and, finally, the real causes of the problems that give rise to a moral panic remain unaddressed. Factors of central importance in understanding an issue as a moral panic are that concerns about behaviour are met with increasing hostility and the issue becomes publicly visible. The issue is represented in disproportionate terms, in that the groups who push social concerns up the political and public agenda do so by constructing the issue as good versus evil and heighten sensitivity by focusing on the worst-case scenario as if it were representative (Thompson, 1998).

Goode and Ben-Yehuda (1994) applied a discussion of moral panic theory to a child trafficking event in Orleans in France in May 1969. Moral panic theory has also previously been drawn on to explain the way in which the 'white slave trade' appeared on the 19th- and 20th-century policy agendas (Doezema, 2001). Methods used by the reform campaigners of the late 19th century had a strong influence on feminist politics and campaigning, particularly those used by the reformer Josephine Butler and her supporters, including the infamous editor of *The Pall Mall Gazette*, William Stead, who ran the infamous exposé: The Maiden Tribute of Modern Babylon Series (Gorham, 1978; Walkowitz, 1992). In more recent work Cree et al (2012) examine this event and the establishment of the UK's Child Exploitation and Online Protection Centre (CEOPS) through a moral panic lens and argue that the emphasis then as now is on the sexual-exploitation aspects of trafficking; other more mundane and less sensationalist reasons for trafficking – domestic care and agricultural work, for example, tend to be overshadowed.

Scale of the problem and proportionality of the response

Despite the development of UK policy responses and the publication of *The UK Action Plan on Tackling Human Trafficking* (Home Office and Scottish Executive 2007) and the practice guidance *Working together to safeguard children who may have been trafficked* (HM Government, 2011), the research literature on the issue of child trafficking in the UK is sparse. A feature of UK NGO publications is a reliance on press reports as evidence of the phenomenon of child trafficking. HM Government (2011) reports that around 300 children are trafficked into the UK annually, and issues a warning that numbers will increase as agencies understand the signs of child trafficking:

there may be little evidence of any pre-existing relationship between the child and the accompanying adult or even no knowledge about the person who will care for the child. There may be unsatisfactory accommodation in the UK, or perhaps no evidence of parental permission for the child to travel to the UK or stay with the sponsor. These irregularities may be the only indication that the child could be a victim of trafficking (HM Government, 2011, pp 7–8).

The issue of children coming to the UK is therefore understood as a problem because children are separated from their parents, families and communities; this distance between and separateness from their origins and immediate family is perceived in policy terms as being laden with risks and vulnerabilities.

The conditions in which it took place

In relation to the causes of child trafficking, the policy approaches are overly reliant on simplistic demand/supply explanations of child trafficking, or familial dysfunction, and are particularly associated with trafficking for commercial sexual exploitation and, as a result, draw heavily on the language of child protection where children are 'groomed' or otherwise constructed as witless victims. This position obscures the need for a more detailed analysis of children's experiences: the ways in which children arrive into the UK, closer examination of the relationships between children and the people who bring them; and the variety of factors that promote children's migrations. UK policy approaches to date towards migrant children coming without or with their families reflect a desire to protect and sustain a rigid asylum and immigration system. These measures are ostensibly designed to stop independent migrations because of the potential risks of trafficking and future exploitation.

These policies were all developed within a wider political context of increased border control and national security, and were enacted in order to address the perceived threat of immigration and international terrorism. Additionally, the economic threats to the UK of unchecked immigration were emphasised. The immigration context of policy making has come in for sharp criticism from anti-trafficking organisations and agencies, and there are widely expressed concerns that these responses do not address the trafficking in children because of the hidden nature of the crime and the exploitation children are said to experience. There have been some notable exceptions in the dominant discourse from individuals and state actors who challenge the view that child trafficking is a massive and hidden social problem, and, while these do bring some measured observations to policy debates, they remain minimised and the emphasis remains on immigration and 'safeguarding' at the expense of providing support to meet needs.

Folk devils

Traffickers are depicted as wicked and evil and the narrative in policy documents suggests that trafficking is a global organised trade run by ruthless criminal gangs. There are baddies (the traffickers) and goodies (the victims and the child rescuers). Conversely, the families in children's countries of origin are also depicted as part of the problem of child trafficking. Witless poor, ignorant parents who sell their children into a life of slavery (at worst) or send them to an unknown future in a foreign country with a distant relative or stranger are common explanations found in policy documents and in media reports about child trafficking. These explanations lack context and simplify what are traditional, complicated and reciprocal international familial relationships, obligations and duties that sustain communities and promote cohesion. Children coming to the UK in such circumstances are not sold and their relationships with their families in their countries of origin remain important. The ideology of the family that is promoted in the anti-trafficking policy narratives and media reports is of a specific form and bears little resemblance to a wider understanding of the constitutions of family forms found in different parts of the world.

Claims makers and moral entrepreneurs

Certain groups gain prestige and status and have 'vested interests' in exposing and exaggerating levels of concern about child trafficking. In the UK the NGOs that are party to national and international governmental anti-trafficking activities could be said to have a vested interest in terms of advancing their agendas, and they have previously advocated protective policy measures based on single and extreme cases (that is, the death of Victoria Climbié in London while in the care of her great aunt, to whom she was entrusted by her Côte d'Ivoire parents). The absence of an informed and academic debate on the subject has left space for the emergence of stories about child trafficking that have little basis in reality. The issuing of policy guidance and Home Office-commissioned training, as well as heightened sensitivity, publicity and awareness campaigns orchestrated by NGOs and the media, combine to raise the profile of child trafficking as a growing moral and child-protection threat that requires immediate and sustained action.

Many of the references to risks found in NGO reports about child trafficking are uncritically reproduced in policy documents and guidance. Statements about the hidden harm and the potentially significant numbers of children thought to be at risk of trafficking are also commonplace in the policy discourses. The true scale of the issue is unknown, but commentators and politicians have argued that it is potentially enormous. For example, in October 2004 during a parliamentary debate on the subject of child trafficking, Mr John Bercow, the MP for Buckingham, suggested that parliamentary attention had been "woefully inadequate to the scale of the challenge that we face" (Bercow, 2004). Bercow illustrates the dangers parents are exposing their children to:

> The high profile case of Victoria Climbié, who was trafficked to the UK by her aunt in order to commit benefit fraud … is the tip of the iceberg.… Parents must be made aware that they are not sending their children to a better life when they put them in the hands of traffickers. (Bercow, 2004)

Consequences of the moral panic about child trafficking

As well as highlighting the more sensationalist aspects of the issue, that is, the exploitation and harm, the construction of risk in this way prioritises certain interventions over others. Potential child-trafficking scenarios gain status and determine interventions that might ordinarily be intrusive and disruptive to families. The means are therefore justified by the ends. In policy and practice, children arriving in the UK attract suspicion and interest from immigration and child-safeguarding officials. It is not viewed as essential to have proof or evidence of child trafficking. The fact that families come into the UK as asylum seekers or refugees and children come into the UK unaccompanied is enough to arouse the interest of officials. In their efforts to stop trafficking, advocates and anti-trafficking campaigners have thus legitimised policy, and practice is focused on all groups of migrant children.

In the UK child-trafficking policy discourses are underpinned with harm-prevention and risk-management narratives. More recently, in welfare policies generally, the victim has become a high priority, while certain highly valued ideologies of childhood persist in wider policy discourses. The values and priorities of the policy discourses in terms of child trafficking are emphasised in the narratives of home and family and loss and betrayal. The crisis narratives evident in child-trafficking policy-making discourses also convey a need for urgent and immediate action: something must be done. In addition, what is known about child trafficking is only the tip of the iceberg.

It is clear in the policy discourses that the migration of children poses individual risks to children and wider risks in terms of the UK's border security, and in terms of their vulnerability to being sexually exploited. Critically, child trafficking has come to be understood as being about wider societal and, particularly, sexual threats to children as well as about 'innocent and helpless victims' (Buckland, 2008). In relation to trafficking in women and children the domination of a 'victim trope' together with the positioning of men as predators, abusers, exploiters or crime bosses, legitimates restrictive and punitive policies, again an approach that underestimates the structural factors that lead to migrations (Buckland, 2008, p 43).

Discussion

Although the activities of the 19th-century social puritans and current anti-trafficking activities might be explained as a moral panic (Cohen, 1972) or as a moral crusade (Goode and Ben-Yehuda 1994), this does not fully account for the way in which the risks have been constructed and reconstructed across the historically different contexts. The amplification of risk is a central and enduring feature in moral-panic writings, and risk is amplified in the case of child trafficking using melodramatic tactics. Melodramatic tactics, according to Hadley (1995), are characterised by portrayals of five key themes: familial narratives of dispersal and reunion; visual rendering of bodily torture and criminal conduct; atmospheric menace and providential plotting; expressions of highly charged emotions; and a tendency to personify absolutes like good and evil. Melodramatic tactics are evident in the 19th-century social-purity campaigning activities, serialised style and pseudo-factual story-telling to convey to an unsuspecting public the tragic situations of victims through emotional appeals and righteous indignation. This was a popularised late 19th-century protest format, peculiar to social purity groups of that period (Walkowitz, 1992), and these tactics are evident in their campaigning publications. The concept of melodramatic tactics has further analytical value as applied to contemporary policy and legislation about the issue of child trafficking.

A common strategy in the melodrama of protest is the attempt to amplify concern through the creation of a 'blameless victim':

> to pinpoint a contemporary evil they set up a blameless hero as the victim of the system, and then subject him to such inhuman persecution that the audience explodes with indignation and demands the immediate repeal of laws which perpetuate such cruelties. (Smith, 1973, p 75)

There is only a limited acknowledgement of the 'harms' and 'risks' associated with intractable problems of war, oppression and poverty that are characteristic features of the countries children originate from. The complexities of child migration seemed to be little understood and do not appear as important or relevant in the policy narratives; what is important is tackling the criminal activities of (criminalised) others. Global structural factors that influence migratory flows are avoided, minimised in the narratives, the emphasis being on tackling the crimes of exploitation, and protecting, indeed rescuing, children from the clutches of wicked criminal gangs. These modern melodramatic tactics are also found in the media exposures of child trafficking that are designed to scandalise and shock audiences. This is hardly surprising, given that the media tend to rely upon anti-trafficking NGOs as 'authoritative' sources of information. These melodramatic tactics are evident in parliamentary papers, which are also informed by NGO evidence and provide campaigners with ammunition to lobby for greater protection and, ultimately, restrictions on the migratory movements of children to the UK. The global social inequalities that push children into migration may be occasionally articulated, although this is often to a much lesser extent in the campaigning materials, and the overwhelming emphasis is on exposing and re-exposing the crime, the villains and a 'suffering children' experience.

Conclusion

There is no doubt that children are brought to the UK and are exploited and abused here. The numbers of children subjected to exploitation in this way are small, and yet policy responses have been swift and all-encompassing in terms of both preventing children from coming into the UK and the depth of official suspicion of those who successfully navigate their way here. The policy responses to child trafficking as discussed in this chapter are disproportionate to the issue and suggest that the problem is widespread and growing, with countless numbers of children at risk or vulnerable to being trafficked.

The UK establishment, media, policy makers and anti-trafficking campaigners in the 21st century have employed well-rehearsed methods for characterising child trafficking as a moral issue, using melodramatic tactics to arouse public indignation and anger at the exploitation of innocent victims, the historical precursors being evident in the 19th-century campaigns against the 'white slave trade'. It is of course also worth remembering that the organisations that lead these campaigns and maintain public awareness of the abuse and exploitation of children more broadly have a vested interest in ensuring that their work remains high profile. Many of these organisations receive huge amounts of funding to train social workers, and develop toolkits to support child victims, and thus their role is not unbiased.

Melodramatic tactics have further analytical value when examining more broadly child welfare and child abuse issues that are becoming a semi-permanent feature of moral panics as stories of the historical abuse of children dominate the news headlines and arouse public anger and politicians' wrath.

References

Bercow, J. (2004) *Hansard*, 21 October, c.1116–c.1117, www.publications.parliament.uk/pa/cm200304/cmhansrd/vo041021/debtext/41021–32.htm#41021–32_spnew8 (accessed 1 June 2014).

Bristow, E. (1978) *Vice and vigilance: Purity movements in Britain since 1700*, Dublin: Gill and Macmillan.

Buckland, B.S. (2008) 'More than just victims: the truth about human trafficking', *Public Policy Research*, vol 15, no 1, pp 42–7.

Cohen, S. (1972) *Folk devils and moral panics*, London: McGibbon and Kee.

Cree, V., Clapton, G. and Smith, M. (2012) 'The presentation of child trafficking in the UK: an old and new moral panic?', *British Journal of Social Work*, vol 44, no 2, pp 418–33.

Critcher, C. (2003) *Critical readings: Moral panics and the media: issues in cultural and media studies*, Buckingham: Open University Press.

Doezema, J. (2001) 'Ouch! Western feminists' "wounded attachment" to the "third world prostitute"', *Feminist Review*, vol 67, pp 16–38.

Goode, E. and Ben-Yehuda, N. (1994) *Moral panics: The social construction of deviance*, London: Blackwell.

Gorham, D. (1978) 'The "maiden tribute of modern Babylon" re-examined: child prostitution and the idea of childhood in late Victorian England', *Victorian Studies*, vol 21, pp 354–79.

HM Government (2011) *Safeguarding children who may have been trafficked*, London: Department for Education and the Home Office, https://www.gov.uk/government/uploads/system/uploads/attachment_data/file/177033/DFE-00084-2011.pdf.

Hadley, E. (1995) *Melodramatic tactics. Theatricalised dissent in the English marketplace, 1800–1885*, California: Stanford University Press.

Home Office and Scottish Executive (2007) *The UK Action Plan on Tackling Human Trafficking*, Norwich: The Stationery Office.

Smith, J.L. (1973) *Melodrama: The critical idiom*, London: Methuen and Co. Ltd.

Thompson, K. (1998) *Moral panics*, Abingdon: Routledge.

Walkowitz, J.R. (1992) *City of dreadful delights. Narratives of sexual danger in late-Victorian London*, London: Virago.

EIGHT

Lost childhood?

Kay Tisdall

Introduction

The trope of 'lost childhood' is a recurring one within UK newspapers. Every few years, a news article, editorial or letter leads with this idea, causing some media interest and connected articles, but then fades away until the next time. For those in childhood studies, the trope is familiar, drawing on adults' idealisations of childhood based around children's 'pricelessness', innocence and vulnerability. A less familiar way to consider the trope is through the lens of moral panic theory. This chapter brings together concepts from moral panics and childhood studies to help analyse this 'lost childhood' trope. As Garland writes, sociologists using the concepts of moral panics start with scepticism that 'permits the initial observation' to give 'way to a different attitude – one that is more analytic, more explanatory, or perhaps better, more diagnostic' (Garland, 2008, p 21).

The chapter uses one particular example of the 'lost childhood' media articles, a letter published on 23 September 2011 in the UK newspaper the *Telegraph*. The article was titled the 'Erosion of childhood', with the sub-title 'Here is the full letter from more than 200 experts about how childhood is being eroded by a "relentless diet" of advertising and addictive computer games'. The letter was concerned about 'too much, too soon' for children, particularly in relation to 'increasing commercial pressures', starting formal education too early and spending time indoors with screen-based technology. The letter cited the UNICEF (2007) publication on children's well-being (where the UK was ranked at the bottom of 21 OECD countries) as key evidence. It made policy recommendations, including information campaigns on children's developmental needs and avoiding a 'consumerist screen-based life-style', establishing a play-based curriculum in nurseries and primary schools, encouraging outdoor play and connection with nature, and banning marketing directed at children up to the age of seven. Two hundred and twenty-eight people signed the letter.

The following discussion brings together relevant concepts from moral panics – that is, the stages of moral panics and, particularly, 'moral entrepreneurs' – to (re)consider the letter. It will end by reflecting on the implications of the letter's moral claims and the usefulness of moral panic theory to consider this media trope of 'lost childhood'.

Stages to moral panics

Critcher suggests eight stages to moral panics, with respective constituents:

1. Emergence	New and threatening development
2. Media inventory	Stereotyping via folk devils/sensationalism/sensitisation
3. Moral entrepreneurs	Moralisation by pressure groups/politicians/religious leaders/press
4. Experts	Expert confirmation of dangers
5. Elite consensus	Public marginalised/opposition weak
6. Coping and resolution	New laws and/or stricter enforcement
7. Fade away	Volatility with possible reoccurrence
8. Legacy	Moral boundaries and established discourse confirmed (Critcher, 2012).

The 'lost childhood' trope can be traced through the UK media in recent years,[1] including this letter of 2011. It does not, however, move through all of Critcher's eight stages. The first stage, emergence, is evident as the trope positions itself against threatening developments: in the case of this letter, a number of concerns like the UK's low score on children's well-being, high levels of teenage distress and disaffection and consumer pressure on children are present. The letter draws strongly on stages 3 and 4, with what appears to be moralising by moral entrepreneurs, claims to expertise and use of experts. But media interest tends to fade away in a day or two; there are no evident links to new laws, nor stricter enforcement. The trope, then, could be seen as a potential moral panic that never happened (Jackson, 2013). Or it could be a micro-panic, drawing on the idea discussed by McRobbie and Thornton (1995): difficulties in mobilising societal fears and concerns, in a multi-mediated world with multiple voices, lead to a multiplicity of micro-issues and micro-panics, rather than 'classic', fully fledged moral panics (see Goode, 2012).

Moral entrepreneurs

Clapton and colleagues (2013) write about 'moral entrepreneurs' and 'claims-makers' as similar concepts, arising from Cohen (1972) and Jenkins (1992), respectively. Moral entrepreneurs or claims makers involve themselves in 'moralising projects, campaigns and crusades that contribute to the genesis of a moral panic' (Clapton et al, 2013, p 804). They seek to extend the reach of their expertise, in a net-widening effect (Clapton et al, 2013, p 805). The letter makes it easy to consider the moral entrepreneurs and the claims makers in this particular example. The text, and the accompanying story, did not originate in the *Telegraph*; a core group of people organised the letter, recruited others to sign and then submitted it to the newspaper.

All signatories use a first name and a surname. They then differ on whether they give a formal prefix (usually only if Professor or Doctor), their position (for example Chief Executive or MP), and/or an organisational affiliation. Many people put forward more than one affiliation or disciplinary connection. Of the 228 signatories, over one-third connect themselves to a university position, while a further number state a university affiliation. Seven people affiliate themselves with teachers' unions, while at least 26 affiliate themselves with a voluntary organisation or charitable trust. But the largest number do not have a clear organisational connection, instead describing themselves as consultants or by profession (for example, general practitioner). In terms of profession or disciplinary focus, at least 20% are connected to psychology, developmental psychology or psychotherapy, while 25% are connected to play, early years or education.

Twenty-six people (11%) describe themselves as authors (and a further two are well-known fiction writers). Some authors write literary fiction (for example, Phillip Pullman), while others write advice books or accessible non-fiction about children. A smattering of other signatories include politicians, police and religious figures. Only three people identify themselves as a parent or grandparent. It is not evident that any child signed the letter.

The identities chosen by signatories suggest particular forms of claims making. The predominance of academic and professional positions subtly stresses expertise and professionalism: here are experts in their fields. The signatories largely do not appeal to political identities, with few signatories describing themselves as politicians: this letter is 'above party politics', 'speaking professional truth to power'.[2] The few signatories who *do* identify themselves as a grandparent or parent highlight that *most* do not. Many more of the 228 signatories are likely to be parents or grandparents, but this is an identity that most do not foreground. Considering the above, the letter puts forward the signatories as authoritative and persuasive *as experts*. This is recognised by the *Telegraph*'s strapline, which refers to '200 experts'.

Yet, the letter also seeks to appeal more widely. The evidence cited in the letter is from UNICEF and 'international league tables' but the letter goes on to make claims about parents being 'deeply concerned' about the erosion of childhood in Britain since 2006. It refers to 'our children' being subjected to increasing commercial pressures. In the final paragraph the letter asserts that 'It is everyone's responsibility to challenge policy-making and cultural developments', and a unified voice 'from the grass roots' is required. The letter thus moves from referring generally to evidence, which does have a research base, to claims about parents and 'our children' that are rhetorical (with no evidence base cited), to positioning itself from the grassroots. The letter thus progresses from a stance of expertise to seeking to depict itself as a grassroots movement. This skilful development in three paragraphs provides an appealing and persuasive narrative.

The morality within the trope

Garland reminds us of the *moral* in 'moral panics', two elements that he argues as essential to Cohen's original concept:

> (i) the moral dimension of the social reaction, particularly the introspective soul-searching that accompanies these episodes; and (ii) the idea that the deviant conduct in question is somehow *symptomatic*. (Garland, 2008, p 11)

What moral concerns are evident in the letter? And how are the concerns, the deviant conduct, symptomatic of broader issues?

To those who read the classics in the childhood studies' literature, the letter makes very familiar appeals. For example, Zelizer wrote a seminal book in 1985, titled *Pricing the Priceless Child: The Changing Social Value of Children*. Writing about the US, she suggests that children's contributions to households are economically worthless but emotionally 'priceless'. Children's value lies in their ability to give meaning and fulfilment to their parents' lives. For parents, protecting their children, protecting the 'preciousness of childhood', seeking to provide their own children with the 'perfect childhood' freed from adult worries and concerns, gives them meaning and fulfilment. Jenks (1996) writes of prevailing, dichotomous perceptions of childhood, which he labels Dionysian and Apollonian. The former considers children as inherently sinful, needing constraint; the latter perceives children as innocent, needing nurturance. The innocent child is frequently associated with Rousseau (writing in the 18th century) and ideas about children being inherently closer to nature, and subsequent ideas about childcare and education (see James et al, 1998).

These well-rehearsed constructions of childhood are evident in the letter. The nostalgic ideas of childhood preciousness and innocence are demonstrated by the concerns about children having 'too much, too soon' and 'growing up too quickly'. Instead, to draw on Rousseau-like ideas, children should be outdoors, playing and 'connected to nature'. The letter expresses a particular concern about modern technology, which in the second paragraph becomes narrowed to 'screen-based technology' and is frequently paired with commercial pressures. Children should be protected from such technology and commercialisation, kept away rather than empowered to engage with it (see Buckingham, 2011 for a discussion of childhood constructions within consumer culture).

Childhood studies makes a distinction between children and childhood. Individual children are at a particular life stage and most will grow out of being children, in due course. They may remain relationally someone's children but, at least in the UK, will become legally and socially 'adults'. Childhood, in contrast, is a permanent feature of social structures, one that can be analysed generationally (Qvortrup, 2009). As described above, the letter is more about a particular notion of childhood than about individual children.

Indeed, the letter can be characterised, following Zelizer and Jenks, as being more about parenthood, adulthood and societal concerns than about childhood itself. For example, Hendrick (1997) writes insightfully about childhood in the 19th century, where health, child development and educational interests focused on children as 'the future of the nation' (influenced by the official discovery of the poor health of potential British recruits to the Boer War). Similarly, the letter refers to international league tables (UNICEF's well-being, teenage distress and disaffection), suggesting children's poor showing in international comparisons – and, presumably, international competition. The second paragraph of the letter starts 'Although parents are deeply concerned about this issue …'; it does not start with children having concerns about this issue, citing no evidence directly from children. In web comments on the letter, contributors write vociferously about the responsibilities and irresponsibility of parents and teachers. In this way, the letter is symptomatic of wider concerns about parenting, societal functioning and 'the future of the nation'.

The letter largely does not appeal to another trope within the UK, that of children's human rights and dignity (see Tisdall, 2014). There is mention in the final paragraph about the need to 'find a more human way to nurture and empower all our children'. Empowerment has connections with social movements and freedom from oppression (see Teamey and Hinton, 2014), but it also has been criticised for being unduly individualistic and failing to confront institutional and structural power sufficiently (Cornwall and Brock, 2005). The particular expression in the letter is 'top-down', suggesting that children will be empowered, rather than empower themselves. The letter does not discuss children's on-going contributions to their families, households and communities, and there is no mention of agency – a key concept within childhood studies that recognises children as social actors (see James, 2009; Oswell, 2013). These moral claims, therefore, are not made.

The letter instead appeals to particular constructions of childhood. These constructions of an *idealised* childhood, a version of which may have existed for some children in some places (and indeed for some of the adults signing the letter). But historical and global evidence of children and childhood shows that childhood was and is often a time of work as well as of play, of experiencing the hardships of poverty, illness and disability, conflict and violence as well as of learning and affection (Cunningham, 2005; Wells, 2009). The letter appeals to a nostalgic view of childhood that may have existed for some, but certainly not across the world, nor over time. By setting up this idealised childhood, however, a childhood that is being 'eroded' and 'lost', the letter sets up 'good' and 'bad' childhood – and 'good' and 'bad' parenting. The letter seems to be as much about monitoring parental choices and behaviour as it is about policy change.

Conclusion

The concepts and theorisations about moral panics are illuminating. Combined with well-rehearsed analyses of how childhood is constructed, historically and more recently, they illuminate the letter's moral work: presenting nostalgic, idealised constructions of childhood that need protection. There is a good childhood – one that is outdoors and connected with nature, focusing on learning through play – and a bad childhood – one that is indoors and obsessed by screen-based technology, pressured by formal learning, tests and targets. The letter is less about children and more about childhood, and less about childhood than about parenthood, especially a category of parent that 'allows' a bad childhood. This analysis underlines the *productivity* of moral panics, the 'culture wars' referred to by Garland (2008), which in this letter redistribute social status between good and bad parents.

A close look at the letter's progression, from paragraph to paragraph, shows an initial appeal to expertise and research evidence, to rhetorical claims to know parental concerns, referring to our children, and placing itself as a grassroots movement in contrast to top-down, political approaches. This both fits and contrasts with the expertise and professionalism expressed within the signatories' identities. The very few claims among the signatories to be parents or grandparents highlight how these are *not* identities listed by most signatories. The moral entrepreneurship may have appealed to the collectivity of parents and grassroots support, but expertise – and even more so, *being* experts – was the strongest claim.

To consider this letter, concepts and theories of moral panic thus help to provide a fresh analysis of familiar ideas within debates about childhood. The lobbying work of a combination of experts and spokespeople, coupled with a particular moral standpoint, could certainly be regarded as claims-making activity and one of the features of the stages of a moral panic. However, Garland reminds us that describing an episode as a moral panic can be merely taking a different moral viewpoint from those who are alarmed. Garland goes further, writing about the 'ethics of attribution', where, empirically, a moral-panic analysis can be applied but 'ethical considerations make the attribution seem tactless, morally insensitive, or otherwise inappropriate' (Garland, 2008, p 24). There is every reason to think that the letter's organisers, and the signatories, were well intentioned, willing to put their energy, their professional standing and their commitment to influencing change. They used familiar tropes and rhetoric, tapping into what the media like to print and tell, which may have made it more likely that the letter would be printed and provided potential for further stories to be generated. If every initiative by civic society is characterised as a moral panic, then this undervalues and undermines people's public action and empties the term of meaning. Whether or not something contributes to a moral panic can often be judged only with the benefit of hindsight, and frequently it is the use to which such expressions are put, rather than the original expression of concern.

This chapter does not want to suggest that the letter, or others like it, are the expressions of, or stimulants to, fully fledged moral panics. They put forward particular ideas of childhood that are, arguably, ahistorical and idealised and convey notions of right and wrong in parenting, but they are seeking to galvanise change to a perceived better goal. The lens of moral panic illuminates the claims being made and the work being done within the text. But the possibility of discussion provides a constructive way forward, where we can look critically at knowledge claims and evidence and debate productively, involving parents, 'experts' – and children – to decide on future policy and practice.

Notes

[1] For example, see M. Narey (2007) '"Toxic childhood" harms British youth', *Telegraph* (13 September), www.telegraph.co.uk/news/uknews/1562980/Toxic-childhood-harms-British-youth.html (accessed 8.7.14); M. Easton (2009) 'Selfish adults "damage childhood"', BBC News (2 February), http://news.bbc.co.uk/1/hi/7861762.stm (accessed 8 July 2014); B. Fenton (2006) 'Junk culture "is poisoning our children"', *Telegraph* (12 September), www.telegraph.co.uk/news/1528642/Junk-culture-is-poisoning-our-children.html (accessed 8 July 2014); Press Association (2014) 'Children's mental health menaced by "unprecedented toxic climate"', *Guardian* (20 January), www.theguardian.com/society/2014/jan/20/children-mental-health-toxic-climate-young-people (accessed 8 July 2014).

[2] Those who organised the letter, with others, moved to develop a group, Early Childhood Action, in February 2012, with the catchphrase on their website 'Fearlessly speaking professional truth to power'. See www.earlychildhoodaction.com/ (accessed 9 July 2014).

References

Buckingham, D. (2011) *The material child: Growing up in consumer culture*, Cambridge: Polity Press.

Clapton, G., Cree, V. and Smith, M. (2013) 'Moral panics, claims-making and child protection in the UK', *British Journal of Social Work*, vol 43, pp 803–12.

Cohen, S. (1972) *Folk devils and moral panics*, St Albans: Paladin.

Cornwall, A. and Brock, K. (2005) 'What do buzzwords do for development policy? A critical look at "participation", "empowerment" and "poverty reduction"', *Third World Quarterly*, vol 26, no 7, pp 1043–60.

Critcher, C. (2012) 'Moral panics and the media: ten years on', presentation at Seminar 1, Moral Panics Seminar Series, 23 September, Edinburgh: Edinburgh University, unpublished.

Cunningham, H. (2005) *Children and childhood in Western society since 1500*, Harlow: Pearson Longman.

Garland, D. (2008) 'On the concept of moral panic', *Crime Media Culture,* vol 4, no 9, pp 9–30.

Goode, E. (2012) 'The moral panic: dead or alive?', presentation at Seminar 1 Moral Panics Seminar Series, 23 September, Edinburgh: Edinburgh University.

Hendrick, H. (1997) 'Constructions and re-constructions of British childhood: an interpretive survey, 1800 to the present', in A. James and A. Prout (eds) *Constructing and reconstructing childhood* (2nd edn), London: Falmer.

Jackson, L. (2013) 'The case of the "good time girl": revisiting the postwar moral panic through the lens of gender', presentation at Seminar 2, Moral Panics Seminar Series, 17 May, Bath: Bath University, http://moralpanicseminars.wordpress.com/seminar-2/ (accessed 9 July 2014).

James, A. (2009) 'Agency', in J. Qvortrup, W.A. Corsaro and M. Honig (eds) *The Palgrave handbook of childhood studies*, Basingstoke: Palgrave, pp 34–45.

James, A., Jenks, C. and Prout, A. (1998) *Theorizing childhood*, Cambridge: Polity Press.

Jenkins, P. (1992) *Intimate enemies: Moral panics in contemporary Britain*, New York: Aldine de Gruyter.

Jenks, C. (1996) *Childhood*, Abingdon: Psychology Press.

McRobbie, A. and Thornton, S. (1995) 'Rethinking "moral panic" for multi-mediated social worlds', *British Journal of Sociology*, vol 46, no 4, pp 559–71.

Oswell, D. (2013) *The agency of children*, Cambridge: Cambridge University Press.

Qvortrup, J. (2009) 'Childhood as a structural form', in J. Qvortrup, W.A. Corsaro and M. Honig (eds) *The Palgrave handbook of childhood studies*, Basingstoke: Palgrave, Basingstoke: Palgrave, pp 21–33.

Teamey, K. and Hinton, R. (2014) 'Reflections on participation and its link with transformative processes', in E.K.M. Tisdall, A.M. Gadda and U.M. Butler (eds) *Children and young people's participation and its transformative potential*, Basingstoke: Palgrave, pp 22–43.

Telegraph (2011) 'Erosion of childhood' (23 September), www.telegraph.co.uk/education/educationnews/8784996/Erosion-of-childhood-letter-with-full-list-of-signatories.html (accessed 9 July 2014).

Tisdall, E.K.M. (2014) 'Children should be seen and heard? Children and young people's participation in the UK', in E.K.M. Tisdall, A.M. Gadda and U.M. Butler (eds) *Children and young people's participation and its transformative potential*, Basingstoke: Palgrave, pp 168–88.

UNICEF Innocenti Centre (2007) *Innocenti Report Card 7: Child poverty in perspective: An overview of child well-being in rich countries*, www.unicef-irc.org/publications/445 (accessed 9 July 2014).

Wells, K. (2009) *Childhood in a global perspective*, Cambridge: Polity Press.

Zelizer, V.A. (1985) *Pricing the priceless child: The changing social value of children*, Princeton, NJ: Princeton University Press.

NINE

Internet risk research and child sexual abuse: a misdirected moral panic?

Ethel Quayle

The collision of recent technological change and fears about sexual risk to children has seemed to polarise debates about online activity by young people and those thought to have a sexual interest in children. Finkelhor (2014) describes the alarmism reflected by scholarly and journalistic literature, which is founded on assumptions about the amplification of deviance, the role and dynamics of the digital environment, and remedies to the problems lying in specialised internet education programmes. He also points out that research findings do not appear to support these assumptions. In many countries, particularly the United States, the rates of child sexual abuse show a decline (Laaksonen et al, 2011; Radford et al, 2011; Finkelhor and Jones, 2012), and only a small proportion of sexual offences against children in the US have an online component (Wolak, Finkelhor and Mitchell, 2009). Bullying, as a form of peer-related aggression, still shows higher rates in face-to-face as opposed to online activity (Livingstone et al, 2011). The US research would also indicate that most online offenders are people who know their victims from offline contexts, and the dynamics of online and offline offenders are similar (Wolak and Finkelhor, 2013), although in the latter analysis the sample reflected two groups that used online communication for sexual communication with a minor. One group was known to the young person in the offline world (family or acquaintances) and the other had first met the young person online, although both used the internet or mobile phone to engage sexually with a minor. In his paper, which was written as a response to Livingstone and Smith (2014), Finkelhor lists many of the positive ways in which technology has facilitated the social development of children, has potentially kept them safe and has provided a buffer to possible harmful risk taking and suggests that it may warrant further exploration 'once the scholarly imagination moves beyond the techno-panic mind set' (Finkelhor, 2014, p 656).

Others have also reminded us that problems such as bullying are serious, and in some cases can lead to suicide, but that this is a serious social problem rather than a technical one (Berg and Breheny, 2014). These authors also note that there have been similar panics in relation to the detrimental effects of subliminal messaging, comic books, cyber pornography and video games on the well-being and behaviour of young people. These concerns do not appear to relate to the demonising of technology per se, but to the fact that in Australia anxieties about harms against children were going to result in a Children's e-Safety Commissioner, with powers to take down material from social media websites, which would represent an increase in government control over the internet and potentially threaten free speech. Other concerns about the impact of technology on the behaviour of young people include fears of ICT-enhanced plagiarism among students (Trushell and Byrne, 2013), as well as companies exploiting a legal loophole to promote unhealthy food and drink consumption through the use of online games (advergames) that include advertisements (www.bbc. co.uk/news/uk-27647445).

Moral panics are generally conceived as a disproportionate public reaction to an event or group that poses a threat to the moral order (Cohen, 1972). The public's fear and unease about the risk of sexual offending against children, and law-enforcement response (or at times a perceived lack of response), have been evident since the 1950s and clearly remain so today. Similarly to the arguments put forward by Finkelhor (2014), it has been suggested that behind all of these constructions there are 'extra-scientific pressures' rather than 'pristine objective reality' (Jenkins, 1998), and that the most recent panics over sex offenders are the consequence of a culture that disproportionately emphasises child protection – and are likely to remain so because of the establishment of the child-welfare movement, health and mental health services and the increased involvement of women in decision making (Fox, 2013). Jenkins (1998) argued that social change has been reinforced by the institutionalisation of the 'child-protection idea' (Jenkins, 1998, p 233) such that it would be unthinkable that any government could seek to return to the status quo of the 1950s or 1960s without facing allegations of 'being soft on child molestation'. Equally, the democratisation of psychiatric and psychological therapies has not only increased access to services but, as suggested by Jenkins (1998), has produced 'a huge constituency with an overwhelming interest in keeping these issues at the center of public concern' (Jenkins, 1998, p 233). Jewkes (2010) suggested that anxieties about crime and safety, and an aversion to risk, have led to a form of social retreat (evidenced in the market for secure housing developments, gated communities, four-wheel-drive vehicles) and that this has resulted, for children and young people, in the denial of freedoms previously enjoyed by their parents. However, paradoxically, the internet is also a form of social retreat, yet potentially provides a freedom of thought, expression and identity presentation unlike anything that young people may have at their disposal in the offline environment. These apparent freedoms may be perceived as a threat to parents' ability to manage their children, particularly in relation to sexual risk taking.

However, Jewkes (2010) has argued that the reason why media stories about child sexual abuse and the internet occupy such a unique place in the collective 'psyche' is because sex, risk and children are three of the twelve cardinal news values that shape news production in the 21st century. This would appear to situate much of the current anxiety about the dangers of the internet for young people in a more overarching anxiety about children and sexual abuse. In the United Kingdom, the last few years have seen a preoccupation with historical and current sexual abuse cases, an obvious example being Operation Yewtree, launched by the police in the wake of the allegations against Jimmy Savile. These stories dominate the popular media and, as suggested by Jewkes, convey the behaviour of adults who are sexually attracted to children and adolescents in extremely negative terms and ignore the complexities of adult–child relations. She argues that constituting the paedophile as the number one folk devil sits oddly with a society that, in areas such as fashion, beauty and art, seeks to fetishise and market youthful bodies. Papadopoulos (2010), author of the Home Office's *Sexualisation of Young People Review* for the British government, presents arguments about the sexualisation of youth that suggest that there is increasing exposure to hyper-sexualised images and that children and young people are also pressured into looking 'sexy' and 'hot'. However, Egan and Hawkes (2012) have argued that the current discourse on sexualisation draws on and reproduces many of the same deeply problematic assumptions regarding the child and its sexuality as purity advocates did over a century ago.

The preoccupation with innocent children and dangerous adults (peer violence outside of bullying does not seem to attract as much attention) sits alongside our excitement and intoxication with the changes brought about by rapid technological development. We are still concerned with sexual abuse, but in some ways (as with celebrity offenders) the internet allows us to position it elsewhere, reinforcing the construction of the dangerous stranger (Jewkes and Wykes, 2012). Ost (2002) suggested a similar moral panic in terms of the threat that child pornography, and those who possess it, is thought to pose to society. As society attempts to tackle the problems of child sexual abuse, tracking down those who possess indecent images of children may be seen as a more attainable goal than eradicating child sexual abuse that may manifest itself in peer circles known to the child or in the family home. Indeed, it may be the very success of law enforcement in successfully arresting those who commit technology-mediated crimes against children that reinforces the likelihood of future investment in this area by both law-enforcement agencies and those who drive policies and legislation. An example from the US of undercover online police operations indicated that interviews with law enforcement about a nationally representative sample of cases ending in arrest for an internet-related sex crime against a minor in 2000 and 2006 suggested a 280% increase in arrests of offenders between the two time periods. The estimated numbers of arrests nationwide grew from 826 to 3,137 (Mitchell et al, 2010).

The success of law enforcement is also mirrored in the increasing number of convictions for possession of indecent images of children (Wolak et al, 2011), which may be a result of higher levels of activity by law enforcement or may reflect a migration of some sexual offending to the online environment. The success of these cases may also relate to the fact that these crimes, unlike many other sexual crimes against children, leave a permanent product in the form of images or texts, which provide clear evidence of a crime's having been committed.

Our concerns about the risks posed by technological change mean that there has been considerable interest in two areas of academic research. The first has examined the similarities and differences between online offenders and contact offenders, and the likelihood of those who possess indecent images of children either having already committed or going on to commit contact offences against children. The second has focused on the vulnerabilities of young people online, and has also led to debates about the prevalence of 'sexting' (sending or receiving sexually explicit images and texts) and its psychological correlates, the majority of them negative (Klettke, Hallford and Mellor, 2014). Only a few voices have argued for a normalcy discourse, suggesting the need for an evidence-based approach to sexting risk prevention that acknowledges both adolescent vulnerability and sexual agency (Döring, 2014). There has been very little interest, outside of victim-identification units within law enforcement, in the children who appear in these indecent images (for example, Svedin and Back, 2003; Quayle and Jones, 2011; Jonsson and Svedin, 2012), other than what they might tell us about the offender (Osborn, Elliott and Beech, 2010; Seto,

Reeves and Jung, 2010). Jenkins (2009) asked the question as to why the issue of child pornography has failed to generate a panic when it appears to fulfil the classic criteria. He suggests that moral-panic theory was founded on a set of implicit value judgements that assumed that the topic under discussion must by definition be bogus or exaggerated. Jenkins argues that 'The understanding of social problems must rely primarily on analysing the rhetorical work of claims-makers and their ability (or lack of it) to appeal to public tastes and prejudices, which may or may not be well founded' (Jenkins, 2009, p 36) and that child pornography offers one instance where there has been a surprising lack of panic. From his own research observing internet bulletin board traffic related to those both using and producing indecent images, he had earlier claimed that the trade in images is considerably greater than had been acknowledged (Jenkins, 2001). This would certainly resonate with the views of many people in law enforcement, although the reality is that we have really no strong basis on which to judge the size of the problem, outside of the databases of known images held by law enforcement. It is difficult to confirm whether the trade in indecent images has increased with the advent of the internet, although one pre-internet study by Schuijer and Rossen (1992) would suggest that at the time of the study the numbers involved in both image production and image use were much smaller, as were the number of children exploited. Jenkins also suggested that many of these images are new or recent and therefore depict the on-going sexual abuse or exploitation of children. His argument of grounds for a moral panic is that the underlying situation is large scale and could easily be portrayed as threatening, particularly because children are central to the problem. It also appears to be an expanding problem (it is difficult for it to be a contracting problem, given that it is a challenge to remove content once it has been widely distributed) and it is certainly global, in that the internet has no obvious geographical boundaries. Jenkins argues that the issue of indecent images also brings in the harmful effects of globalisation, the undermining of national laws and sovereignty, and offers all kinds of additional issues including popular fears about technology and the exploitation of children by sinister men: 'And the demon figures are ready and waiting' (Jenkins, 2001, p 38).

Jenkins (2009) accounts for the lack of moral panic because of the general lack of technical understanding on the part of many people in law enforcement, resulting in an annexing of the problem to the already known issues of child abuse. In addition, there is comprehensive official control of the issue and, as Mirkin (2009) has indicated, access to these images for the purpose of research is problematic, and this may have limited study of this area. There appear to be much bigger concerns about children being exposed to sexual content (for example, Flood, 2009) rather than appearing in images of their abuse. One possibility is that the moral panic that exists in relation to technology and sexual risk has become tangential to sexual abuse with and through the production of indecent images. The majority of people will never have been exposed to such images, and Cooper (2011) has argued that even specialist medical professionals tasked with the care of children have shown a reluctance to engage with law enforcement in the examination of these cases. She suggests that this reluctance relates to many possible factors such as: feelings of aversion to the images; a disbelief that these represent real children; the difficulties of establishing a professional relationship with the images; a failure to appreciate that they represent a crime scene; and the lack of guidelines concerning the procedures for examining such material. The unease expressed in this assessment is mirrored in an observed discomfort on the part of, for example, the judiciary to examine the images related to prosecution cases. While there are strong ethical grounds for limiting access to these images, the result is that for most of us they remain unknown and unknowable. Our gaze is then drawn to those convicted of their possession, and the language used by popular media to describe the 'horrific' collections seized by the police (Travis, 2014) or even the possibility that our children might be exposed to them, while there is much less attention paid to the children depicted in them. The internet is therefore positioned as a place where predators wait to share images of abuse and, more saliently for most people, to catch our children when they are online. Perhaps what fuels these anxieties is the rapid expansion of technology in our everyday lives, with the competitive gallop of companies to produce not just phones but a range of connected devices, from home appliances to door locks and watches, that are able to communicate with each other (Taipei Times, 2014). Atzori, Iera and Morabito (2014) discuss the next development in this 'Internet of Things', which will include social-like capabilities that allow a network to enhance the level of trust between objects that are 'friends' with each other. At one level we are excited by these developments that quickly become embedded in routine activities, such as searching for information, buying tickets, paying bills and expanding our social networks. At another level, we imbue this technology with destructive power and fear for the safety (and control) of our children (Altobelli, 2010) in the face of those who use the internet as a playground for sexual perversion. Lim (2013) points out that the internet is neither a technology of hope nor a weapon of moral destruction; rather, the social impacts of the internet result from an organic interaction between technology and existing social, political and cultural structures. There are consequences to problematising the impact of technological change on the well-being and sexuality of young people. It potentially diverts attention away from the possibilities of technology as protective, providing a forum for risk taking that potentially has fewer consequences (Finkelhor, 2014), and instead results in considerable investment in protective strategies that may have little impact on the behaviour of young people (Mitchell et al, 2010). It may also lead to a diversion of resources away from service provision for children who have been sexually abused, along with less attention being paid to resourcing the identification of children in indecent images, which has not appeared to capture the public imagination or to have produced a claims maker to champion their cause.

References

Altobelli, T. (2010) 'Cyber-abuse – a new worldwide threat to children's rights', *Family Court Review*, vol 48, no 3, pp 459–81.

Atzori, L., Iera, A. and Morabito, G. (2014) 'From "smart objects" to "social objects": the next evolutionary step of the internet of things', *IEEE Communications Magazine*, vol 52, no 1, pp 97–105.

Berg, C. and Breheny, S. (2014) 'The cyberbullying moral panic', *IPA Review*, vol 66, no 1, pp 24–7.

Cohen, S. (1972) *Folk devils and moral panics: The creation of the Mods and Rockers*, London: McGibbon & Kee.

Cooper, S.W. (2011) 'The medical analysis of child sexual abuse images', *Journal of Child Sexual Abuse*, vol 20, no 6, pp 631–42.

Döring, N. (2014) 'Consensual sexting among adolescents: risk prevention through abstinence education or safer sexting?', *Cyberpsychology*, vol 8, no 1, pp 1–18.

Egan, R. and Hawkes, G. (2012) 'Sexuality, youth and the perils of endangered innocence: how history can help us get past the panic', *Gender & Education*, vol 24, no 3, pp 269–84.

Finkelhor, D. (2014) 'Commentary: cause for alarm? Youth and internet risk research – a commentary on Livingstone and Smith (2014)', *Journal of Child Psychology and Psychiatry*, vol 55, no 6, pp 655–8.

Finkelhor, D. and Jones, L.M. (2012) *Have sexual abuse and physical abuse declined since the 1990s?*, Durham, NH: Crimes against Children Research Center, University of New Hampshire.

Flood, M. (2009) 'The harms of pornography exposure among children and young people', *Child Abuse Review*, vol 18, no 6, pp 384–400.

Fox, K.J. (2013) 'Incurable sex offenders, lousy judges and the media: moral panic sustenance in the age of new media', *American Journal of Criminal Justice*, vol 38, pp 160–81.

Jenkins, P. (1998) *Moral panic: Changing concepts of the child molester in modern America*, New Haven, CT: Yale University Press.

Jenkins, P. (2001) *Beyond tolerance: Child pornography on the internet*, New York: New York University Press.

Jenkins, P. (2009) 'Failure to launch: why do some social issues fail to detonate moral panics?' *British Journal of Criminology*, vol 49, pp 35–47.

Jewkes, Y. (2010) 'Much ado about nothing? Representations and realities of online soliciting of children', *Journal of Sexual Aggression*, vol 16, no 1, pp 5–18.

Jewkes, Y. and Wykes, M. (2012) 'Reconstructing the sexual abuse of children: "cyber-paeds", panic and power', *Sexualities*, vol 15, no 8, pp 943–52.

Jonsson, L. and Svedin, C.G. (2012) 'Children within the images', in E. Quayle and K. Ribsil (eds) *Internet child pornography: Understanding and preventing on-line child abuse*, London: Routledge.

Klettke, B., Hallford, D.J. and Mellor, D.J. (2014) 'Sexting prevalence and correlates: A systematic literature review', *Clinical Psychology Review*, vol 34, pp 44–53.

Laaksonen, T., Sariola, H., Johansson, A., Jern, P., Varjonen, M., Von Der Pahlen, B. and Santtila, P. (2011) 'Changes in the prevalence of child sexual abuse, its risk factors, and their associations as a function of age cohort in a Finnish population sample', *Child Abuse & Neglect*, vol 35, no 7, pp 480–90.

Lim, M. (2013) 'The internet and everyday life in Indonesia: A new moral panic?', *Bijdragen tot de Tall-, Land-en Volkenkunde*, vol 169, pp 133–47.

Livingstone, S. and Smith, P.K. (2014) 'Annual research review: harms experienced by child users of online and mobile technologies: the nature, prevalence and management of sexual and aggressive risks in the digital age', *Journal of Child Psychology and Psychiatry*, vol 55, pp 635–54.

Livingstone, S., Haddon, L., Gorzig, A. and Olafsson, K. (2011) *Risks and safety on the internet: The perspective of European children: full findings*, London: LSE, EU Kids Online, http://eprints.lse.ac.uk/33731/.

Mirkin, H. (2009) 'The social, political, and legal construction of the concept of child pornography', *Journal of Homosexuality*, vol 56, pp 233–67.

Mitchell, K., Finkelhor, D., Jones, L. and Wolak, J. (2010) 'Growth and change in undercover online child exploitation investigations, 2000–2006', *Policing & Society*, vol 20, no 4, pp 416–31.

Osborn, J., Elliott, I.A. and Beech, A.R. (2010) 'The use of actuarial risk assessment measures with UK internet child pornography offenders', *Journal of Aggression, Conflict and Peace Research*, vol 2, no 3, pp 16–24.

Ost, S. (2002). 'Children at risk: legal and societal perceptions of the potential threat that the possession of child pornography poses for society', *Journal of Law and Society*, vol 29, no 3, pp 436–60.

Papadopoulos, L. (2010) *Sexualisation of Young People Review*, London: Home Office.

Quayle, E. and Jones, T. (2011) 'Sexualized images of children on the internet', *Sexual Abuse: A Journal of Research & Treatment*, vol 23, no 1, pp 7–21.

Radford, L., Corral, S., Bradley, C., Fisher, H., Basset, C., Howat, N. and Collishaw, S. (2011) *Child abuse and neglect in the UK today*, London: NSPCC.

Schuijer, J. and Rossen, B. (1992) 'The trade in child pornography', *IPT forensics*, 4, cited in Y. Jewkes and M. Yar (eds) *The handbook of internet crime*, Cullompton: Willan.

Seto, M.C., Reeves, L. and Jung, S. (2010) 'Motives for child pornography offending: The explanations given by the offenders', *Journal of Sexual Aggression*, vol 16, pp 169–80.

Svedin, C.G. and Back, K. (2003) *Why didn't they tell us? Sexual abuse in child pornography*, Stockholm: Save the Children Sweden.

Taipei Times (2014) 'Samsung unwraps Tizen for "Internet of Things"', www.taipeitimes.com/News/biz/archives/2014/06/05/2003592005 (accessed 24 July 2014).

Travis, A. (2014) 'Online child abuse images becoming "more extreme, sadistic and violent"', *Guardian* (11 March), www.theguardian.com/society/2014/mar/11/online-child-abuse-images-more-extreme-sadistic-violent.

Trushell, J. and Byrne, K. (2013) 'Education undergraduates and ICT-enhanced academic dishonesty: A moral panic?', *British Journal of Educational Technology*, vol 44, no 1, pp 6–19.

Wolak, J. and Finkelhor, D. (2013) 'Are crimes by online predators different from crimes by sex offenders who know youth in-person?', *The Journal of Adolescent Health*, vol 53, pp 736–41.

Wolak, J., Finkelhor, D. and Mitchell, K.J. (2009) *Trends in arrests of 'online predators'*, Durham, NH: Crimes against Children Research Center, University of New Hampshire.

Wolak, J., Finkelhor, D., Mitchell, K. and Jones, L. (2011) 'Arrests for child pornography production: data at two time points from a national sample of U.S. law enforcement agencies', *Child Maltreatment*, vol 16, no 3, pp 184–95.

TEN

The Rotherham abuse scandal

Anneke Meyer

Introduction

This chapter examines the Rotherham abuse scandal, which centres on the exploitation and abuse of (mostly) teenage girls between 1997 and 2013 in the South Yorkshire town of Rotherham and the publication of an official inquiry report (Jay, 2014) into the abuse and, more specifically, into agencies' response to it. The report was released on 26 August 2014 and sparked intense media coverage. It is not difficult to see why. The report details the violent and sexual abuse and trafficking of minors, often over a number of years, carried out by groups of men who had befriended these children 'on the streets'. This pattern of abuse is described as 'child sexual exploitation' (CSE). The report identifies 1,400 victims, emphasising that this is a 'conservative estimate'. Around a third were in local council care or known to social services. The report is highly critical of the two key agencies in charge of CSE, namely the police and the council and its social and children's services. It paints a picture of serious failings and repeated inaction; Jay particularly criticises senior staff and management who actively ignored concerns about CSE.

This chapter considers the Rotherham abuse scandal from a moral panic perspective. It explores in detail media representations of the scale of the problem and the framing of blame, two key elements through which moral panics are instigated (Cohen, 2002). To this end, a limited press analysis was carried out in which the coverage of four newspapers was examined during the five days following the release of the Jay report. The newspapers were chosen to capture opposite ends of the political spectrum and the market: the legalist and moderately conservative broadsheet, *The Times*; the populist conservative tabloid, the *Sun*; the staunchly and morally conservative, mid-market paper, the *Daily Mail*; and the liberal left-wing broadsheet, the *Guardian*. A search of the LexisLibrary database produced a total of 180 articles for the time-period, between 30 and 38 per day, confirming that this was indeed a scandal of considerable proportion.

The Rotherham abuse scandal and moral panic theory

The nature and scale of the problem

In his analysis of moral panics Cohen (2002) argues that heightened societal interest and outrage are driven by media representations of the subject as a serious and large-scale problem, indicative of the moral malaise of society as a whole. Strategies for creating this picture include the use of emotive and moralistic language, sensational and alarming claims, distortion and exaggeration, prediction and symbolisation.

Newspaper reporting of the Rotherham scandal demonstrates this clearly, and labelling is key to this. Jay (2014) defines what happened in Rotherham as 'CSE', although what is meant by this term is not always clear, either in the report or in the wider coverage, perhaps not surprisingly, since the term is a relatively recent invention to include both child sexual abuse and child trafficking (Cree et al, 2014). In spite of the lack of clarity about the label CSE, the abuse itself is graphically described, in both the report and in the newspapers that covered it; and in each case the specific scandal around CSE in Rotherham is turned into a nationwide problem. For example, the scale of CSE is described as 'endemic' (*Guardian*, 28 August); 'grooming' is presented as at a 'Horrific scale' (*Daily Mail*, 31 August); and Rotherham is only the tip of the iceberg, as the 'same abuse is continuing to happen across the country' (*Guardian*, 28 August). The *Daily Mail* predicts that the problem is increasing, describing is as 'overwhelming' and growing 'out of control' (31 August) and claims in prominent headlines that 'THE ABUSE IS STILL GOING ON – AND NOW IT'S EVEN WORSE' (27 August). Meanwhile, the *Guardian's* editorial (28 August) asserts that hard evidence is no longer needed because, 'Absence of evidence is not evidence of absence, and a pattern of abuse that has now resulted in convictions in towns from Torbay to Rochdale is very likely to be happening in other places not yet identified.' The scandal itself is seen as indicative of a wider moral malaise in which society has become so brutal and amoral that something like this could occur: 'HOW CAN THIS HAPPEN IN A CIVILISED COUNTRY?' the *Daily Mail* (27 August) asks.

All newspapers prominently and repeatedly refer to the official figure of 1,400 victims. There is no critical analysis of this figure. Moreover, the media sensationalises the number through emotive language and front-page headlines such as '1400 lost girls' (*The Times*, 27 August). And the net is cast widely to include even potential victims: '[A]n extensive report into the nature of child sexual exploitation [...] estimated that 16,500 children were at risk of a specific type of abuse that can see gangs of abusers grooming children as young as 11' (*Guardian*, 28 August).

The scale of CSE is further constructed through the theme of nationwide 'grooming gangs'. Three out of the four newspapers (*The Times*, the *Daily Mail* and the *Sun*) focus on the issue of organised groups of Asian men who systematically befriend, exploit and abuse white teenage girls. A wide range of shorthands is used to refer to this phenomenon, either with or without an ethnic prefix: for example, '(Asian) grooming gangs'; '(Asian) sex gangs'; '(Asian) grooming networks'; 'groups of Asian (or Pakistani) men grooming'; 'Asian (or Pakistani) gangs' and so on. This over-wording indicates preoccupation (Fairclough, 1989) and because 'sex gangs' are reported to be active in towns across the UK – the most commonly cited examples including Rochdale, Oxford, Derby and Telford (*Daily Mail*, 27 August; *Sun*, 31 August) – the Rotherham scandal is turned into a nationwide problem. *The Times* also gives a sense of these networks being a significant problem across Britain, particularly the North of England and the Midlands (28 August), but this is not reported with any sense of panic. In contrast, the *Sun* and the *Daily Mail* are much more alarmist. Sex gangs are represented as a problem of huge proportions. The *Sun* features headlines such as 'ABUSE GANGS UK; CHILD SEX SCANDAL POLICE TO REOPEN 1,000 MORE FILES' and claims that an 'industrial scale gang-rape and trafficking of children' exists; 'similar large-scale exploitation of young girls by gangs is happening right across the UK' (31 August). The *Sun* meanwhile demands a nationwide inquiry and urges readers to sign a petition for this (31 August).

Blame, folk devils and the issue of ethnicity

Blame is an essential part of moral panics, as culprits are demonised to the extent of becoming folk devils. The culprits are usually the perpetrators of deviance, but many moral panics around child abuse have also demonised social workers for failing to protect children in their care (for example, Franklin and Parton, 1991; Critcher, 2003). In the Rotherham abuse scandal, the focus is on the public sector system and its failings, as well as on Asian men.

All four newspapers are highly critical of the authorities in charge of CSE in Rotherham, notably Rotherham council, with its social services, and South Yorkshire police. The two broadsheets describe in detail the authorities' failure to act and term errors 'blatant' and 'catastrophic'. There is a moralistic theme of lack of response amounting to the 'betrayal of children', which renders the authorities callous. An editorial in *The Times* (28 August) writes that victims 'were not just tortured by criminals but betrayed by child protection professionals and ridiculed by police', while the *Guardian* judges that the authorities in Rotherham were responsible for 'the most shameful mass betrayal of young people in the history of children's safeguarding' (27 August). The *Times* also personalises blame by sensationally labelling staff a 'disgrace' and 'as bad as the perpetrators' (28 August). However, large parts of the broadsheet coverage are neutral in tone and fact based. For example, both *The Times* and the *Guardian* make a distinction between senior managers and front-line staff. In line with Jay's (2014) report, they accuse senior figures in the council and the police of systematically ignoring knowledge of CSE.

The *Daily Mail* and the *Sun* are far more emotive and sensational in their critique of the authorities. The *Sun* criticises Rotherham council for a 'sickening dereliction of duty towards 1,400 victims of paedophile rape' and says about the police that 'their incompetence and callousness towards these children simply boggles the mind' (28 August). The editorial the previous day describes the failure to act as a deliberate, calculated strategy:

> They knew about it for years. But the Left-wing council let it go on because the rapists were Asian. Senior officials ordered worried staff to downplay it for fear of being accused of racism. Think about that. They prioritised political correctness over the gang-rape of children. [...] The council and police did nothing. But not through oversight or incompetence. This was policy. (*Sun*, 27 August)

This quotation thus renders senior council staff as truly inhuman, because they did not care about the suffering of children. But more than this, they chose to protect themselves from accusations of racism. Racism and ethnicity shape the dynamics of blame in the Rotherham scandal; this issue has been given so much media attention as to become synonymous with the scandal itself. The *Sun* and the *Daily Mail* shape this discourse into an attack on what they pejoratively term 'PC culture'. They argue that left-wing politics dominate local government and create a climate of political correctness in which 'the truth' cannot be spoken. The blame, then, is laid less with individual social workers and more with a way of thinking, demonised on front-page headlines such as the *Sun*'s '1,400 VICTIMS OF PC BRIGADE; CHILDREN ABUSED FOR 16YRS' and its editorial, 'Left's blind eye to child rapes' (27 August). The first *Daily Mail* editorial on the scandal also identifies 'PC culture' as the culprit:

> But perhaps most chilling is the reason why so many officials were reluctant to get to the bottom of these vile crimes. [...] Several staff described being nervous about identifying the ethnic origins of perpetrators for fear of being thought 'racist'; others remembered clear directions from managers not to do so. [...] The inescapable conclusion is that the dictates of political correctness were placed above the duty to protect children against violent abuse. (*Daily Mail*, 27 August)

The essence is that this culture is 'letting evil thrive' (*Daily Mail*, 28 August), rendering it guilty and evil by implication. As the scandal is seen as indicative of a wider moral malaise, 'PC culture' becomes responsible for the lack of decency, virtue and morality that blights contemporary society. Yet Jay's (2014) report concludes that a complex puzzle of many contributory factors led to authorities' reluctance to act; focusing only on 'PC culture' ignores the wider context in which agencies were operating and misrepresents Jay's conclusion. Furthermore, when the 'PC culture' argument is linked to multiculturalism and the ethnic and religious backgrounds of perpetrators, the *Daily Mail* and the *Sun* become racist. A lack of morality is identified as the cause of CSE: only evil people could have perpetrated such horrific crimes. This lack of morality is not limited to specific perpetrators but attributed to the entire Asian and Muslim community. The *Sun* states in an article headlined 'ANYONE who thinks the Rotherham sex abuse was not about race is kidding themselves':

> British Pakistani Muslims saw white children as trash. And now there should be a million British Muslims marching in the street saying – not in our name. [...] When some new controversy surrounds British Muslims we always hear about the 'overwhelming majority' of British Muslims who are proud to share British values. Why do we never see them? (*Sun*, 31 August)

The final question insinuates that it is a myth that most Muslims subscribe to British values, meaning that they have either different values or none at all. Given the context – the Rotherham scandal, the Asian background of offenders, their supposed hatred of white children and a headline that tells readers that 'race' was a causal factor – the logical conclusion is set up for readers that this lack of British (read 'proper') values in the Asian Muslim community is the cause of CSE (Fairclough, 1989). This then becomes an attack on multiculturalism:

> [T]his show[s] the terrible damage done by the ideology of multiculturalism which, in Rotherham, was elevated above the requirements of law enforcement and compassionate morality. [...] Thanks to this dogma, we no longer have a universal moral code or national identity, and the consequences can be seen all around us, whether in the rise of home-grown Islamic extremism or in the failure of too many migrant groups to learn even basic English. The advance of multiculturalism across our civic life has been fuelled by the deepening official fixation with anti-racism. (*Daily Mail*, 28 August)

The problem with multiculturalism is thus its refusal to enforce the British moral code on all ethnic groups. Of course, neither the *Sun* nor the *Daily Mail* says this directly, but they strongly cue their readers into these conclusions as the only logical ones (Fairclough, 1989). In contrast, the two broadsheets mention a number of causal factors highlighted by the Jay report, including poverty, budget cuts, gender and class issues. As a consequence, even when *The Times* highlights the 'fear of being labelled as racist' argument, this does not appear as a stand-alone explanation. The *Guardian* likewise emphasises that members of all ethnic groups carry out CSE (28 August) and, with *The Times* (30 August), voices the opinion that the social class of the victims, rather than ethnicity of the perpetrators, was the main reason for authority inaction. Both newspapers point to statistics indicating that the vast majority of sex offenders are white males.

Discussion and conclusion: the Rotherham scandal, the media and social work

All newspapers' treatment of the issue demonstrates the 'politics of outrage' that routinely accompanies child-protection controversies (Parton, 2014): they portray Rotherham as a scandal, agree that

CSE is a serious and widespread problem, share common themes such as authority failure and use dramatic language. But considerable differences were found between the newspapers, attributable to market category and political orientation. The two broadsheets used more factual language, provided significantly more information, and were therefore less simplistic and more accurate. Given this diversity and complexity of newspaper positions, it is impossible to identify the kind of media consensus Cohen envisages as occurring during a moral panic. This is especially true for the issue of blame.

Franklin and Parton (1991) note that moral panic theory has never been able to fully explain why, in cases of child abuse, the media do not turn on the perpetrators, the obvious 'folk devils', but instead blame social workers. In the Rotherham scandal, social services are frequently criticised, but this does not turn into the full-blown social worker demonisation typical of other child-abuse cases (Critcher, 2003). This is despite the case's possessing all the necessary ingredients, such as children being abused, many victims being known to social services and abuse not being detected or successfully dealt with for years. Aldridge (1999) argues that this is due to social work's diminished significance as a political symbol; however, the vilification of social work during the high-profile 'Baby P' case in 2007–08 clearly undermines this idea (Parton, 2014). Rather, it appears that social workers did not feature as folk devils in the Rotherham scandal because of several interacting factors, namely newspaper politics, the Jay report, the nature of the case and the sensitivity of the topic of ethnicity.

The two most sensational newspapers in the study, the *Sun* and the *Daily Mail*, turned their anger on 'PC culture', which shifted the focus away from social work per se. The two papers blamed a wider culture that they suspect to dominate the entire public sector. In the early 1990s, Franklin and Parton wrote that social workers are often presented in the media as a 'symbol for the entire public sector, personifying "evil" which the political new right presumes to be inherent therein' (Franklin and Parton, 1991, p 9). In the Rotherham case, right-wing newspapers like the *Sun* and the *Daily Mail* used 'PC culture' rather than social work as a metaphor to wage war on the public sector they detest. The focus on 'PC culture' may be grounded in Jay's (2014) report, which identifies that front-line workers (social workers, youth workers) repeatedly tried to raise awareness with senior officials, who failed to act. In the light of this, stereotyping social workers as soft, ineffectual, ignorant and uncaring (Franklin and Parton, 1991) would have required quite a discursive sleight of hand. The serial nature of child-protection scandals means that, over time, certain discourses are entrenched and come to serve as ready-made interpretive frameworks for further scandals; the explanatory discourse of 'institutional failure' is a particularly important one (Parton, 2014). Child abuse is always the domain of the police as well as social services, but the media tend to focus on and blame social services (Franklin and Parton, 1991). Arguably, the type of abuse at the centre of the Rotherham scandal was so obviously criminal that it was difficult for the media to ignore the role of the police. As a consequence, the discourse of 'institutional failure' had to be applied to the police and any full-blown vilification of the authorities would have had to focus on the police as well as social services. This may have contributed to the reluctance of conservative papers to engage in outright demonisation, because they tend to be supportive of the police, whom they see as maintaining law and order on behalf of the moral majority.

In the end, no single folk devil emerges in the Rotherham scandal. A vague entity such as 'PC culture' does not lend itself to demonisation, as labels of evil are difficult to attach in a meaningful way. Asian men forming 'sex gangs' were obvious folk-devil candidates, but the *Guardian* does not support the theme and *The Times* is rather reluctant, despite its conservative leaning, possibly because of the sensitivity of the issue of ethnicity. As a consequence, the blame game is marked by complexity and diversity. A moral-panic lens helps to illuminate the media treatment of the Rotherham scandal, allowing insights into the framing of CSE as a national problem through distorted claims and emotive language, but it may overestimate consensus, and so cannot fully capture the discursive complexity of the case.

References

Aldridge, M. (1999) 'Poor relations: state social work and the press in the UK', in B. Franklin (ed) *Social policy, the media and misrepresentation*, London: Routledge, pp 89–103.

Cohen, S. (2002) *Folk devils and moral panics: The creation of the Mods and Rockers* (3rd edn), London and New York: Routledge.

Cree, V.E., Clapton, G. and Smith, M. (2014) 'The presentation of child trafficking in the UK: an old and new moral panic?', *British Journal of Social Work*, vol 44, pp 418–33.

Critcher, C. (2003) *Moral panics and the media*, Milton Keynes: Open University Press.

Fairclough, N. (1989) *Language and power*, Harlow: Longman.

Franklin, B. and Parton, N. (1991) 'Media reporting of social work: a framework for analysis', in B. Franklin and N. Parton (eds) *Social work, the media and public relations*, London: Routledge.

Jay, A. (2014) *Independent inquiry into child sexual exploitation in Rotherham (1997–2013)*, Rotherham: Rotherham Metropolitan Borough Council.

Parton, N. (2014) *The politics of child protection: Contemporary developments and future directions*, Basingstoke: Palgrave Macmillan.

Afterword

Mark Hardy

Endings are commonplace within life and work and yet can often be neglected among the demands of front-line social work practice. There can be pressure to close cases once acute risks have been addressed. A difficult meeting or phone call is still on your mind in the evening or over the weekend. Ideally, an ending supports the transition between one state and another and often this is best achieved when it is prepared for in advance. While reading Part Two, you may have been thinking of your own work and asking yourself what difference an understanding of moral panics might make to your research, study or practice. Within this afterword, I hope to help in this transition from theory to practice by identifying what I feel are some of the key themes addressed by the contributors and discussing their relevance to the current context of social work policy and practice.

I am employed as a social worker in a local authority Children and Families practice team in Scotland and have previous experience of youth work and residential childcare. My current role encompasses child protection, children in need, looked after and accommodated children, and adoption and permanency work. This places my perspective within a specific context. Scotland has its own legal system and distinctive Children's Hearing System (see Hothersall, 2014). However, many of the issues facing social workers in Scotland have much in common with other child welfare systems in Anglophone countries (Lonne et al, 2009). I would like to concentrate on two broad themes, both of which are indicated in the quote from Stanley Cohen (1972) at the beginning of Chapter Six by Ian Butler, and which in my opinion are particularly relevant for social work policy and practice: firstly, the way in which social problems are represented in moral panics; and secondly, the responses to those social problems.

Each of the contributions in this part describes how a phenomenon, individual or group becomes defined as a social problem and represented through the media, politicians and other 'claims makers', or 'moral entrepreneurs', in ways that are over-simplified, stereotyped and distorted. Specific strategies are used by claims makers to foreground their opinions and construct problems according to particular ideologies. In Chapter Eight Kay Tisdall uses the example of the 'lost childhood' trope and a letter printed in the media to show how claims makers represent themselves as holding relevant expertise and appeal to idealised constructions of childhood that construct good/bad dichotomies of childhood and parenting. Similar characterisations are described by Ethel Quayle in Chapter Nine in relation to 'innocent children' and the dangers of technology. Joanne Westwood (Chapter Seven) discusses the use of melodrama tactics to portray child trafficking and Anneke Meyer (Chapter Ten) highlights how language can be used to construct problems in particular ways. A common thread through these examples is the way that young people, children and childhood are constructed. Childhood is represented as a time of innocence and vulnerability to risk. The discourse of child protection is highly prevalent in relation to both children's use of the internet and child trafficking. Children and young people are represented as passive victims who require protection from dangerous adults. Their vulnerabilities are focused upon at the expense of their strengths. The agency of children and young people is rarely considered in these representations (Cree et al, 2014), denying them a voice regarding their own circumstances and futures.

In Chapter Six Ian Butler describes how particular child deaths become scandals that then influence the formation of child-protection policy and practice. Specific child deaths are laden with new meanings as they are chosen by claims makers to advance particular agendas. The phenomenon of child abuse is represented to society by reference to only its most extreme examples, rather than its more prevalent and systemic forms. This distorted emphasis has led to a stereotyping of child abuse that places child abusers as 'others', beyond the moral pale, leading to a neglect of structural and social factors in the aetiology of child abuse. Within a scandal or moral panic the characteristics of the phenomenon, individual or group come to be regarded as symptomatic of something more widespread. This can lead to whole classes or types of people, and often young people, being demonised as 'folk devils', such as Stanley Cohen's (1972) 'Mods and Rockers' and Hall et al's (1978) 'muggers'. In the example of the tragic death of Peter Connelly ('Baby P'), it was the kinds of families who are often the clients of social work that were vilified and used as evidence of the failure of the welfare state, marking an ideological shift in the politics of welfare. This served the particular neoliberal agenda to move responsibility for social problems away from the state and onto individuals and families who could then be held as at fault for the problems they faced, rather than the problems being the consequence of structural or social factors, and thus permitting increasingly punitive approaches to families. Social work and social workers have also at various times been portrayed as a social threat, and failures to protect children have been blamed on the shortcomings of individual social workers rather than on the political or social context in which they operate.

Disproportionate responses and stigmatisation are characteristic of moral panics and create difficulties in understanding more deeply the nature of social problems. Moral panics tend both to be engendered by and to lead to further, disproportionate or inappropriate responses. In Chapter Nine Ethel Quayle describes the increase in social control and greater restrictions placed on children using the internet, due to increased anxiety and aversion to risk. Resources are diverted towards control measures and away from researching the protective potential of technology. In relation to child trafficking, there is an emphasis on harm prevention and risk management, tending to increase social control. According to Ian Butler (Chapter Six), responses to child welfare scandals have tended to promote the development of a compliance culture within the child-protection system. Social workers become the target of control measures. Many of the changes stemming from inquiries into child deaths have tended to focus on regulation and controlling the workforce, rather than on directly addressing the causes of child abuse. While some improvements in the child-protection system have been made in the past 30 years, much has also been counter-productive, due to the tendency towards over-prescription and bureaucratisation. At the time of writing, the report of the *Independent Inquiry into Child Sexual Exploitation in Rotherham* (Jay, 2014) was released. This is the latest in a series of scandals relating to sexual abuse that have been in the headlines since the exposure of Jimmy Savile as a paedophile. It has prompted renewed calls for a system of mandatory reporting of child abuse, with criminal sanctions (Starmer, 2014; Townsend and Doward, 2014), although in this case it is also asserted that concerns were reported by front-line social workers and youth workers but not subsequently acted upon at a senior level. In such a climate within the UK, an understanding of moral panics is very relevant. This is well illustrated by Anneke Meyer's analysis (Chapter Ten) of the media response to the scandal, although she suggests that the idea of moral panic does not necessarily capture all the complexity of specific cases and media reporting is not necessarily homogeneous. Another analysis of this can be seen in a blog by Cree (2014).

Themes from the analyses of moral panics resonate strongly with findings from the Munro (2011) *Review of Child Protection*. This comprehensive review of the child-protection system in England and Wales was requested by the UK government, due to the perceived lack of improvements in the system despite numerous inquiries into child deaths. In the first part of the review (Munro, 2010), it was noted that previous reforms to the child-protection system have led to an 'imbalance and distortion of practice priorities' (Munro, 2010, p 5). Professional practice has become driven by compliance with rules and regulation, rather than based upon professional relationships with children, young people and their families (Munro, 2010, p 8). Child-protection referrals in England and Wales had been on a steadily increasing trend but this had risen sharply following the death of Peter Connelly, suggesting that net-widening was having a significant impact on the child-protection system. According to Munro (2011, pp 134–5), 'The false hope of eliminating risk has contributed significantly to the repeated use of increasing prescription as the solution to perceived problems. Consequently, this has increased defensive practice by professionals so that children and young people's best interests are not always at the heart of decisions.' The problems experienced by children and families that contribute to child-protection concerns are due to multiple and complex factors that cannot be reduced to simplistic or superficial explanations. Munro (2011) states that the combination of a bureaucratised compliance culture and high caseloads has placed pressure on the time that practitioners have to spend with children, building relationships with them, understanding their views and getting to know their families and networks. This has negatively impacted upon the knowledge that practitioners have of the children and families they work with, consequently undermining the quality of assessment and decision making (cf Thomas and Holland, 2010). In an attempt to cope with these pressures, the child-protection system has become focused upon investigation in order to eliminate the likelihood of children's being killed or seriously injured, taking attention and resources away from preventative practice. This has led to what Clapton et al (2013) describe as 'fortress social work', in which there has been a coarsening of attitudes towards families and a deterioration in relationships: the role of social services has become that of monitoring and surveillance rather than the provision of support. It is hardly surprising, in these circumstances, that recruitment and retention of social workers has remained a significant issue when social workers struggle to practise in ways that are congruent with what motivated them to join the profession in the first place (Social Work (Scotland), 2014).

The Munro Review recommends that children should be at the heart of the child-protection system, and promoting the best outcomes for children and young people requires that social workers develop meaningful relationships with them and their families. Professional practice has to be underpinned by sound knowledge of theory and research, and barriers to professional judgement have to be removed. Social work expertise needs to be developed through the creation of learning (rather than compliance) cultures within child-protection work. These recommendations have generally been warmly received by social work practitioners not only in England and Wales but also in the rest of the UK. While there appears to be a willingness within the social work profession to move in the direction that Munro proposed, there are concerns that the impetus for change has been undermined by austerity cuts to public services in the UK. Many consider these cuts themselves to be ideologically driven, in line with Ian Butler's analysis (Chapter Six). This leaves the likelihood of positive change uncertain, and the Munro Review may acquire the status of another well-meaning report, unless its recommendations are put into practice (Edmondson et al, 2013).

Moral-panic writings provide a lens through which a significant part of the story of the difficulties currently being faced within child-welfare and child-protection systems can be understood. It provides conceptual tools and analyses that can help to explain some of the macro-level drivers influencing social work policy and practice. The contributions in Part Two have highlighted that 'moral panics do harm in the "real" world' (Cree et al, 2014, p 32): they influence the understanding of social problems, the distribution of resources, the way in which individuals and groups of people are treated and the context within which social workers practise and social policy is made. An understanding informed by moral panic perspectives is therefore valuable to practitioners in order to critically reflect on social problems and challenge social injustice (Cree et al, 2014). The concept of moral entrepreneurs or claims makers also provides a useful concept by which social workers can question their own practice and the claims they make regarding the children and families with whom they work. It is not only the media and politicians who can be swept up by moral panics (cf Wastell and White, 2012). As a profession we need, I believe, to ground social work expertise, in terms of knowledge, values and skills, on the relationships we have with children and their families, and not fall into the trap of reductionism and stereotyping to impose a false sense of certainty over the complexity of people's lives: 'The problems with which social work engages are ancient and recalcitrant. Only the most nuanced arguments hold any real promise, yet these are often conspicuous by their absence' (Featherstone et al, 2014, p 53). Social workers need time and discretion to build relationships with children, young people and their families if they are to develop the kind of 'nuanced arguments' required. We also need time to think and learn, and a moral panic perspective can be a valuable conceptual tool for practitioners' reflections on policy and practice.

References

Clapton, G., Cree, V. and Smith, M. (2013) 'Critical commentary: moral panics, claims-making and child protection in the UK', *British Journal of Social Work*, vol 43, no 4, pp 803–12.

Cohen, S. (1972) *Folk devils and moral panics. The creation of the Mods and Rockers*, London: MacGibbon and Kee Ltd.

Cree, V. (2014) 'The Rotherham inquiry – an alternative view', ESRC Moral Panic Seminar Series 2012–2014 (5 October), http://moralpanicseminarseries.wordpress.com/2014/10/05/the-rotherham-inquiry-an-alternative-view/.

Cree, V., Clapton, G. and Smith, M. (2014) 'The presentation of child trafficking in the UK: an old and new moral panic?', *British Journal of Social Work*, vol 44, no 2, pp 418–33.

Edmondson, D., Potter, A. and McLaughlin, H. (2013) 'Reflections of a higher specialist PQ student group on the Munro recommendations for children's social workers', *Practice: Social Work in Action*, vol 25, no 3, pp 191–207.

Featherstone, B., White, S. and Morris, K. (2014) *Re-imagining child protection*, Bristol: Policy Press.

Hall, S., Critcher, C., Jefferson, T., Clarke, J. and Roberts, B. (1978) *Policing the crisis. Mugging, the state and law and order*, London: Macmillan.

Hothersall, S. (2014) *Social work with children, young people and their families in Scotland* (3rd edn), London: Sage.

Jay, A. (2014) *Independent inquiry into child sexual exploitation in Rotherham (1997–2013)*, www.rotherham.gov.uk/inquiry (accessed 27 August 2014).

Lonne, B., Parton, N., Thomson, J. and Harries, M. (2009) *Reforming child protection*, Abingdon: Routledge.

Munro, E. (2010) *The Munro Review of Child Protection Part One: A systems analysis*, London: Department of Education.

Munro, E. (2011) *The Munro Review of Child Protection Final Report: A child-centred system*, London: Department of Education.

Social Work (Scotland) (2014) 'Massive rise in vacant posts in England – but what's the cause?', *Professional Social Work*, September, p 8.

Starmer, K. (2014) 'How can we prevent another Rotherham?', *Guardian* (28 August), www.theguardian.com/commentisfree/2014/aug/28/how-can-we-prevent-another-rotherham.

Thomas, J. and Holland, S. (2010) 'Representing children's identities in core assessments', *British Journal of Social Work*, vol 40, pp 2617–33.

Townsend, M. and Doward, J. (2014) 'Rotherham: Yvette Cooper calls for change of law after abuse scandal', *Observer* (30 August), www.theguardian.com/uk-news/2014/aug/30/rotherham-yvette-cooper-call-law-change.

Wastell, D. and White, S. (2012) 'Blinded by neuroscience: social policy, the family and the infant brain', *Families, Relationships and Society*, vol 1, no 3, pp 397–414.

Part Three
The state

Edited by Viviene E. Cree

Introduction

Viviene E. Cree

In common with the other parts of this book, a key theorist within the 'moral panic' genre is now introduced. Stuart Hall's ideas have been pivotal to the development of a more overly political analysis of moral panics. Many of his ideas are reflected in the chapters in this and the other parts, while others have been taken forward in other writing in the field.

Stuart Hall

Stuart McPhail Hall was born on 3 February 1932 in Kingston, Jamaica and first came to the UK in 1951 to study English at Oxford University, after winning a Rhodes scholarship. He described himself as a 'familiar stranger' at Oxford, steeped in English traditions and yet very different socially, culturally and ethnically to the other students and staff. He found politics (Marxism), and became part of the *Universities and Left Review*, which later merged with the *New Reasoner* to form the *New Left Review*, with Hall as its founding editor. Hall completed his MA and began a PhD on the Anglo-American novelist Henry James, before giving up his studies and moving to London, where he worked as a supply teacher in Brixton and a magazine editor. In 1961 he was appointed Lecturer in Film and Media at Chelsea College, London University; in 1964, at the invitation of Richard Hoggart, he moved to the newly formed Centre for Contemporary Cultural Studies (CCCS) at Birmingham University as its first research fellow. He remained until 1979, when he went on to become Professor of Sociology at the Open University, a post that he held until 1998.

Stuart Hall is widely acknowledged as someone who played a significant part in bringing cultural studies from the margins into the centre of academic and public analysis and debate. He collaborated with colleagues in the CCCS on a number of volumes, including *Resistance through Rituals* (1975); *Culture, Media, Language* (1980); *Politics and Ideology* (1986); *The Hard Road to Renewal* (1988); *New Times* (1989); *Critical Dialogues in Cultural Studies* (1996); and *Different: A Historical Context: Contemporary Photographers and Black Identity* (2001). Perhaps his best-known book, *Policing the Crisis. Mugging, the State, and Law and Order* (1978) was a collaboration between academics at the CCCS. The book begins in 1972 with the story of 'a mugging gone wrong' – this was a police officer's description of a street robbery in London that resulted in the death of an elderly widower. Hall and others go on to explore what happened next, including the appropriation of a new scare-word into the British lexicon, that is, 'mugging'. They are at pains to point out that they do not condone street robbery, which they see as a 'manifestation of powerlessness' (1978, p 396). But they argue that the furore around mugging must be understood as a moral panic, focusing as it does on the representation of young, black, working-class men as 'dangerous'. They go on to draw attention to the deliberate focus on 'race' in Thatcherite politics, especially in the characterisation of the 'law and order' agenda. Hall went on to explore this further in *The Politics of Thatcherism* (1983), in which he criticised the Left for making Thatcherism possible because of its traditional statism.

Hall contributed to many non-academic activities during his lifetime. He served on the Runnymede Commission on the Future of Multi-Ethnic Britain between 1997 and 2000; and chaired Autograph (the Association of Black Photographers) and the International Institute of Visual Arts. He helped to secure funding for Rivington Place, in East London, a centre dedicated to public education in multicultural issues.

This volume, even without being consciously aware of it, reflects something of the spirit of Stuart Hall, not just in its sceptical approach or its interest in issues of 'race' and class, but because it is interdisciplinary. It tries to 'think outside the box', and is a tribute to Stuart Hall's creativity, imagination and honesty.

Stuart Hall died on 10 February 2014.

Content of Part Three

The chapters in Part Three all explore, in some way, moral panics and the state. Of course, 'the state' is itself a very broad concept, and therefore it should be no surprise to find chapters here on everything from internet pornography to internet radicalisation, from 'chavs' to 'troubled families', and finally, patient safety. As in the other parts, authors are writing from different disciplinary backgrounds, though on this occasion all are located in the UK. If there is any consensus across the chapters, it is that moral panics have potentially detrimental consequences for all of us; they can be used by the state, as Hall et al (1978) demonstrated clearly, to justify policies and legislation that are, at the very least, repressive and regressive.

Chapter Eleven, by Jim Greer, tackles a social anxiety that is currently raging across the developed and developing worlds alike, namely, internet pornography and, in particular, the risk of children's access to and use of internet porn. Greer argues that we are all panicking about this, in large part because we hold very contradictory ideas about children, who are at the same time seen both as innocent and naïve and as 'capable of being corrupted'. He argues that the long-term consequences of the crusade against internet pornography are likely to be both censorship and a loss of freedom of speech; he urges that those of us who value the internet's creative and collaborative potential should take note of this now and campaign against it.

The internet remains the focus of concern in Chapter Twelve, but this time, the subject is the danger of radicalisation through the internet. David McKendrick picks up the story of the murder of off-duty soldier Lee Rigby by two Muslim men on a London street in 2013, an event that was all the more shocking because it (and its aftermath) was filmed by passers-by and the video uploaded to YouTube. McKendrick outlines what he describes as a moral panic that followed this brutal killing as politicians, journalists and policy makers queued up to blame 'cyber jihad' for the murder. This is a story that has echoes of Hall et al's earlier study of 'race' and crime, but the new element of the 'out-of-control' internet adds a new, 21st-century dimension to the panic.

Chapters Thirteen and Fourteen take us in different directions, although both are fundamentally concerned with issues of social class. In Chapter Thirteen, Elias le Grand outlines the creation of the 'chav' stereotype in the UK: the chav is a current-day 'folk devil', young, white, working class and male (there are female chavs, or chavettes, too, often portrayed as pregnant or pushing a pram). The chav is a welfare 'scrounger', a threat to the respectable working class because of their choice to remain unemployed and on benefit. Importantly, le Grand argues that the creation of the chav as folk devil allows the rest of us ('respectable' working-class people and the middle classes) to rest easy in our beds, absolved of any responsibility for increasing poverty levels and inequality in society.

Steve Kirkwood's Chapter Fourteen takes a very different moral panic, although it seems likely that there were some 'chavs' within this story too. He examines the riots that erupted in cities and towns in England during August 2011, following on from the shooting dead of a 29-year-old black man, Mark Duggan, by the police in Tottenham in London. Kirkwood unpicks the process of moral panic as it developed, and asks why it was that the government was able to blame the riots on poor parenting and, most especially, on families without fathers. He argues that the government's focus on 'troubled families' offered a convenient way out – it depoliticised the structural nature of the problems that were brought to a head in the riots in 2011. In that sense, this chapter, perhaps more than any other in this volume, owes allegiance to the work of Stuart Hall and others.

The final chapter in Part Three considers a very different case-study example of a moral panic, this time the panic around patient safety. William Fear argues that while this might have become a state-led movement, in practice, the campaign for greater patient safety has actually been run from within the medical profession. By retaining an institutional hold on the issue, the medical profession has been able to set the agenda and dictate terms. As a consequence, although vast empires have been built around patient safety, the power of the medical establishment has been reinforced, not undermined. This is an interesting example of what happens when the powerful make use of a moral-panic model for their own ends.

References

Chen, K.-H. and Morley, D. (1996) *Stuart Hall, critical dialogues in cultural studies*, London: Routledge.

Donald, J. and Hall, S. (1986) *Politics and ideology: A reader*, Virginia: Open University Press.

Hall, S. (1988) *The hard road to renewal. Thatcherism and the crisis of the Left*, London: Verso Books.

Hall, S. and Jacques, M. (eds) (1983) *The politics of Thatcherism*, London: Lawrence and Wishart Ltd.

Hall, S. and Jacques, M. (eds) (1989) *New times: Changing face of politics in the 1990s*, London: Lawrence and Wishart Ltd.

Hall, S. and Jefferson, T. (1975; 2nd edn, 2006) *Resistance through rituals: Youth subcultures in post-war Britain* (Cultural Studies Birmingham), London: Routledge.

Hall, S. and Sealy, M. (2001) *Different: A historical context: contemporary photographers and Black identity*, Michigan: University of Michigan Press.

Hall, S., Critcher, C., Jefferson, T., Clarke, J. and R. Bryan (1978; 2nd edn, 2013) *Policing the crisis: Mugging, the state and law and order*, London: Macmillan.

Hall, S., Hobson, R., Lowe, A. and Willis, P. (1980) (2nd edn) *Culture, Media, Language, Trade in Culture, Media, Language: Working Papers in Cultural Studies, 1972–79* (Cultural Studies Birmingham), London: Routledge.

ELEVEN

Children and internet pornography: a moral panic, a salvation for censors and Trojan horse for government colonisation of the digital frontier

Jim Greer

Introduction

This chapter will argue that we are currently experiencing a moral panic around children accessing internet pornography. This issue will be introduced within the context of society's views of young people, echoing previous moral panics about the influence of popular media on children. The chapter will then go on to consider what evidence (if any) exists for the extent of the problem of young people accessing and being influenced by internet pornography. This will be followed by scrutiny of 'moral entrepreneurs', that is, academics and others who are likely to benefit or prosper from internet regulation and the groups and communities who may be collateral damage in the 'war on porn'. Finally, the chapter will evaluate the chances of internet porn initiatives succeeding in their stated aims and the wider implications for society and its relationship with the 'wired worlds' of the internet.

The nature of the panic

On the weekend of 9 and 10 November 2013, the colour supplements of both *The Times* and the *Sunday Times* featured stories about concerns regarding what children do online. *The Times* cover featured a posed shot of a schoolgirl alone in darkened room, her face lit by only her mobile phone, her slightly chilling (or was it fearful?) gaze fixed on the reader. This photograph illustrates well the current moral panic around children and the internet. Children are simultaneously understood to be innocent, yet capable of being corrupted; in control of bewildering technology, yet somehow vulnerable to its dark side;

networked to the world, yet also alone and vulnerable. Articles like these have proliferated in print and online media; meanwhile, new scares have been identified and named, including cyberbullying, children sexting, online grooming, adults accessing child pornography and children accessing legal (adult) pornography. These phenomena are often discussed together and almost always interchangeably. The confusion between these issues is evident in, for example, articles that advocate for the use of internet filters to tackle child pornography, when in fact such material is mainly confined to the so-called 'deep web' (Pagliery, 2014).

The relationship with previous moral panics

Concerns about young people and the negative effects of media technology are not new. In the 1950s there was a campaign in the UK against American and 'American-style' comics on the basis of the horrific and violent content they contained. The campaign involved teachers' organisations, women's organisations, trade unions and churches, and, as in the current internet pornography campaign, the evidence that children were being adversely affected was largely anecdotal. In a detailed analysis of the 1950s campaign, Barker (1984a) argued that children were portrayed as innocent on the surface, yet containing a dangerous aspect that could be awoken by exposure to the wrong type of media. This parallels more recent fears about pornography 'distorting [children's] view of sex and relationships' (Cameron, 2013). In common with the current moral panic about children and the internet, strong concern was expressed in the 1950s about long-term damage to children's emotional and psychological development. Barker (1984a) expressed the view that the highly emotive nature of concerns about children's development led to there being no effective opposition to the campaign, and it resulted in the passing of legislation, despite a lack of empirical evidence. The legislation, the Children and Young Persons (Harmful Publications) Act 1955, is still in force.

The 1980s saw another moral panic that focused on children and technology. This time the concern was about children watching violent and horrific films on home video cassettes (so-called 'video nasties'); the rise in recorded crime was blamed on the easy availability of these films (Barker, 1984b). A parliamentary inquiry was quickly organised, the outcome of which was the Video Recordings Act 1984, which made it illegal to sell or distribute most videos without prior censorship by the British Board of Film Classification (BBFC) (Barker, 1984b; Brown,

1984). Barker (1984b, p 2) described the Video Recordings Act as 'the biggest growth in censorship in this country for very many years'.

The extent of the problem

One of the reasons frequently given for concern about young people accessing pornography on the internet is the sheer volume of pornographic websites and web pages that are reputed to exist on the internet. However, there is a lack of reliable information on the amount of pornography on the internet.

One recent attempt to assess what is known about children and their access to pornography is found in the report, 'Basically, Porn is Everywhere': Report of Children's Commissioner: A Rapid Evidence Assessment on the Effect that Access and Exposure to Pornography Has on Children and Young People (Horvath et al, 2013). This report was commissioned by the Office of the Children's Commissioner (OCC) in England as part of its Inquiry into Child Sexual Exploitation in Gangs and Groups (CSEGG). The study was limited in time and scope (as its title suggests) and was based mainly on a literature review of published papers, very few of which were from the UK. Nevertheless, the report does contain some findings that are instructive. Most notably, the report found very little research anywhere on the effects on children and young people of exposure to pornography. It points out that comparable research on the effects on children of violence in the media elicits contradictory evidence. The report states (Horvath et al, 2013, p 51) that 'For every study which concludes that viewing violence causes aggression in young people, there seems to be one which contradicts this.' The report raises concerns about the ethics of trying to look for causal relationships between exposure to pornography and harm and suggests that future research should consider questions such as: 'what are young people seeing when they are exposed to pornography?' and 'what roles do culture and socialisation play ... on young people's attitudes to pornography?' The report also looked at evidence in relation to children, the media and sex. One study found that the mass media explained only 13% of variance when looking at young people's attitudes towards sex; parents, religion, peers, grades at school and demographic factors were equally influential (L'Engle et al, 2004). Another study found a correlation between the amount of sexually explicit media consumed by boys and an increased tendency to see women as sex objects (Peter and Valkenburg, 2007). However, the report concluded that sexual stereotyping is not necessarily indicative of how young people view their relationships, or of their actual behaviour. Looking at the picture overall, there was little to justify the title '*Basically Porn is Everywhere*' or to justify David Cameron (2013) in proposing that internet service providers should install 'default on' internet filtering in every household. Rather, the report recommends that the Department for Education needs to drive improvement of sex and relationships education, including an awareness of pornography (recommendations 1–3) and that the government has to increase parents' awareness of their responsibilities towards children in this area (recommendation 4).

So why has the threat to children from internet porn captured popular and political attention?

One possible reason for the popular and political attention on the threat to children from internet porn is the cascade effect (Kuran and Sunstein, 1999), in which media attention creates public interest, which in turn creates more media attention. Media attention in this way feeds the availability heuristic (Tversky and Kahneman, 1974), by which people will over-estimate the size of risks that are easier to bring into recall. Another reason, identified by Boyd and Marwick (2009), is that technology makes risky behaviours 'more conspicuous'. Sexting and accessing pornography leave a trail in ways that behaviours like 'show me yours and I'll show you mine' wouldn't. Furthermore, the way in which an issue is framed affects how it is perceived (Tversky and Kahneman, 1986). Most of the discussions in the UK media about children and internet pornography (see, for example, Orr, 2013) have been framed in terms of how we can protect children, rather than how we can maintain the educational and political benefits of free access to the internet.

As with the previous moral panics of horror comics and video nasties, the emotive nature of the issue has silenced debate; any potential loss of freedom of speech seems to us a small price to pay in comparison with something as serious as children and children's moral development.

Cultural differences in how much value is given to free speech and free expression play a role. In general, the British media's reporting of the issue has lacked any real defence of free speech, with even liberal media such as the *Guardian*'s website running opinion pieces in favour of internet filters (for example, Orr, 2013). By contrast, US reporting on UK internet filtering has focused on freedom of speech issues (for example, the *New York Times* commentary by Ong, 2013)) and lampooning of the UK establishment (for example, an American liberal video podcast which had David Cameron portrayed as a Town

Crier (The Young Turks, 2013). Sunstein (2005) argues that it is widely believed that Europe operates from a precautionary principle in relation to risk, whereas in the US there is a normally held to be a need for evidence of harm before risks will be regulated for. However, Sunstein adds that this can be seen as an over-generalisation and that the US and Europe differ in the types of risk that are perceived to be greatest. In the UK, the very possibility that children may be being harmed by pornography is enough to justify the use of governmental directives. As Furedi writes: 'While many of the moral transgressions of the past have lost significance, those directed at children are policed more intensively than at any time in human history' (Furedi, 2013, p 45). Thus, the topic of children and internet pornography brings together two contemporary areas of fear – the fear of novel technology out of control and the fear of harm to children.

Claims makers/moral entrepreneurs

Government policy on children and the internet was taken forward by the Conservative MP Clare Perry via an *Independent Parliamentary Inquiry into Online Child Protection* (Perry, 2012). Despite the title, this inquiry did not focus, as we might have expected, on online grooming, abuse or bullying, but instead looked at children's internet consumption and the need to filter it. The report was also not, as the title suggests, 'independent'. Instead, it was (as stated on the report), sponsored by Premiere Christian Media (a UK Christian broadcaster and campaigning charity) in partnership Safer Media for a Safer Society (a charity 'seeking to reduce the harmful effects of the media on our children, families and society'), two organisations with a clear vested interest in promoting a climate of concern around the effects of online media.

The key findings of the report included the fact that most parents did not use existing filters because they trusted their children to use the internet safely and responsibly. Furthermore, parents who did use filters were more concerned with filtering suicide sites than pornography. This could have been seen as a positive reflection on the character of the nation's children and the trust that their parents have in them. However, the report recommended that internet service providers (ISPs) should be instructed to roll out internet filters to all homes, supported by legislation if necessary. Following Perry's review, the Department for Education in England was tasked with carrying out a wider consultation on how internet filters might be rolled out. The findings of that consultation (Department for Education, 2013) were that a majority of parents who took part felt that child internet safety was a shared responsibility between parents and ISPs, not government, and that a majority did not want any of the filtering options on offer. Despite this, David Cameron decided to go ahead with a requirement for 'default on' filtering. The filtering systems that are to be introduced in the UK require citizens (irrespective of whether they have children or not) to make an active decision to turn these filters off. A failure to respond to an online prompt will result in the filters being set at 'on'. The account holder is then presented with a menu of categories that they can have filtered out. It seems likely that the 'default on' approach will place psychological pressure to accept the filters through what Kahneman, Knetsch and Thaler (1991) have termed 'status quo bias'; someone will accept the default setting because it is a suggestion/ recommendation by the policy maker, who may be seen as an expert. Parents may also be concerned about being identified as someone who is an irresponsible parent or perhaps as someone who is interested in terrorism or pornography. They may be concerned that their filtering choices may become known to the authorities or be 'leaked' onto the web, or have negative consequences for them if they were ever suspected of any kind of offence, abuse or neglect in relation to children.

The House of Commons Culture, Media and Sport Committee's report on *Online Safety* (2014, section 4.87) asserts that the internet is currently a 'free for all' in which anyone with a computer could be a publisher. The unstated implication is that this is an unsatisfactory state of affairs that needs to be curbed. This theme is echoed in the Department for Culture, Media and Sport (2013) policy paper, *Connectivity, Content and Consumers: Britain's Digital Platform for Growth*. This document again has a strong emphasis on 'consumer safety', signalling a policy direction that, I would argue, represents a move towards government colonisation and control of the internet: rather than being common land where international citizens can share ideas and collaborate freely and take part in free commerce, the internet is to be controlled by national governments. Censorship bodies such as the BBFC and the Authority for Television on Demand (ATVOD), who feared that the internet would make them redundant, are now waiting for their share of the regulatory bonanza that fears about children and pornography seem likely to open up. The ATVOD has recently issued its own 'research report' (ATVOD, 2014). Page 15 has large banner text stating that '44,000 children aged 6–11 visited an adult website from a PC or a laptop in December 2013'. However, a footnote in tiny writing on the same page states that 'these demographics do not meet minimum sample size standards'. Reporting of the ATVOD report has tended to focus on the alarmist headline findings, rather than notes of methodological caution. ATVOD's strong presence seems likely to increase as we move ahead and the regulator seeks to increase its role in online protection.

The wider implications of the panic for social work and wider society

There is much to fear from a closed, regulated internet for social work and for those who are concerned about the rights of oppressed people all around the world. The policy of 'default on' internet filtering has already caused damage, because filtering programmes are relatively unsophisticated and cannot distinguish between harmful material and educational or informative material. There have been examples of access to LGBT information sites being lost (Cooper, 2013), and also of access to sex education and sexual health websites being curtailed (Blake, 2013). There is also a danger that access to sites that carry independent news and information on issues such as global affairs and terrorism, female genital mutilation, abuse and human trafficking, forced prostitution and so on will be closed off. It is possible to ask for blocked sites to be 'white listed'. However, it is not clear how easy this process might be and people may not realise that they want to access a site if they cannot see what is on it in the first place. Young people who wish to access information about concerns such as anorexia may also find access blocked to sites that would actually be helpful to them. Teenagers who want to discuss issues to do with relationships can easily have their access to these sites curtailed if their parents deny household access to web forums.

For those who care about child protection issues such as online grooming, exploitation and cyberbullying, internet filtering gives the illusion that the government is doing something to protect children online, when in fact it isn't addressing these problems. Of course, there will be a small number of young people who may become hooked into watching online porn, just as a small number will become addicted to gambling or other potentially harmful activities. Some children and young people may see things online that are at the very least unattractive, if not downright abusive. But Ferguson (2014) suggests that we should think about the relationship between the media and consumers as an interactive, rather than a passive one (the young person is as much 'doing' as being 'done to'). Furthermore, if a young person is spending a lot of time accessing online pornography, then they probably have wider problems that would exist even if pornography was not available to them in this way.

Conclusion

Early results from the roll-out of filters are that uptake has been poor, despite the 'default on' approach. An Ofcom (2014) report on the level of activation of filters by new internet account customers is 5% for BT, 8% for Sky, 36% for TalkTalk and 4% for Virgin. The low take-up by Virgin customers has been partly explained by engineers' installation by-passing the option and not giving customers the choice to activate filters at installation. It is perhaps not surprising that the overall take-up is so low, in the light of previous public consultation on the issue. However, it will be interesting to see whether the government will accept that the public has responded negatively to network-level filtering as an option, or whether this will be seen as a justification for forcing families without children to use filters.

Another recent piece of legislation, the Data Retention and Investigatory Powers Act 2014, has been passed amid claims by technology law experts that it has been 'unnecessarily rushed through Parliament' and 'represents a serious expansion of surveillance' (Kiss, 2014). The 'video nasties' moral panic was associated with fears that violent media in a new technology could fuel civil unrest and crime as well as corrupting children. The existing moral panic again plays of fears about new technology, corruption of childhood and a new threat of violence – this time from terrorism and religious extremism, as will be discussed more fully in subsequent chapters.

Government regulation and control of the internet could lead to legal and financial barriers to both the publication and consumption of information. For those who value the capacity of the internet to offer an unfettered space for protest, minority views and the challenging the powerful interests, this is a discomforting direction of travel for government policy.

For social workers who are concerned about the risks to children from new technologies there are plenty of alternatives to censorship, as demonstrated by Childline's (2014) 'Zipit' app, which enables young people to send smart retorts to close down sexting or requests by phone for inappropriate photographs. Initiatives like these offer a child-centred alternative to blanket internet censorship.

References

ATVOD (2014) *For Adults Only? A Research Report by the Authority for Television on Demand*, 28 March 2014, www.atvod.co.uk/uploads/files/For_Adults_Only_FINAL.pdf.

Barker, M. (1984a) *A haunt of fears: The strange history of the British Horror Comics campaign*, London: Pluto Press.

Barker, M. (1984b) 'Nasty politics or video nasties', in M. Barker (ed) *The video nasties: Freedom and censorship in the media*, London: Pluto Press, pp 7–38.

Blake, S. (2013) 'Porn or better sex education', www.pinknews.co.uk/2013/08/21/comment-porn-or-better-sex-education/ (accessed 17 March 2013)

Boyd, D. and Marwick, A. (2009) 'The conundrum of visibility', *Journal of Children and Media*, vol 3, no 4, pp 410–14.

Brown, B. (1984) 'Exactly what we wanted', in M. Barker (ed) *The video nasties: Freedom and censorship in the media*, London: Pluto Press, pp 68–87.

Cameron, D. (2013) 'The Internet and pornography: Prime Minister Calls for Action', speech, 24 July, www.gov.uk/government/speeches/the-internet-and-pornography-prime-minister-calls-for-action (accessed 17 March 2015).

Childline (2014) Zipit app, www.childline.org.uk/Play/GetInvolved/Pages/sexting-zipit-app.aspx.

Cooper, C. (2013) 'David Cameron's plan for internet-porn filters "risks hurting LGBT community"', *Independent* (21 August), www.independent.co.uk/news/uk/politics/david-camerons-plan-for-internetporn-filters-risks-hurting-lgbt-community-8778956.html .

Department for Culture, Media and Sport (2013) *Connectivity, Content and Consumers: Britain's digital platform for growth*, https://www.gov.uk/government/publications/connectivity-content-and-consumers-britains-digital-platform-for-growth.

Department for Education (2013) *The Government Response to the Consultation on Parental Internet Controls*, http://webarchive.nationalarchives.gov.uk/20130903121526/http:/media.education.gov.uk/assets/files/pdf/c/20130122%20gov%20response%20to%20parental%20internet%20controls.pdf.

Ferguson, C. (2014) 'Is video game violence bad?', *The Psychologist*, vol 21, no 5, pp 324–7.

Furedi, F. (2013) *Moral crusades in an age of mistrust: The Jimmy Savile scandal*, Basingstoke: Palgrave Macmillan.

Horvath, M.A.H., Alys, L., Massey, K., Pina, A., Scally, M. and Adler, J.R. (2013) *'Basically, porn is everywhere': A rapid evidence assessment on the effect that access and exposure to pornography has on children and young people*, London: Children's Commissioner.

House of Commons Culture Media and Sport Committee (2014) *Online Safety*, 6th report of session 2013–14, www.publications. parliament.uk/pa/cm201314/cmselect/cmcumeds/729/72902.htm.

Kahneman, D., Knetsch, J.L. and Thaler, R.H. (1991) 'Anomalies: the endowment effect, loss aversion, and status quo bias', *Journal of Economic Perspectives*, vol 5, no 1, pp 193–206.

Kiss, J. (2014) 'Academics: UK "Drip" data law changes are "serious expansion of surveillance"', *Guardian* (15 July), www.theguardian. com/technology/2014/jul/15/academics-uk-data-law-surveillance-bill-rushed-parliament.

Kuran, T. and Sunstein, C. (1999) 'Availability cascades and risk regulation', *Stanford Law Review*, vol 51, pp 683–768.

legislation.gov.uk (2014) Data Retention and Investigatory Powers Act 2014, www.legislation.gov.uk/ukpga/2014/27/contents/enacted.

L'Engle, K.L., Brown, J.D. and Kenneavy, K. (2004) 'The mass media as an important context for adolescents' sexual behaviour', *Journal of Adolescent Health*, vol 38 pp 186–92.

Ofcom (2014) *Report on Internet Safety Measures*, July 2014.

Ong, J. (2013) 'Internet Filtering Should be "Opt –In"', *New York Times* (19 August), www.nytimes.com/roomfordebate/2013/08/19/can-free-speech-and-internet-filters-co-exist/internet-filtering-should-be-opt-in.

Orr, D. (2013) 'Why such outrage over porn filters ? The idea seems perfectly reasonable to me', *Guardian* (26 July), www.theguardian. com/commentisfree/2013/jul/26/why-such-outrage-porn-filters (accessed 17 March 2015).

Pagliery, J. (2014) 'The Deep Web you don't know about', http:// money.cnn.com/2014/03/10/technology/deep-web/ (accessed 17 March 2015).

Perry, C. (2012) 'Premiere Christian Media and Safer Media for a Safer Society', *Independent Parliamentary Inquiry into Online Child Protection*, www.claireperry.org.uk/downloads/independent-parliamentary-inquiry-into-online-child-protection.pdf.

Peter, J. and Valkenburg, P.M. (2007) 'Adolescents' exposure to a sexualized media environment and their notions of women as sex objects', *Sex Roles*, vol 56, pp 381–95.

Sunday Times (2013) Colour magazine, 10 November.

Sunstein, C.R. (2005) 'Precautions against what? The availability heuristic and cross-cultural risk perception', *Alabama Law Review*, vol 75, pp 2–3.

The Young Turks (2013) 'Internet porn blocked all over Britain', https://www.youtube.com/watch?v=ACrrGTiV1VI 2013 (accessed 6 February 2015).

Times (2013) Colour magazine, 9 November.

Tversky, A. and Kahneman, D. (1974) 'Judgement under uncertainty: heuristics and biases', *Science*, vol 185, pp 1124–31.

Tversky, A. and Kahneman, D. (1986) 'Rational choice and framing of decisions', *Journal of Business*, vol 59, no 4, pp 251–78.

TWELVE

Internet radicalisation and the 'Woolwich Murder'

David McKendrick

Introduction

Lee Rigby was murdered in London on 22 May 2013. He was returning to the army barracks in Woolwich where he was living when he was hit by a car and then murdered by two men wielding knives and a cleaver. This event took place in broad daylight on a busy street in the capital city. The brutality of the murder seemed incomprehensible, as was the apparent randomness of the attack: Lee Rigby was targeted because he was a soldier – his attackers knew nothing more about him. They even took time after the assault to talk to passers-by, some of whom recorded the interaction on their mobile phones before uploading the footage to social networking sites, including YouTube. Both men were subsequently shot and wounded by armed police officers and taken to hospital. In February 2014, Michael Adebolajo and Michael Adebowale were found guilty of murder and given sentences of whole-life and 45 years, respectively. Video footage of the event was used repeatedly by the mainstream media after the murder and again at the time of the trial, bringing a 'real time' dimension to the attack and increasing its shock value considerably. An anti-Muslim backlash erupted in various parts of the UK in 2013 and 2014, with a series of assaults on mosques and on men and women assumed to be Muslim.

It is not surprising, given the seriousness and the unexpected nature of this event, that there has been intense speculation as to why it might have happened, and what might be done to prevent it happening again. A familiar story has emerged, picked up and carried in all of the major news outlets, that the attackers had been 'radicalised on the internet', supporting a narrative of the internet as a place where extreme views are contained and where people who harbour vicious, murderous intent have a safe and secure home. The internet, and more specifically social media channels such as YouTube, Twitter and Facebook, are portrayed here as the sites through which vulnerable young men (and women) are radicalised. The phrase 'cyber jihad' has been coined to describe aspects of internet activity. At the same time, Lee Rigby's murder was used to strengthen the argument for the passing of a Communications Data Bill aimed at giving the police and others more powers to investigate citizens' use of the internet, the so-called 'Snoopers' Charter'. Although this Bill failed to progress in Parliament, a subsequent Act was rushed through in July 2014, the Data Retention and Investigatory Powers Act 2014 (also discussed in Chapter Eleven).

Radicalisation and the internet

It is important now to take a step back from this and to ask: what is going on here? Should we view Lee Rigby's murder as part of a wider campaign of terror or as an isolated, horrific event? In seeking explanation and understanding of the event in Woolwich, there is a natural desire to seek to distance it from ourselves and our everyday lives. The remote nature of the internet provides a ready vehicle for this: we can reassure ourselves that, lurking somewhere deep in the shadows of the internet, social media channels exist where young, disenfranchised minority groups become 'radicalised' (a few years ago we might have called it 'brainwashed'). By creating this spectre that empowers our 'folk devils' (Cohen, 1972), we create a comfort space between ourselves and their actions. In other words, developing a narrative of 'extremism' means that you have decreased responsibility for the actions and motivations of the extremist. Your safety is secure. But is it? Or is it more likely that the reaction to extreme events like this may actually lead to a worse (and less safe) situation for all of us, as classic moral panic theory suggests? History shows us that moral panics about religious extremism are nothing new; the current social anxiety about young radical men is also familiar because it reminds us of earlier moral panics centred on the behaviour of young people (Cohen, 1972; Pearson, 1983; Thompson, 1998).

To help us think this through more carefully it might be helpful to look at the government's policy on radicalisation. Classic moral panic theory requires the participation of 'claims makers', those who would seek to claim relationships between issues or events that are unrelated, which then stokes fear over a particular subject in order to support a particular agenda, often their own. This can be achieved by stealth, through associating fear of particularly extreme behaviour with more general everyday concerns. In this particular case, the then Conservative Minister for Security, James Brokenshire (now Immigration Minister), in a speech on 27 June 2013 described what he saw as a link between internet radicalisation, terrorism and the government's initiatives for supporting children and families in difficulty:

> One particular interest of mine is the importance of ensuring that our counter radicalisation strategy sits alongside other key areas of public sector work ... I think it's important that we articulate our counter radicalisation strategy within the context of safeguarding ... In a similar vein, I am keen to ensure that the Government's work to support troubled families is aligned to our work to support vulnerable individuals at risk of being drawn into terrorist activity. (Brokenshire, 2013)

The counter-radicalisation strategy being discussed here is CONTEST (HM Government, 2011), a wide-ranging strategy that sought to provide an 'end to end' approach to tackling the issue of terrorism, radicalisation in general and, specifically, internet radicalisation. The four strands to the strategy are outlined here:

- pursue: to stop terrorist attacks
- prevent: to stop people becoming terrorists or supporting terrorism
- protect: to strengthen our protection against a terrorist attack
- prepare: to mitigate the impact of a terrorist attack.

The Prevent section of the strategy aimed to challenge the development of radicalisation in local communities by providing financial support for community projects in particular areas where the government had identified there being a risk of radicalisation. (It is of interest to note that the word 'terrorism' features heavily in the title of the document and not 'radicalism' or 'radicalisation'; the emphasis is plainly on terrorism.) Community projects such as these would work in areas that the government had identified as being at increased risk of radicalisation; social workers, nurses and teachers were to be in the 'front line' of the strategy to counter radicalisation. Prevent was initially developed in 2005 as part of the government's CONTEST strategy, following the London bombings. It underwent a number of revisions in 2011 and 2013 but it remains the government's primary social policy for challenging any form of domestic terrorism and extremism.

Perhaps unsurprisingly, there has been significant criticism of the approach taken in both Prevent and Channel. In 2009, the Institute of Race Relations first published Kundnani's *Spooked: How Not To Prevent Violent Extremism*, an evaluation of the strategy, which argued that this was overly focused on Muslim communities and was an attempt to insert counter-terrorist police officers into communities where there was a high Muslim population. *Spooked*, and a follow-up article in 2011 entitled 'Still Spooked', argued that the approach targeted vulnerable populations such as young Muslims and saw them through a lens of 'at risk of radicalisation'. Moreover, the monies and resources provided to develop preventative and diversionary services were decided at a central government level with little or no communication with the local areas where they were to be delivered. Because of this, the strategy never engaged effectively with the populations it aimed to support and local communities felt that there was an unprecedented level of intrusion into their daily lives.

Spooked also took issue with the characterisation in Prevent and Channel of radical and extreme views as inevitably dangerous, as if holding radical views meant that you were automatically a risk to others. The danger inherent in such an attitude is that simply holding radical views becomes something that requires a response from counter-terrorist police officers and other government agencies that seek to reduce and challenge domestic terrorism. This securitisation of those who hold radical views has been criticised as stifling and undermining fundamental democratic rights to free speech; by making the link between extremism and terrorism explicit in this way, the state gives permission for greater surveillance of increased numbers of the population and gradually advances itself into the private lives of citizens. The strategy also runs the risk of driving away from the democratic process the very young people that it purports to wish to engage with. As *Spooked* identified, the social and economic factors in people's lives that may contribute to a sense of isolation, anger and frustration are largely ignored, as the dominant emphasis is on significant risk to society that gives permission for the state to act in increasingly severe ways.

While *Spooked* focused on the experiences of young Muslim people in respect of the strategy, there is a further concern that should be explored. The strategy seeks to identify radicalism across the spectrum of 'troubled families' and 'safeguarding', thus affecting all countries of the UK, because counter-terrorism is a reserved Westminster power. The Troubled Families programme (TFP) is described thus:

> The aim of the programme is to 'turn round' the lives
> of the 120,000 most troubled and 'troublesome' families
> in the UK, by the end of the current Parliament in May
> 2015. Troubled families are defined nationally as those who

commit crime and/or anti-social behaviour, whose children are not attending school, and where at least one adult is on out of work benefits. If a family meets all three of these criteria they are classified as a 'troubled family', although the figure of 120,000 originally came from research looking at the extent of multiple disadvantages and not 'problematic behaviours'. (Levitas, 2012)

Local authorities, who are tasked with implementing the programme, can use 'local filter criteria' if a family meets two out of the three criteria. The TFP operates on a payment-by-results basis, where local authorities 'claim' payments from central government once they have achieved certain milestones relating to the family's behaviour and/ or labour market participation. The programme was voted the 'top government policy in a poll of local authority chief executive officers' in 2013 (Department for Communities and Local Government, 2013).

'Safeguarding' has an even broader definition:

- protecting children from maltreatment
- preventing impairment of children's health or development
- ensuring that children are growing up in circumstances consistent with the provision of safe and effective care
- taking action to enable all children and young people to have the best outcome.

[...] the action we take to promote the welfare of children and protect them from harm – is everyone's responsibility. Everyone who comes into contact with children and families has a role to play. (HM Government, 2009)

If Prevent and Channel are delivered through the prism of universal services that engage with all members of the community, this locates the risk of radicalisation, and indeed of domestic terrorism, in the widest possible arena; the net to challenge terrorism and radicalisation is now wide enough to include everyone within it. The Channel literature makes this abundantly clear:

Channel uses existing collaboration between local authorities, statutory partners (such as the education and health sectors, social services, children's and youth services and offender management services), the police and the local community to:

- identify individuals at risk of being drawn into terrorism
- assess the nature and extent of that risk
- develop the most appropriate support plan for the individuals concerned.

Channel is about safeguarding children and adults from being drawn into committing terrorist-related activity. It is about early intervention to protect and divert people away from the risk they face before illegality occurs. (HM Government, 2012)

These are powerful concepts. Equating 'early intervention' – a service seen as benign and supportive and that aims to support vulnerable people in a manner that negates the need for further statutory intervention – with prevention of terrorist attacks that threaten the fabric of society inserts the most restrictive elements of the state into services that are seen as offering support and encouragement to vulnerable families.

Deviancy amplification

The idea of deviancy amplification is at the heart of moral panic literature (see Cohen, 1972; Young, 1971). Writing as far back as 1964, the sociologist Leslie Wilkins introduced the concept of deviancy amplification. Wilkins argued that deviancy amplification was a deliberate strategy to exaggerate small individual acts of deviance and to amplify them in order to support a wider set of goals – goals that sought to label increasingly wider groups within society as being risky or concerning. In so doing, the existing powers maintained their position and were able to justify increasingly restrictive and intrusive responses. State hegemony was thereby secured, using the various instruments of the state (in this case, public services, the police and the intelligence service) and by the effective use of deviancy amplification. Brokenshire's earlier comments can be seen as classic deviancy amplification tactics; they have led not only to a securitisation of social policy but to an increased emphasis on securitising public servants, particularly when this is considered in respect of safeguarding or the TFP. To support this, the evidence of interventions under Prevent and Channel makes for interesting reading. In *Still Spooked,* we discover that:

According to Freedom of Information Act requests submitted to the twelve police forces involved in Channel, 1,120 individuals were identified by Channel project practitioners as on a pathway to radicalisation between 2007 and 2010. Of these, 290 were under sixteen years old and fifty-five were under 12. Over 90 per cent were Muslim; the rest were identified for potential involvement in far-right extremism. Of these 1,120 individuals, 286 were deemed to be in need of a further intervention of some kind. (Kundnani, 2011)

There is a stark difference between the 286 who are seen as requiring 'further intervention' and the widest possible number of children known through the TFP, safeguarding and early intervention. There is a lack of analysis as to why these young people have come to be at risk of radicalisation; ordinary life events such as adolescence, transitions, the death of a loved one or indeed the general trials and tribulations that we all experience as part of daily experiences can cause us to think differently about life and can lead to decision making that would not otherwise be considered if the conditions we find ourselves in change in an unexpected or damaging way.

In this sense, the notion of 'internet radicalisation' can be understood as a classic moral panic. Similar to Cohen's original 1972 work, the focus is once more on young people who are cast as 'folk devils'. The 'claims makers' in this case are the state, specifically the minister James Brokenshire, and deviancy amplification is used to perpetuate the ruling cultural hegemony, by subjugating those whom it has labelled as being at risk of radicalisation. The inherent danger is that we concentrate our efforts on the concept of radicalisation without developing an acute understanding of the other factors that are at play. The work of Stuart Hall (1975, 1978, 1980) is especially instructive here.

To return to Lee Rigby's murder. Latour (1993) suggests that to understand people, we must place them in their networks – that is, in the social, political, economic and technological world that they inhabit and interact with. On the YouTube footage, we hear the explanation/justification of one of the attackers as he rails against government policy, war, bombing of countries, racial and religious intolerance and the anger of young people. He clearly locates his actions in a network, which he understands in his own unique way. To get close to understanding his actions, we need to understand his network, in all its complexity and all its brutality. The young people targeted through the Prevent policy have similarly complex, but presumably very different, networks, each one navigating their own way through them, often in typically excessive teenage ways. Some of them will be drawn towards extremism; however, the deliberately engineered proximity of extremism, radicalism and terrorism draws them into a securitised world of threat and danger. Adolescents are at a formative stage in their life, and many are beginning to experiment with the content of the adult world. It is a time of exploration and discovery and a time when young people are influenced by the complex content of the networks they are a part of. As moral panic theory suggests, if we view the experiences of young people through a narrow paradigm of radicalisation and extremism we may increase the danger we are exposed to by failing to take into account the diversity of their lived experience. Narrow populist responses, often inflated by the media, can contribute to young people's feeling excluded or alienated and can encourage them to seek others who feel the same. While the reality for some young people may be that they are attracted to extremist views, this should not prompt a response that sees them as either 'at risk' or worse still 'a risk'; we need to have mechanisms that see young people in their fullest, most global sense and appreciate the complexities that make them so. If we are seeking to reduce risk and danger while encouraging a more nurturing, caring and understanding environment, we need to develop a more holistic understanding of young people and the issues they are facing.

I would like to suggest that the internet is only one potential aspect of the young person's network; it is akin to suggesting that publishers are responsible for what happens after people read books, or that violent films lead to violent actions. This is a dangerous path: content is not created by the medium; rather, content is created, in this case, by the actions, thoughts and beliefs of human beings. It may well then be conveyed in a variety of mediums, but the crucial point is that the vehicle is a container for the message that is created by the thoughts, feelings and opinions of individuals. This then interacts with the networks of individual actors in a similarly complicated journey, in a process that we must try to understand in all of its unique, multifaceted complexity. The true extent of any part played by the internet in the terrible crime committed at Woolwich has yet to emerge; only then can we learn the lessons that it will offer us.

References

Brokenshire, J. (2013) 'Countering violent extremism through communications', speech to the Global Counter Terrorism Forum (27 June), https://www.gov.uk/government/speeches/security-minister-james-brokenshire-countering-violent-extremism-through-communications (accessed 6 February 2015).

Cohen, S. (1972) *Folk Devils and Moral Panics*, London: MacGibbon & Kee.

Department for Communities and Local Government (2013) 'Troubled Families programme receives extra £200 million boost', www.gov.uk/government/news/troubled-families-programme-receives-extra-200-million-boost (accessed 17 March 2013).

Hall, S. and Jefferson, T. (1975; 2nd edn 2006) *Resistance through rituals: Youth subcultures in post-war Britain* (Cultural Studies Birmingham), London: Routledge.

Hall, S., Critcher, C., Jefferson, T., Clarke, J. and R. Bryan (1978; 2nd edn 2013) *Policing the Crisis: Mugging, the State and Law and Order*, London: Macmillan.

Hall, S., Hobson, R., Lowe, A. and Willis, P. (1980) (2nd edn) *Culture, Media, Language, Trade in Culture, Media, Language: Working Papers in Cultural Studies, 1972–79* (Cultural Studies Birmingham), London: Routledge.

HM Government (2009) *Working Together to Safeguard Children Consultation Document, A guide to inter-agency working to safeguard and promote the welfare of children* (December), https://www.education.gov.uk/consultations/downloadableDocs/Working%20Together%20to%20Safeguard%20ChildrenV2.pdf.

HM Government (2011) *CONTEST: The United Kingdom's Strategy for Countering Terrorism* (July), https://www.gov.uk/government/uploads/system/uploads/attachment_data/file/97994/contest-summary.pdf.

HM Government (2011) *Prevent Strategy* (June), Cm 8092, https://www.gov.uk/government/uploads/system/uploads/attachment_data/file/97976/prevent-strategy-review.pdf.

HM Government (2012) *Channel: Protecting vulnerable people from being drawn into terrorism: A guide for local partnerships* (October), https://www.gov.uk/government/uploads/system/uploads/attachment_data/file/118194/channel-guidance.pdf.

Kundnani, A. (2009) *Spooked: How not to prevent violent extremism*, Institute of Race Relations, www.irr.org.uk/publications/issues/spooked-how-not-to-prevent-violent-extremism/.

Kundnani, A. (2011) 'Still Spooked; How Not To Prevent Violent Extremism', Institute of Race Relations, www.irr.org.uk/news/still-spooked/.

Latour, B. (1993) *We have never been modern*, trans. C. Porter, Boston, MA: Harvard University Press.

Levitas, R. (2012) 'There may be "trouble" ahead: what we know about those 120,000 "troubled" families', www.poverty.ac.uk/sites/default/files/attachments/WP%20Policy%20Response%20No.3-%20%20%27Trouble%27%20ahead%20%28Levitas%20Final%2021April2012%29.pdf (accessed 17 March 2015).

Pearson, G. (1983) *Hooligan: A history of respectable fears*, Basingstoke: Macmillan.

Thompson, K. (1998) *Moral panics*, London: Routledge.

Wilkins, L. (1964) *Social deviance*, London: Routledge & Kegan Paul.

Young, J. (1971) *The drugtakers: The social meaning of drug use,* London: Paladin.

THIRTEEN

Moralising discourse and the dialectical formation of class identities: the social reaction to 'chavs' in Britain

Elias le Grand

Introduction

> They are the non-respectable working-classes: the dole-scroungers, petty criminals, football hooligans and teenage pram-pushers. (Lewis, 2004).

Since the early 2000s, the 'chav' has become a widely spread stereotype, well-institutionalised into British public and everyday discourse (le Grand, 2013). The term is tied to strong forms of hostility and moral-aesthetic distinction, and commonly applied to white working-class youths appropriating a certain style of appearance, including what is known as 'streetwear' clothing and jewellery. Drawing on an analysis of news media, websites and popular culture, this chapter discusses the social reaction to chavs and how it is bound up with the formation of class identities.

Following calls to extend the conceptual reach of moral panic analysis (Hier, 2002, 2008, 2011; Critcher, 2009, 2013; Hier et al, 2011; Hunt, 2011), I conceptualise moral panic as a strong and volatile type of social reaction rooted in long-term processes of moral regulation. Both moral panic and moral regulation are conceived as moralisation processes that entail the formation of moralising discourses that act upon the conduct of both self and other. Moralisation therefore involves a dialectical relationship between those actors who moralise certain issues and those who are the object of such moralising discourses and practices. However, Critcher (2009) states that while moral panic discourses focus on constructing the 'folk devil' as a threat to the moral order and an object of social control measures, moral regulation projects typically involve processes of moral governance, or the reformation of 'character' or the adaptation of behaviour.

In this chapter, I explore the ways in which such dialectical processes of moralisation are tied to the formation of class identities, and to this end I draw on a multi-dimensional, relational notion of class informed by Bourdieu (1984 [1979], 1986, 1987). Bourdieu argues that classed forms of identification and distinction are tied to individuals' unequal access to economic, cultural and social capital; individuals from different classed social locations have differing possibilities to construct identities that are valued and recognised in society. Class formation is therefore tied to hierarchies of moral worth (Skeggs, 1997; Sayer, 2005).

The social reaction to chavs

The emergence and diffusion of the chav stereotype in many ways follows that of a classic moral panic. The term appeared suddenly, 'as if from nowhere', at the beginning of the 20th century. In particular, the 'humorous' website Chavscum, set up in December 2003, was instrumental in constructing and diffusing images of chavs on the internet. By the beginning of 2004, news media caught on and soon chavs were all over the public realm. A LexisNexis database search of the term 'chav' in the 16 UK newspapers with nationwide distribution shows that there were no mentions of the term in 2003, but in 2004 it was mentioned in 374 articles. The same year it also became a dictionary term and was named the buzzword of the year (Dent, 2004). The term 'chav' has continued to be used in news media. In 2013, as many as 481 newspaper articles mentioned the term. It can therefore be argued that the term has been well institutionalised into British public discourse.

Like many moral panics, however, the phenomenon over which the social reaction emerged has existed for much longer. Young working-class people in streetwear clothing associated with low social status and loutish behaviour have existed throughout the UK since the 1990s (Hayward and Yar, 2006). Moreover, the term 'chav' has been used in South-East England since at least the 1970s, although it was not tied any particular group of youths and largely lacked derogatory meanings (for a discussion of the origins of the term, see le Grand, 2010).

The chav as folk devil

In public discourse, chavs have frequently been the object of moral outrage, ridicule and disgust. The image of the chav is largely constructed through practices of consumption (Hayward and Yar, 2006) and often denotes poverty and deprivation. Chavs are said to live on council estates and to gather in gangs, occupying public spaces such as street corners, shopping centres and McDonald's restaurants. They smoke, binge drink and live on a diet of cheap and unhealthy food, especially fast food. In general, the appearance and lifestyles of chavs are coded as excessive, hedonistic, unhealthy, wasteful and vulgar. For instance, the *Telegraph* sneers at chavs' style of appearance, describing them as 'dripping in bling', that is, 'cheap, tasteless and usually gold-coloured jewellery' (Tweedie, 2004).

Moreover, chavs are portrayed as loud mouthed and aggressive. Male chavs in particular are often associated with violence and petty crime, such as football hooliganism, vandalism, assaults and muggings. This is captured by the notion that the term is an acronym for 'council housed and violent'. Chavs are also described as promiscuous and sexually irresponsible, and this is especially the case for 'chavettes', that is, female chavs, who are depicted as 'sluts' with no control over their sexuality. They are also associated with teenage pregnancy and motherhood. Thus, in a *Daily Mail* article entitled 'A-Z of chavs', one can read: 'PRAM: Any Chavette who isn't pushing one of these by the age of 14 is obviously frigid, infertile or a "lezza" [lesbian]' (Thomas, 2004). Moreover, chavs have often been portrayed as uneducated, lazy, unemployed welfare cheats lacking any willingness to work, who are happily using the welfare system paid for by 'us' hard-working respectable people. As the *Sun* put it:

> They just want to leech off the sweat of the rest of us ...
> These freeloaders are not too thick to realise they can get more by scrounging on the dole rather than working. They've sussed that even with a minimum wage they can lie in their pits until the afternoon and still pick up a nice wedge, especially if they keep pushing out their soon-to-be-feral offspring. (Gaunt, 2008)

Thus, chavs have been constructed as non-respectable, white, working-class 'folk devils' who threaten the moral order of society through their sexual and reproductive activities, willing joblessness, antisocial behaviour and vulgar taste. Here a marginal class position, that is, a lack of economic and cultural capital, is tied to a 'dirty' and therefore racialised form of whiteness (see also Hall and Jefferson, 1975; Webster, 2008).

A contested public issue about class

An important aspect of the chav discourse is that it has made social class the subject of public discussion. This is significant, given the earlier silence around the topic in the British public sphere (Savage, 2000; Skeggs, 2004). Some cases of class contempt directed against chavs have become widely debated. One example is a YouTube video clip entitled 'Class Wars' made by pupils of Glenalmond College, one of Britain's foremost public schools. The video is a supposedly humorous take on a fox hunt, but one that involves the shooting of chavs instead of foxes. Another example is the media debate following the publication of a promotional e-mail sent by travel company Activities Abroad that offered 'chav free holidays'. It based this claim on the fact that names associated with chavs were absent from its database. The company's managing director, Alistair McLean, later defended the e-mail, stating:

> "I simply feel it is time the middle-classes stood up for themselves. We make a positive contribution to our economy and watch it all be frittered away by people who simply can't be bothered ('bovvered'). /../ So regardless of whether it is class warfare or not I make no apology for proclaiming myself to be middle-class and a genuine contributor to our society." (Digitalspy, 2009)

In this statement, McLean contrasts respectable, hard-working middle-class people with chavs who threaten to destroy everything that the former built up. The huge volume of such strongly derogatory content directed against chavs in public discourse, not the least when articulated by journalists representing 'serious' news media, suggests that in many contexts, such language is legitimate.

Yet many commentators, especially from the Left, have criticised 'chav-bashing' as a form of classism or class-racism. This reflects the fact that in contemporary, fragmented public spheres, moral panics and other public issues are frequently contested (McRobbie and Thornton, 1995). One notable illustration of this was in 2008 when Tom Hampson, editor-in-chief of the *Fabian Review*, the journal published by the left-wing think-tank the Fabian Society, wrote an editorial that generated much debate. In this he argued that the term 'chav' should be banned, and that its usage 'is deeply offensive to a largely voiceless group and – especially when used in normal middle-class conversation or on national TV – it betrays a deep and revealing level of class hatred' (Hampson, 2008). This article was repeated in an opinion piece in the *Guardian* online (Hampson and Olchawski, 2008) and has been further explored in an influential book entitled *Chav: The Demonization of the Working Class* by writer and journalist Owen Jones (2011). The book created extensive debate and put issues of social class and the chav phenomenon further onto the public agenda, not only in Britain but also internationally.

Social control measures

In the wake of moral panics, measures of social control are typically instated in order to 'protect' the public from the threat posed by the 'folk devils' (Cohen, 2002 [1972]). This was also the case for the anxieties that surround chavs, who became the target of new and existing forms of policing. One such form of policing dealt with regulating access to public space. Shopping malls, pubs, night clubs and internet cafes started banning the wearing of garments or brands associated with chavs, including baseball caps, hoodies, tracksuits and clothes in Burberry check. One of the cases most covered by the media was the ban on 'hoodies' (hooded tops) in the Bluewater Shopping Centre in Kent in 2005 (see Hier et al, 2011).

Chavs have also been strongly associated with Anti-Social Behaviour Orders (ASBOs). First issued by the Labour government in 1997, but strengthened and broadened during 2003–04, an ASBO is a civil order serving 'to restrict the behaviour of a person likely to cause harm or distress to the public' (Oxford Dictionaries, nd). In common parlance, ASBO also refers to the kind of people against whom such civil orders are issued. Chavs are often conceived as ASBOs, as in the following definition of the term on Urban Dictionary (nd): '[ASBO is] an essential qualification for all chavs and general idiots who think that beating the shit out of random people walking down the street/ throwing bricks through people's windows/generally displaying how few brain cells they have, makes them look "hard"'. Chavs are often seen as glorifying ASBOS, and are supposed to believe that getting one is seen as a 'badge of honour'.

Conclusion: moralisation and the dialectics of class identity

In what way can the moralisation of chavs be considered a moral panic? The social reaction to chavs emerged suddenly and involved significant hostility. Thus, chavs were constructed as a folk devil threatening the moral and aesthetic order of British society. Chavs also became the targets of different forms of social control. However, contra fully fledged moral panics, there has been no discrete group of moral entrepreneurs organising campaigns against chavs in any systematic or extended fashion. Rather, the social reaction emerged and diffused spontaneously throughout the 'grassroots' of the public sphere. I would therefore argue that the chav phenomenon constitutes a sudden, strong form of social reaction with elements of a moral panic that is bound up with longer-term moralisation processes of white working-class people in Britain.

Through these moralisation processes the chav has been constructed as a non-respectable figure of the white British working class. This works dialectically: on the one hand, the chav becomes a stigmatising social identity in which certain white working-class people are positioned. On the other hand, these processes simultaneously enable middle-class and working-class people to position themselves as respectable and morally righteous. Notions of respectability have been central in constructing classed hierarchies of moral worth (Skeggs, 1997; Sayer, 2005). In Britain, this has entailed the long-standing moral denigration of certain groups of white working-class people as non-respectable (Stacey, 1960; Bott, 1964; Skeggs, 1997, 2004; Watt, 2006).

The emergence of the chav stereotype can be linked to the neoliberal economic restructuring and deindustrialisation of the last decades, which led to the rise of 'flexible' and poor work (McDowell, 2003), as well as to the increasing marginalisation, poverty and fragmentation of working-class communities, particularly in the North of England (see also Charlesworth, 2000; Turner, 2000). By the late 1990s, when New Labour came into power, there was no room for the marginalised white working-class in its vision of 21st-century Britain. As Haylett (2001) has shown, the political rhetoric of New Labour envisioned a multicultural, modern and progressive Britain in which white, poor working-class people simultaneously became cast as the unmodern, racist and backward 'other'. I would argue that the youth of this group has come to be further demonised and pathologised under the label 'chav'. It is also in this context of marginalised whiteness that the moralising discourse directed against chavs has become a widely legitimate form of class racism, which it would be impossible to direct against any ethnic or sexual minority with the same force (le Grand, 2013).

References

Bott, E. (1964) *Family and social network: Roles, norms and external relationships in ordinary urban families*, London: Tavistock Publications.

Bourdieu, P. (1984 [1979]) *Distinction: A social critique of the judgement of taste*, Cambridge, MA: Harvard University Press.

Bourdieu, P. (1986) 'The forms of capital', in J.G. Richardson (ed) *Handbook of theory and research for the sociology of education*, Westport, CT: Greenwood Press, pp 241–58.

Bourdieu, P. (1987) 'What makes a social class? On the theoretical and practical existence of groups', *Berkeley Journal of Sociology*, vol 22, pp 1–17.

Charlesworth, S.J. (2000) *A phenomenology of working-class experience*, Cambridge: Cambridge University Press.

Cohen, S. (2002 [1972]) *Folk devils and moral panics: The creation of the Mods and Rockers* (3rd edn), London: Routledge.

Critcher, C. (2009) 'Widening the focus: moral panics as moral regulation', *British Journal of Criminology*, vol 49, no 1, pp 17–34.

Critcher, C. (2013) 'New perspectives on anti-doping policy: from moral panic to moral regulation', *International Journal of Sport Policy and Politics*, vol 6, no 2, pp 153-69.

Dent, S. (2004) *Larpers and shroomers: The language report*, Oxford: Oxford University Press.

Digitalspy (2009) '"Chav-free" holidays offered by travel firm!!!', http://forums.digitalspy.co.uk/showthread.php?t=980152 (accessed 17 March 2015)

Gaunt, J. (2008) 'Karen's in a class of her own', *Sun* (18 April).

Hall, S. and Jefferson, T. (1975; 2nd edn 2006) *Resistance through Rituals, Youth Subcultures in Post-War Britain* (Cultural Studies Birmingham), London: Routledge.

Hampson, T. (2008) 'Drop the word "chav"', *Fabian Review*, vol 120, no 2, pp 19.

Hampson, T. and Olchawski, J. (2008) 'Ban the word "chav"', *Guardian* (15 July), www.theguardian.com/commentisfree/2008/jul/15/equality.language.

Haylett, C. (2001) 'Illegitimate subjects? Abject Whites, neoliberal modernisation, and middle-class multiculturalism', *Environment and Planning D: Society and Space*, vol 19, no 3, pp 351–70.

Hayward, K. and Yar, M. (2006) 'The "chav" phenomenon: consumption, media and the construction of a new underclass', *Crime, Media, Culture,* vol 2, no 1, pp 9–28.

Hier, S.P. (2002) 'Conceptualizing moral panic through a moral economy of harm', *Critical Sociology,* vol 28, no 3, pp 311–34.

Hier, S.P. (2008) 'Thinking beyond moral panic: risk, responsibility, and the politics of moralization', *Theoretical Criminology*, vol 12, no 2, pp 173–90.

Hier, S.P. (2011) 'Tightening the focus: moral panic, moral regulation and liberal government', *British Journal of Sociology,* vol 62, no 3, pp 523–41.

Hier, S.P., Lett, D., Walby, K. and Smith, A. (2011) 'Beyond folk devil resistance: linking moral panic and moral regulation', *Criminology and Criminal Justice,* vol 11, no 3, pp 259–76.

Hunt, A. (2011) 'Fractious rivals? Moral panics and moral regulation', in S.P. Hier (ed) *Moral panic and the politics of anxiety,* London: Routledge, pp 53–70.

Jones, O. (2011) *Chavs: The demonization of the working class,* London: Verso.

le Grand, E. (2010) *Class, place and identity in a satellite town,* Stockholm: Acta Universitatis Stockholmiensis.

le Grand, E. (2013) 'The "chav" as folk devil', in J. Petley, C. Critcher, J. Hughes and A. Rohloff (eds) *Moral panics in the contemporary world,* London: Bloomsbury, pp 215–34.

Lewis, J. (2004) 'In defence of snobbery', *Telegraph* (31 January).

McDowell, L. (2003) *Redundant masculinities? Employment change and white working class youth,* Oxford: Blackwell.

McRobbie, A. and Thornton, S. (1995) 'Rethinking "moral panic" for multi-mediated social worlds', *British Journal of Sociology,* vol 46, no 4, pp 559–74.

Oxford Dictionaries (nd) 'Asbo', www.oxforddictionaries.com/definition/ english/ASBO (accessed 3 May 2013).

Savage, M. (2000) *Class analysis and social transformation,* Buckingham: Open University.

Sayer, A. (2005) *The moral significance of class,* Cambridge: Cambridge University Press.

Skeggs, B. (1997) *Formations of class and gender: Becoming respectable,* London: Sage.

Skeggs, B. (2004) *Class, self, culture,* London: Routledge.

Stacey, M. (1960) *Tradition and change: A study of Banbury,* Oxford: Oxford University Press.

Thomas, D. (2004) 'A-Z of chavs', *Daily Mail* (20 October).

Turner, R.L. (2000) *Coal was our life: An essay on life in a Yorkshire former pit town,* Sheffield: Sheffield Hallam University Press.

Tweedie, N. (2004) 'Cheltenham ladies and the chavs', *Telegraph* (14 December).

Urban Dictionary (nd) 'ASBO', ww.urbandictionary.com/define.php?term=ASBO (accessed 17 March 2015).

Watt, P. (2006) 'Respectability, roughness and "race": neighbourhood place images and the making of working-class social distinctions in London', *International Journal of Urban and Regional Research*, vol 30, no 4, pp 776–97.

Webster, C. (2008) 'Marginalized white ethnicity, race and crime', *Theoretical Criminology*, vol 12, no 3, pp 293–312.

FOURTEEN

The presence of the absent parent: troubled families and the England 'riots' of 2011

Steve Kirkwood

Introduction

The 'riots' in England during August 2011 involved a level of public disturbance and destruction rarely seen in the United Kingdom. These events resulted in widespread speculation as to the causes of, and solutions to, the violence and looting. The public and media responses could be seen as constituting a 'moral panic' in relation to the people involved, particularly in terms of the scapegoating of the young people who took part in the 'riots'. In this regard, Prime Minister David Cameron argued that the involvement of many young people was related to poor parenting and absent fathers, and stated that he would seek to 'turn around the lives of the 120,000 most troubled families in the country'. This chapter explores the way in which 'troubled families' were portrayed as a cause of people's involvement in the 'riots' and critically examines the implications of such understandings of and responses to public unrest. In particular, it demonstrates how the discourse and related initiatives depoliticise 'riots'; how 'problem families' are portrayed as being a target for policy; and how the 'riots' were used to expand a policy direction already in place.

The 'riots'

On 4 August 2011, Mark Duggan, a 29-year-old black man from Tottenham, was shot dead by police. On 6 August, a group of approximately 200 people gathered at Tottenham police station seeking further information regarding the incident. There is evidence that police used aggressive tactics that provoked a reaction from the crowd (Reicher and Stott, 2011), which was followed by some members of the public setting police cars on fire, throwing various objects at the police and causing damage to certain commercial buildings. From 6 to 10 August, public disturbance spread to various parts of England and appeared to involve a variety of motivations, including protesting against discriminatory police practices, reacting to general inequalities in society and elements of opportunism (Reicher and Stott, 2011).

On 11 August 2011, Prime Minister David Cameron made a parliamentary speech on the events and the actions that were being taken to address them (Cameron, 2011a). He highlighted the death of Mark Duggan and the 'peaceful demonstrations' that initially followed, and asserted that these were 'then used as an excuse by opportunist thugs in gangs', leading to behaviour that constituted 'criminality pure and simple', thus illustrating Potter and Wetherell's (1987) idea that 'splitting' people into 'good' and 'bad' protestors is a way of condemning certain groups and behaviours while still appearing, on the surface, to be reasonable and understanding. In this case, people involved in the 'peaceful demonstrations' were portrayed as legitimate whereas those involved in other activities could be vilified as 'criminals', while avoiding dealing with the ways in which wider social issues and police relations might, in practice, structure both categories of behaviour.

Cameron also referred to the 'deeper problems' that provided the context for the 'riots':

> I have said before that there is a major problem in our society with children growing up not knowing the difference between right and wrong. This is not about poverty, it's about culture. A culture that glorifies violence, shows disrespect to authority, and says everything about rights but nothing about responsibilities. In too many cases, the parents of these children – if they are still around – don't care where their children are or who they are with, let alone what they are doing. (Cameron, 2011a)

Here the problem was portrayed as lying with young people – 'children' – and the way in which they had been raised. Importantly, the 'riots' were presented as immoral behaviour perpetrated by those who did not know any better and were thereby depoliticised. Furthermore, the inequalities in society – and the government's role in maintaining or exacerbating these inequalities – were dismissed, thus reinforcing an image of the riots as non-political. Rather, the 'problems' were presented as relating to 'culture' and the ways that this might facilitate or endorse 'rioting' behaviours. If Cameron's account functioned to provide a broader 'context' or source of the riots, rather than pointing to structural issues or problems of inequality, it thus shifted blame onto the parents and families of the 'rioters'.

'Troubled families'

On 15 August, David Cameron gave a more extended account regarding the 'riots'. He discounted explanations relating to 'race', 'government cuts' or 'poverty' and stated:

> No, this was about behaviour ...
> ... people showing indifference to right and wrong ...
> ... people with a twisted moral code ...
> ... people with a complete absence of self-restraint.
> (Cameron, 2011b)

As with the accounts provided in his previous speech, here he explicitly rejected explanations for the 'riots' that focused on the actions of the government or on inequality. This depoliticised the 'riots' and suggested solutions that focused on individual rather than structural issues. He specifically emphasised the role of families and parents:

> Let me start with families. The question people asked over and over again last week was 'where are the parents? Why aren't they keeping the rioting kids indoors?' Tragically that's been followed in some cases by judges rightly lamenting: 'why don't the parents even turn up when their children are in court?' Well, join the dots and you have a clear idea about why some of these young people were behaving so terribly. Either there was no one at home, they didn't much care or they'd lost control.
> Families matter. I don't doubt that many of the rioters out last week have no father at home. Perhaps they come from one of the neighbourhoods where it's standard for children to have a mum and not a dad ... where it's normal for young men to grow up without a male role model, looking to the streets for their father figures, filled up with rage and anger. So if we want to have any hope of mending our broken society, family and parenting is where we've got to start. (Cameron, 2011b)

Here the parents are condemned for not taking enough interest in their children, specifically for being absent, uncaring or incompetent.

The implication is that 'rioting' behaviour was a result of parents who were not present, not interested or not capable of raising their children appropriately. More specifically, the account condemns fathers for their absence and asserts a causal link between a father's absence and children's violent behaviour.

A key element of Cameron's stated approach related to the notion of 'troubled families':

> And we need more urgent action, too, on the families that some people call 'problem', others call 'troubled'. The ones that everyone in their neighbourhood knows and often avoids. […] Now that the riots have happened I will make sure that we clear away the red tape and the bureaucratic wrangling, and put rocket boosters under this programme … with a clear ambition that within the lifetime of this Parliament we will turn around the lives of the 120,000 most troubled families in the country. (Cameron, 2011b)

An important aspect of Cameron's description of these families is the use of the terms 'problem' and 'troubled'. More specifically, labelling them as 'problem families' suggests that they are the source of the problem and that they constitute a problem for other people. In contrast, 'troubled families' implies that they face troubles and that they are the ones having to deal with difficulties that affect them from external sources. Although he uses the term 'troubled families' later in the extract, the way in which he introduces these two labels suggests at least an ambivalence towards the families and the ways of conceiving of them. The idea that they may be 'problem families' more than 'troubled families' is reinforced by his suggestion that they are '[t]he ones that everyone in their neighbourhood knows and often avoids'. Cameron clarified his use of the phrase in a subsequent speech:

> Officialdom might call them 'families with multiple disadvantages'. Some in the press might call them 'neighbours from hell'. Whatever you call them, we've known for years that a relatively small number of families are the source of a large proportion of the problems in society. (Cameron, 2011c)

The account suggests that Cameron's view is that these families are the cause of the problems rather than merely those who are on the receiving end of such problems (that is, 'problem families' more than 'troubled families').

As Cameron makes clear, his approach towards these 'troubled families' had begun several months before the riots occurred. A key part of Cameron's approach is the goal to 'turn around the lives of the 120,000 most troubled families in the country'. This aim had resulted in the development of the Troubled Families Unit within the government to oversee the work on this matter. One of the interesting issues relates to the '120,000' families identified in Cameron's speech. The Department for Communities (nd) released a document explaining the origins of this figure. Levitas (2012) challenged the figure, including the £9 billion the government suggested these families cost the taxpayer, due to their 'troubles'. An important aspect of Levitas' critique is that the estimate is based on a figure from a study that found that 2% of the study sample met at least five of the following seven criteria, and were therefore multiply disadvantaged:

> No parent in the family is in work;
> Family lives in overcrowded housing;
> No parent has any qualifications;
> Mother has mental health problems;
> At least one parent has a long-standing limiting illness, disability or infirmity;
> Family has low income (below 60% of median income);
> Family cannot afford a number of food and clothing items. (Levitas, 2012)

It is clear that these criteria relate to issues of unemployment, poverty, illness and disability. This is very different from the issues of absent parents, violence, criminality, gang involvement, poor parenting and lack of morals identified by Cameron in his speeches. As Levitas (2012, p 10) points out, the government's account of these families constitutes an instance of 'slippage from the criteria of multiple deprivation to those of anti-social behaviour'. Far from a mere error of transposition, this shift is evident in Cameron's (2011c) speech, where he suggests that there is no substantial difference between 'families with multiple disadvantages' and 'neighbours from hell'. To the contrary, these different criteria could mark the difference between families that *face* trouble and families that *make* trouble. Of course, the ambiguity inherent in the notion 'troubled families' allows for such slippage, while introducing a negative moral evaluation of families that experience a variety of problems.

Moral panic?

I will now explore whether this issue can be understood from the perspective of the concept of 'moral panic' (Cohen, 1972), drawing on Goode and Ben-Yehuda's (2009) model. This argues that the following characteristics are likely to be in place for a moral panic to ensue: concern, hostility, consensus, disproportion and volatility. There is clear evidence that the 'riots', as discussed already and as demonstrated by Hedge and MacKenzie (2012), resulted in widespread concern and hostility. I will therefore focus on the remaining criteria.

Consensus

Reicher and Stott (2011) claim that: 'Within a week of the riots there was a clear consensus that the riots were all about criminality [...] Within a month, that consensus had crystallized into policy.'

But how far was there 'a clear consensus'? In an earlier publication, Reicher and Hopkins (2001) suggest that the greater the consensus in terms of the significance of an event in a nation's history, the more potential disagreement over its meaning. In the case of the riots, Ed Miliband (2011), Leader of the Opposition, explicitly rejected David Cameron's account and argued that the types of values reflected in the actions of 'looters' were modelled through the 'greedy, selfish and immoral' behaviour of elite sections of society, including bankers, MPs and journalists. Furthermore, a public survey by eDigitalResearch (nd) found various levels of support for different explanations, including greed and lack of respect, poor parenting, police tactics and lack of opportunities for young people. Importantly, Newburn et al (2011) argue that many of the 'rioters' characterised their own behaviour as 'protesting', thus challenging other accepted accounts. All of this suggests that consensus was not just absent, but an impossibility. Rather than establishing consensus, I believe that it may be more helpful to consider the extent to which elites are able to produce legitimacy in relation to a social issue.

Disproportion

Turning to the question of the proportionality of the response, the cost of damage from the 'riots' was estimated at over £500 million (Riots, Communities and Victims Panel, 2012). David Cameron (2011c) suggested that the '120,000 troubled families' cost the taxpayer approximately £9 billion a year, and allocated £448 million to address the situation. Sentences for those convicted of crimes during the riots were criticised by some commentators as being too harsh, although others suggested they were appropriate (BBC, 2011). Although it is possible to compare damage costs to the cost of 'solutions' or to compare sentences for similar crimes, this will not resolve the issue of proportionality, as the extent and nature of the problem, and the appropriate response, are exactly the issues under dispute. Defining a response as 'proportionate' as opposed to 'disproportionate' must, I would argue, be understood as a rhetorical accomplishment in itself.

Volatility

How far can the riots be considered, in moral panic parlance, to have been volatile? They did 'erupt fairly suddenly' (Goode and Ben-Yehuda, 2009, p 41), but how far were they a unique, identifiable phenomenon in their own right? Hier et al (2011, p 260) argue that 'moral panics represent episodes of contestation and negotiation that emerge from and contribute to or reinforce broader processes of moral regulation'. In this regard, both main political parties have focused on the responsibilisation of parents, with Labour's Family Intervention Projects for the '50,000 most chaotic families' (Gregg, 2010), followed up by David Cameron's commitment to address the '120,000 most troubled families'. This would suggest that the response to the 'riots' constituted a continuation and emphasis of the attention on such families, rather than merely a 'knee jerk' reaction to the 2011 'riots'.

Discussion

The way the 'riots' were portrayed and linked to 'troubled families' functions to depoliticise the 'riots' and shifts attention away from structural causes, while 'slippage' between families that *face* problems and families that *cause* problems leads to stigmatisation. Whether they provide an example of the unfolding of a classic moral panic, as characterised by Goode and Ben-Yehuda (2009), seems doubtful. It has been demonstrated that consensus was not only unlikely, but an impossibility. Similarly, proportionality is exactly the issue at stake and there are no 'objective' criteria to resolve the dispute. Following Hier et al (2011), although the 'riots' themselves appeared to be an indication of volatility, the governmental response regarding a focus on responsibility, out-of-control youth and poor parenting constituted relative continuity in policy. This analysis thus illustrates the way in which a significant event can be used to bring attention and resources to an issue and policy strategy that is already in place, despite tenuous causal links.

As highlighted by Pearce and Charman (2011), research on moral panics has involved a range of theoretical perspectives, including Cohen's (1972) focus on labelling, Hall et al's (1978) Marxist influences and Goode and Ben-Yehuda's (2011) social constructionist approach. The present discussion suggests that a discursive approach (Potter and Wetherell, 1987), which focuses on the way that language functions to actively construct social realities, may be helpful in understanding certain aspects of events that could be deemed 'moral panics'. Such an approach should help to extend the scope of such research while potentially addressing some of the common criticisms of the ways in which moral panics are conceived. In relation to Goode and Ben-Yehuda's criteria, such an approach could examine: how concern is manifested and justified; the nature of the hostility; the way people legitimise their responses and claim consensus; how responses are portrayed as being proportionate or disproportionate; and how the apparent volatile nature of the response may be understood within a context of relative continuity in terms of the discursive construction of 'folk devils' and related policy responses.

Conclusions

The England 'riots' of 2011 illustrate an instance where the UK government mobilised a policy for intervening with 'troubled families', based on tenuous connections between the targets of the intervention and the original 'riots'. Furthermore, it is helpful to understand this situation in the context of continuity – in the sense of a policy direction that was already underway – rather than merely as a reactive response to extreme events. When analysing the situation, it is useful to see how the situation and appropriate responses were discursively constructed by key players in the government, as well as by alternative voices. This approach highlights that 'slippage' in language ('troubled families' versus 'problem families'), the construction of consensus and arguments over proportionality function to legitimise or criticise policy responses. The concept of 'moral panics' helps to understand extreme events such as 'riots'; however, some of the key criteria for a 'moral panic' are exactly the things that are most contested in this context and 'objective' measures will remain elusive. For this reason, it is important to go beyond the moral-panic heuristic (Rohloff and Wright 2010), drawing on alternative ideas such as those from discourse analysis, in order to strengthen our understanding.

References

BBC (2011) 'Some England riot sentences "too severe"', www.bbc.co.uk/news/uk-14553330 (17 August).

Cameron, D. (2011a) 'PM's speech on Big Society', www.gov.uk/government/speeches/pms-speech-on-big-society (accessed 17 March 2015).

Cameron, D. (2011b) 'PM's speech on the fightback after the riots', www.gov.uk/government/speeches/pms-speech-on-the-fightback-after-the-riots (accessed 17 March 2015).

Cameron, D. (2011c) 'Troubled families speech', www.gov.uk/government/speeches/troubled-families-speech (accessed 17 March 2015).

Cohen, S. (1972) *Folk devils and moral panics*, London: MacGibbon & Kee.

Department for Communities (nd) Troubled family estimates explanatory note, http://webarchive.nationalarchives.gov.uk/20120919132719/www.communities.gov.uk/documents/newsroom/pdf/2053538.pdf (accessed 17 March 2015)

eDigitalResearch (nd) *England riots survey – August 2011: Summary of findings*, https://www.edigitalresearch.com/files/sky/news_panel/riot_survey_summary_of_findings.pdf.

Goode, E. and Ben-Yehuda, N. (2009) *Moral panics: The social construction of deviance* (2nd edn), Chichester, UK: Wiley-Blackwell.

Gregg, D. (2010) *Family Intervention Projects: A classic case of policy-based evidence*, www.crimeandjustice.org.uk/sites/crimeandjustice.org.uk/files/family%20intervention.pdf (accessed 17 March 2015).

Hall, S., Critcher, C., Jefferson, T., Clarke, J. and Roberts, B. (1978) *Policing the crisis: Mugging, the state, and law and order*, London: Macmillan.

Hedge, N. and MacKenzie, A. (2012) 'Riots and reactions: Hypocrisy and disaffiliation?', Philosophy of Education Society of Great Britain Annual Conference, New College, Oxford, 30 March–1 April, www.yumpu.com/en/document/view/25297348/riots-and-reactions-hypocrisy-and-disaffiliation-philosophy-of- (accessed 17 March 2015)

Hier, S.P., Lett, D., Walby, K. and Smith, A. (2011) 'Beyond folk devil resistance: Linking moral panic and moral regulation', *Criminology and Criminal Justice*, vol 11, pp 259–76.

Levitas, R. (2012) 'There may be "trouble" ahead: What we know about those 120,000 "troubled" families', www.poverty.ac.uk/sites/poverty/files/WP%20Policy%20Response%20No.3-%20%20%27Trouble%27%20ahead%20%28Levitas%20Final%2021April2012%29.pdf.

Miliband, E. (2011) 'Full transcript – speech on the riots', *New Statesman*, www.newstatesman.com/politics/2011/08/society-young-heard-riots.

Newburn, T., Lewis, P., Addley, E. and Taylor, M. (2011) 'David Cameron, the Queen and the rioters' sense of injustice', in D. Roberts (ed), *Reading the riots: Investigating England's summer of disorder*, London: Guardian Books. [Kindle Edition]

Pearce, J.M. and Charman, E. (2011) 'A social psychological approach to understanding moral panic', *Crime, Media, Culture*, vol 7, pp 293–311.

Potter, J. and Wetherell, M. (1987) *Discourse and social psychology: Beyond attitudes and behaviour*, London: Sage.

Reicher, S. and Hopkins, N. (2001) *Self and nation*, London: Sage.

Reicher, S. and Stott, C. (2011) *Mad mobs and Englishmen? Myths and realities of the 2011 riots*, London: Constable & Robinson Ltd.

Riots, Communities and Victims Panel (2012) *After the riots: The final report of the Riots Communities and Victims Panel*, http://riotspanel.independent.gov.uk/wp-content/uploads/2012/03/Riots-Panel-Final-Report1.pdf.

Rohloff, A. and Wright, S. (2010) 'Moral panic and social theory: beyond the heuristic', *Current Sociology*, vol 58, no 3, pp 403–19.

FIFTEEN

Patient safety: a moral panic

William James Fear

Introduction

This chapter introduces a new subject into the moral panic literature – patient safety – and in doing so explores the ways in which moral panics around patient safety have been used by physicians as part of a deliberate strategy in order to bring about institutional transformation. It is important to note that the term 'moral panic' has a much longer lineage than is commonly thought to be the case. It first appeared in the *Quarterly Christian Spectator* in 1830, and then again in *The Journal of Health Conducted by an Association of Physicians* in 1831. In this journal, a French physician visiting Sunderland (in England) praised the English government for its approach to the cholera epidemic. He congratulated the government for not surrounding the town with a cordon of troops which as 'a physical preventive would have been ineffectual and would have produced a moral panic far more fatal than the disease now is' (unknown, 1831, p 180). The term was picked up much later, in 1964, with the Canadian sociologist Marshall McLuhan's ground-breaking work on the influence of the media, and later expanded by Jock Young (1971) and Stan Cohen (1972). Given the historical nature of the phenomenon, it seems both unrealistic and unlikely to assume that moral panics are inherently media driven. However, it seems equally realistic and likely to assume that the media plays, at times, a key role, as we will see in the case-study examples that follow.

The chapter focuses on two case-study examples, anaesthesia as a specific medical intervention and healthcare more broadly, noting that there are many more possible cases of which 'injury to the person' is a subfield that could have been considered, including, for example, automotive safety, consumer-product safety and medical insurance.

Moral panic and institutionalism

A moral panic may be described simply as a perceived threat to society and its cultural values, based on a hitherto unacknowledged or taboo subject. There may be a perceived individual, group or class of individual who is held to be responsible for the threat, usually portrayed in the media as 'folk devils'; those who identify the threat are often known as 'moral entrepreneurs' (Cohen, 1972). However, as the historical examples demonstrate, there is no reason to assume that a moral panic requires either folk devils or moral entrepreneurs. Instead, what we saw in the *Journal of Health Conducted by an Association of Physicians* reference was the early seeds of institutional, if not moral, entrepreneurship in relation to epidemics, and the strong inclination on the part of physicians to wrest control of perceived and potential epidemics from government and policy makers.

Patient safety provides, in my view, an illustration of a phenomenon where there is evidently moral entrepreneurship, but no clear folk devils. Moral entrepreneurship is exercised as a means to build an institution within healthcare. Simply put, the moral entrepreneur identifies a quantifiable number of deaths associated with a practice (for example, anaesthesia) or the practice of medicine (for example, hospital care). These deaths are then calculated as far in excess of what could, and should, be reasonably expected; the problem is not any one individual or group but, rather, the very nature of the practice itself. Following this, an argument is made that there is a resource requirement needed to address this problem, and the problem is couched in terms of an epidemic. Comparisons are made to other areas of practice, or other epidemics, where unnecessary deaths have been reduced ('saved lives') following the provision of resources. The saving of lives (sometimes phrased as the reduction of injury to the person) is mooted as a measurable and identifiable outcome, should the necessary and sufficient resources be made available. Not only that, the saving of lives is couched as a moral imperative – a necessary response to the dire state of affairs now made known.

We turn now to the two case-study examples: anaesthesia and healthcare. An important distinction must be made at the outset. In the case of anaesthesia, I will argue that a moral panic was suppressed and contained within the medical community; as a result, it did not lead to any substantive acquisition and redistribution of resources, and the only outcome was that insurance premiums were reduced. In contrast, in the case of healthcare, attempts at suppression were overcome and a moral panic ensued, and continues to ensue, on a global scale. This has led to substantive acquisition and redistribution of resources, but no measurable outcome as yet.

Patient safety in anaesthesia

Anaesthesia provides one of the clearest examples of moral entrepreneurship that was contained within a community. As early as 1954, Beecher and Todd published a paper in the *Annals of Surgery* that deplored the number of deaths occurring in anaesthesia, comparing it to an epidemic and arguing for further resources. They wrote:

> Anaesthesia might be likened to a disease which afflicts 8,000,000 persons in the United States each year. More than twice as many citizens out of the total population of the country die from anaesthesia as die from poliomyelitis. Deaths from anaesthesia are certainly a matter for 'public health' concern. When one thinks of the millions of dollars rightly spent each year on research to combat poliomyelitis and the next-to-nothing, comparatively, spent in research to overcome the hazards of anaesthesia, a very great need is evident. (Beecher and Todd, 1954, p 28)

Other medics disagreed; an article in the same journal the following year by Abajtan, Arrowood, Barret et al (1955) took issue with Beecher and Todd's claims, and since then the subject has been regularly revisited within the profession. Over time, the problem of avoidable harm was recognised within anaesthesia, resulting in the establishment in the US of the Anesthesia Patient Safety Foundation (APSF, nd) in late 1985. The APSF describes itself on its website as an 'independent, non-profit corporation with representation from anesthesiologists, nurse anesthetists, nurses, manufacturers of equipment and drugs, regulators, risk managers, attorneys, insurers and engineers'; its vision is that 'no patient shall be harmed by anesthesia' (APSF, nd). Meanwhile, the UK's Safe Anaesthesia Liaison Group is also firmly institutionalised within the remit of the Royal College of Anaesthetists of Great Britain and Ireland. The scale of preventable harm and related deaths from anaesthesia remains disputed and disputable today. This can, in summary, be seen as a panic that never really took off; patient safety in relation to anaesthesia remains located firmly within the boundaries of the medical profession. We will see a very different picture in relation to the moral panic around healthcare.

Patient safety in healthcare

The origins of the concept of 'patient safety' in healthcare are often erroneously assumed to lie with the publication of the Institute of Medicine's report *To Err is Human* (Kohn, Corrigan and Donaldson, 1999). In fact, this concept can be traced back to a publication by Schimmel (1964) on the problems of preventable harm in hospitalised care. This work was later extended to include medical malpractice litigation in the *Harvard Studies* (Brennan, Leape, Laird et al, 1991; Leape, Brennan, Laird et al, 1991). From here on, moral entrepreneurship was exercised within the physician community, to much criticism from within the community. The matter was resolved in 1994/95 with a paradigm shift within the community. However, the moral entrepreneurship continued and the report *To Err is Human* is effectively a rewrite of *Human Error in Medicine* (Bogner, 1994). It is suggested that it is no accident that the writing of *To Err is Human* was undertaken by a journalist and the report was 'leaked' to the press the day before its official publication.

The basis of the claim made in *To Err is Human* is: 'at least 44,000 Americans die each year as a result of medical errors. The results of the New York study suggest the number may be as high as 98,000 ... deaths due to medical errors exceed the number attributable to the 8th-leading cause of death. More people die in a given year as a result of medical errors than from motor vehicle accidents (43,458), breast cancer (42,297), or AIDS' (Kohn et al, 1999, p 1). The report went on to argue for substantial resources to address this concern and it subsequently successfully attracted a substantial level of resource. More importantly, the report marked a global shift in policy and legislation in healthcare as governments and related organisations rushed to address this seeming problem. For example, the World Health Organization (WHO) launched the World Alliance for Patient Safety (2004) in response to a World Health Assembly Resolution (2002) that urges member states to pay the closest possible attention to the problem of patient safety. In 2005, the European Commission published the Luxemburg Declaration on Patient Safety and there has been legislation such as the US Patient Safety and Quality Improvement Act of 2005 and the Danish Patient Safety Act 2003. Throughout this, there has been a strong 'recognition' of the 'need' for a body of research to inform practice and procedures, and a 'need' for centralised, blame-free error-reporting mechanisms (see, for example, Jensen, 2008; Fischbacher-Smith and Fischbacher-Smith, 2009; and Waring, Rowley, Dingwall et al, 2010). Since the early 2000s national patient safety monitoring organisations have been created in many countries, for example, in the US (the National Center for Patient Safety and the National Patient Safety Foundation), the UK (the National Patient Safety Agency and the National Reporting and Learning Service), Australia (the Australian Patient Safety Foundation), Denmark, Canada, Spain, Sweden and Switzerland, in the form of both public bodies and charitable organisations. In the UK, quality is held to be the prime focus of the NHS and patient safety is the 'first dimension' within this; senior management have quality and patient safety as key responsibilities (Department of Health, 2000; House of Commons Health Committee, 2009; National Patient Safety Agency, 2009).

So far, so good. Who could possibly disagree with a focus on patient safety? Examining this more closely, we find that some of the principal actors in this process of institution building openly recognise that the new concern for patient safety has not led to improvements in either safety or quality of care (for example, Leape, Berwick, Clancy et al, 2009; Jha, Prasopa-Plaizier, Larizgoitia et al, 2010; Woodward, Mytton, Lemer et al., 2010). To be clear, specific changes in practice for identified interventions have led to improvements for that practice in that intervention in the hospitals where the change in protocol has been correctly implemented. But a recent report (*Making Health Care Safer II*, Agency for Healthcare Research and Quality, 2013), noted that of 100 patient safety interventions reviewed, only 10 had sufficient evidence of effectiveness and implementation to be 'strongly encouraged' for adoption. Indeed, we can equally argue that if the quality of healthcare in the UK post-1999 is anything to go by, then a logical conclusion from the same arguments operationalised by the moral entrepreneurs is that patient safety initiatives have increased preventable harm in healthcare, not reduced it, by encouraging attention and resources to be focused too narrowly on specific targets. And of course, this also depends largely on whether or not we can purport to have an accurate and unbiased measure of preventable harm or an equally unbiased and accurate proxy. In sum, the foundations of patient safety in healthcare rest firmly on a moral panic that has little resemblance to the problem identified by Schimmel (1964). The act of moral entrepreneurship was extended beyond the bounds of the professional community and into the wider public domain. Once this happened, a full-blown moral panic ensued and continues to this day.

Discussion

Patient safety is a global institution and a global industry (Fear and Azambuja, 2014); this should come as no surprise when we consider the broader and deeper history of medicine and healthcare (Starr, 1982). The profession has developed and honed its institution-building capabilities over centuries, and this is but one readily identifiable demonstration of this.

The use of moral panic as a means to facilitate institution building in healthcare calls into question some of our existing understandings of moral panic in a number of key ways. Firstly, it challenges any notion that moral panics are always driven by the media; what we see instead is the media picking up and publicising a cause célèbre already articulated by the medical community (the moral entrepreneurs, in moral panic parlance). Secondly, there were no 'folk devils' in either of the case-study examples discussed here. There was, however, a clear 'episode' within healthcare that was couched in terms of an epidemic, which physicians have tried to institutionalise as their domain of policy at various times since at least 1830, and, in their doing so, the end result has been sizeable political and social change, just as moral panic theory (for example, Cohen, 1972) suggests. There is little evidence that 'moral crusaders', as outlined by Hall, Critcher, Jefferson et al (1978), joined forces in the process. Rather, physicians engaged directly in control of the entrepreneurial process. The contention that 'moral entrepreneurs launch crusades, which occasionally turn into panics, to make sure that certain rules take hold and are enforced' (Goode and Ben-Yehuda, 2009, p 67) is thus clearly supported. Of course, moral panic is not the only way of conceptualising this story; patient safety could also be seen as illustrative of a crisis in risk society (Ungar, 2001). However, given the historic reference to moral panic in the early medical journal in 1831, I believe that there is good reason to continue to frame this as a moral panic. Perhaps most importantly of all for our discussion, patient safety demonstrates that a moral panic can itself be an object, not merely a societal response to an external threat. Moral entrepreneurs use moral panics as tools to bring about institutional change; their use of 'evidence-informed' argument and publication in 'scientific' journals only adds weight to their claims. Put another way, publication in a leading scientific journal does not preclude the operationalisation of a moral panic – this is a caution to all of us (academics, researchers and policy makers) who engage in claims making.

Conclusion

There is no question that the moral panic of 'patient safety' has had an enormous impact on policy and practice, including in the form of legislation in most 'Western democracies'. There are lessons here about the way in which moral panics are taken account of; we need to go beyond explanations that locate causes with the media and folk devils. Beyond this, I have argued that professional and other collectives make use of a moral panic as a means for acquiring resources. This can take place over substantial periods of time and may result in institution building. The moral panics presented here led to substantial global institutions being built and the transformation of existing institutions; this had further impact on resource distribution. While there has been post-hoc justification of the process, there has also been some acknowledgement that the process did not always result in improvements 'on the ground'. We might conclude, therefore, that while a moral panic may result in resource distribution, this may not necessarily lead to the desired improvements.

References

Abajtan Jr, J., Arrowood, J., Barret, G., Dwyer, R.H., Eversole, C.S., Fine, U.H., Hand, J.H. and Woodbridge, L.V. (1955) 'Critique of "A Study of the Deaths Associated with Anaesthesia and Surgery"', *Annals of Surgery*, vol 142, no 1, pp 138–41.

Agency for Healthcare Research and Quality (2013) *Making Health Care Safer II: An Updated Critical Analysis of the Evidence for Patient Safety Practices*, Evidence Reports/Technology Assessments, no 211, Report no: 13-E001-EF, Rockville, MD: Agency for Healthcare Research and Quality (US), www.ncbi.nlm.nih.gov/books/NBK133363/ (accessed April 2014).

APSF (nd) About APSF, www.apsf.org/about_history.php.

Beecher, H.K. and Todd, D.P. (1954) 'A Study of the Deaths Associated with Anaesthesia and Surgery', *Annals of Surgery*, vol 140, no 1, pp 2–34.

Bogner, S. (ed) (1994) *Human error in medicine*, Hillsdale, NJ: Lawrence Erlbaum Associates.

Brennan, T A., Leape, L.L., Laird, N.M. et al (1991) 'Incidence of adverse events and negligence in hospitalized patients: Results of the Harvard Medical Practice Study I', *New England Journal of Medicine*, vol 324, pp 370–6.

Cohen, S. (1972) *Folk devils and moral panics: The creation of the Mods and the Rockers,* London: MacGibbon and Kee.

Department of Health (2000) *An organisation with a memory*, Norwich: The Stationery Office.

Fear, W.J. and Azambuja, R. (2014) 'Narrative and deliberative instauration: The use of narrative as process and artefact in the social construction of institutions', *Learning, Culture and Social Interaction*, online publication complete: 14 May, doi: 10.1016/j.lcsi.2014.04.002.

Fischbacher-Smith, D. and Fischbacher-Smith, M. (2009) 'We may remember but what did we learn? Dealing with errors, crimes and misdemeanours around adverse events in healthcare', *Financial Accounting and Management*, vol 25, no 4, pp 451–74.

Goode, E. and Ben-Yehuda, N. 2009 (1994) *Moral panics: The social construction of deviance*, 2nd edn, Malden: Wiley-Blackwell.

Hall, S., Critcher, C., Jefferson, T., Clarke, J. and Roberts, B. (1978) *Policing the crisis: Mugging, the state, and law and order*, Critical Social Studies, London: Macmillan.

House of Commons Health Committee (2009) *Patient safety*, London: The Stationery Office.

Jensen, C.B. (2008) 'Sociology, systems and (patient) safety: Knowledge translations in healthcare policy', *Society, Health and Illness*, vol 30, no 2, pp 309–24.

Jha, A.K., Prasopa-Plaizier, N., Larizgoitia, I. and Bates, D.W. (2010) 'Patient safety research: an overview of the global evidence', *Quality and Safety in Health Care*, vol 19, no 1, pp 42–7.

Kohn, L.T., Corrigan, J.M. and Donaldson, M.S. (eds) (1999/2000) *To Err is Human: Building a Safer Health System*, Committee on Quality of Health Care in America, Institute of Medicine, Washington, DC: National Academy Press, www.nap.edu/catalog.php?record_id=9728 (accessed May 2010).

Leape, L.L., Berwick, D., Clancy, C. et al (2009) 'Transforming healthcare: a safety imperative', *Quality of Safety and Healthcare*, vol 18, pp 424–42.

Leape, L.L., Brennan, T.A., Laird, N.M. et al (1991) 'The nature of adverse events in hospitalized patients: Results of the Harvard Medical Practice Study II', *New England Journal of Medicine*, vol 324, no 6, pp 377–84.

McLuhan, M. (1964) *Understanding media: The extensions of man*, New York: Signet.

National Patient Safety Agency (2009) *Seven steps to patient safety in general practice*, London: National Patient Safety Agency.

Schimmel, E.M. (1964) 'The hazards of hospitalization', *Quality and Safety in Healthcare*, vol 12, pp 58–64 (repr 2003).

Starr, P. (1982) *The social transformation of American medicine: The rise of a sovereign profession and the making of a vast industry*, New York: Basic Books.

Unknown (1831) 'Safeguards against the cholera', *The Journal of Health*, vol 3, no 2, 179–83, https://archive.org/stream/journalofhealth03slsn/journalofhealth03slsn_djvu.txt (accessed 17 March 2015).

Ungar, S. (2001) 'Moral panic versus the risk society: the implications of the changing sites of social anxiety', *British Journal of Sociology*, vol 52, no 2, pp 271–91.

Waring, J., Rowley, E., Dingwall, R., Palmer, C. and Murcott, T. (2010) 'Narrative review of the UK Patient Safety Research Portfolio', *Journal of Health Services Research Policy*, vol 15, no 1, pp 26–32.

Woodward, H.I., Mytton, O.T. , Lemer, C. et al (2010) 'What have we learned about interventions to reduce medical errors?' *Annual Review of Public Health*, vol 31, no 1, pp 479–97.

Young, J. (1971) *The drugtakers: The social meaning of drug use*, London: Judson, McGibbon and Kee.

Afterword

Neil Hume

I remember first coming across Cohen's ground-breaking work on moral panics when I was an undergraduate sociology student; featuring evocative accounts of leather-clad rockers clashing with sharp-suited soul aficionados on the beaches of Brighton, Cohen analysed the process by which certain groups came to be deemed as threats to the social order by the media and establishment figures, and how public attitudes were manipulated to generate a groundswell of intolerance. It was irresistible stuff for the younger, left-lurching, Che Guevara-worshipping incarnation of myself. Yet, during my post-graduate training to become a social worker, and the several years I have spent working in the criminal justice system and children's services, it is not a body of work that I have ever returned to. When I read the contributions in this volume, which focus on the complex relationship between moral panics, the state and the profession of social work, I realise how many of the ideas and issues presented here speak to my day-to-day experience of being a front-line practitioner.

As the Introduction to Part Three acknowledges, the concept of the state is somewhat nebulous and notoriously difficult to nail down. Unsurprisingly, many different sociologists have wrestled with the subject. One of the most influential was Weber (1994 [1919]), who sought to explain how the nature of the state has evolved throughout history. He suggested that the success of early forms of social organisation hinged on the charismatic influence of certain leaders. Feudal monarchies would later invoke the power of tradition and custom to maintain their subjects' loyalty. In liberal democracies the state commandeers the technical expertise required to operate a complex system of laws, regulations and public institutions, but also monopolises the legal use of any violent force. The key contribution of Hall et al (1978) was to recognise how the state could suppress political challenges to its authority in more subtle ways: through exploiting public concerns about certain social issues, such as crime, the state can justify the introduction of policies that effectively erode civil liberties. As many social workers involved in some form of safeguarding role in relation to children and adults are employees of the state, I felt that Hall's theories posed some unsettling questions for our profession, which I explore below.

In Kirkwood's Chapter Fourteen, on the riots that took place in North London over the summer of 2011, he draws on the idea of moral panic to suggest that the government pushed a particular perspective on the situation that portrayed the participants as the products of poor parenting (and feckless fathers); and in its so doing the complex economic and social factors that contributed to this explosive expression of collective disaffection were side-lined within the public discourse. Moreover, to question this official – but highly politicised – account of what caused this disturbance was, in the eyes of the various claims makers and moral entrepreneurs, tantamount to approving arson. In a similar fashion, McKendrick (Chapter Twelve) describes how certain politicians sought to connect public concerns around the radicalisation of young Muslim men in the wake of the unprovoked murder of an off-duty soldier to the government's social policy initiative of providing intensive support to families that it deemed were in (or a source of) trouble. Thus, a flagship welfare programme designed, ostensibly, to help the most vulnerable children in society was explicitly linked to a raft of anti-terrorist initiatives, and the complex reasons why specific young people might come to identify with particular extremist organisations became conflated with a moral claim that there was a need to tackle dysfunctional families across society. So the contradictory messages that the state is sending to many families – that they are entitled to support from social work to overcome their difficulties but that they are also regarded as the source of many social problems, including future civil disobedience and potential terrorist acts – is likely to make them far less inclined to engage with state agencies, which in turn could make them more vulnerable. As practitioners we recognise that families either choose or are compelled to engage with social workers for a whole variety of reasons, in a wide range of circumstances. Yet within this morally charged atmosphere there is a real danger that the public will view the involvement of the state in a person's family life as confirmation that they must therefore be a threat to law and order.

On a similar theme, le Grand's article (Chapter Thirteen) suggests that through our profession's identification with the state we could be contributing to the continuation of some negative stereotypes by simply doing our jobs. Le Grand writes that the 'chav' persona – as it has come to be constructed by the media – is defined by their unwillingness to financially support themselves (or their dependents), and their wish to rely on social welfare agencies. So by being the profession that works closest with those poor, white, working-class young men and women and their families who are labelled as 'chavs', we are – in the public's mind – confirming the caricature. But as social workers, we are accustomed to working alongside those people who are misunderstood, and often maligned by the media or powerful sections of society: we are adept at uncovering the complex human stories that exist behind the malicious myths. During my career, I have met the proud but harried single mother struggling to get by on 'too generous' state benefits who, in desperation, resorts to a pay-day loan company; I have listened to the man who explained that after being released from prison he lived in homeless accommodation for two years and, overwhelmed by a sense of hopelessness, returned to using heroin; I too was told to 'f★★★ off' by the young person hanging around the shopping centre during the school day, hood closed tightly over her face, projecting an image of menace to hide her vulnerability.

As somebody who has worked in local government for over 10 years, I see a virtue in public service; I am enormously proud of the positive difference the state has made, and continues to make, to millions of people's lives through the National Health Service, the education system, plus targeted services like statutory social work. It was therefore troubling to read how the state's reaction to a moral panic can actually create further harm for individuals. In Chapter Eleven Greer highlights that, in response to public fears about seemingly irresponsible teenagers accessing inappropriate material on the internet, the government endorsed the increased use of filters to block certain content. However, this move meant that some young people became unable to visit websites that provided valuable information about suicide, safe sex or LGBT identity issues. As moral panics often scapegoat one particular social, cultural or ethnic group in society, seeking to portray them as the source of a perceived crisis, how the state decides to respond in such high-profile situations can significantly affect the quality of relationships between different communities. One could argue that the reactions of certain politicians to Lee Rigby's murder, as discussed by McKendrick in Chapter Twelve, were intentionally provocative, and that they aggravated, rather than allayed, wider public distrust of those individuals who subscribe to the Islamic faith.

Yet in my mind there appears to be an important distinction between suggesting that the state deliberately uses moral panics to restrict the freedom of individuals and to generate social discord – as is perhaps suggested by Hall – as opposed to viewing these responses as lapses in good governance, sometimes leading to unintended consequences. It would seem to me that there are many instances highlighted in this part where state officials have responded to media pressure or a perceived change in public mood, arguably in a rash or ill-considered manner, but with no more sinister a motive than wanting to sway the electorate in the desired direction. But one's opinion on such issues may well depend on whether one regards the state's influence within society as something to be supported or to be viewed with suspicion: is the state our benevolent parent, trying to act with positive intentions to promote our collective best interest, or is it a nefarious tyrant, naturally prone toward negative forms of social control? In reality it is probably neither fully the one nor the other; encompassing many diverse and competing institutions, interests and ideas, the modern state seems both biased towards preserving existing power structures while also trying to protect some semblance of a humane and civilised society within a ruthless, global capitalist system (with arguably limited success).

In order for the state to respond more effectively to moral panics, we must begin with an acknowledgement that many ordinary people will (and are entitled to) feel unease with various types of social change; and, left unaddressed, such anxieties can morph into something more sinister. Parton (2005) has written about the controversial 'name and shame' campaign undertaken by the *News of the World* newspaper in 2000 following Sarah Payne's murder by a predatory sex offender, and how this triggered a wave of vigilante-style attacks on the suspected homes of alleged paedophiles. Though it was apparent that the actions of the media were fuelling public alarm and influencing the political agenda – and thus a moral panic was seemingly in progress – Parton also argues that we should not lose sight of the fact that those parents living with their families in the predominantly working-class communities where the state had chosen to resettle a number of convicted sex offenders, without any prior public consultation, were likely to feel shocked and scared. It is a depressing fact that headlines that play on parents' fears about their children's safety are likely to sell more newspapers. However, in these circumstances the media did not conjure up a moral panic 'out of nothing', so to speak; they responded, perhaps irresponsibly, to pre-existing concerns.

It is no longer good enough to dismiss moral panics as being the irrational over-reaction of a naïve public, duped by unscrupulous media moguls or power-hungry politicians. This stance runs the risk of denying ordinary people a voice. Drawing on the lessons of the Left Realist school of criminology, pioneered by Kinsey et al (1986), we should accept the public's fears as legitimate and meet them head on. It is vital that the state should begin to listen, learn and lead a response to people's views on the many difficult and divisive social issues that characterise modern society. I would see social work as being at the forefront of this bold and proactive strategy: dispensing with the moral rhetoric and political posturing that dominate much public discussion, practitioners can engage people in honest, straightforward conversations on subjects such as who actually commits sexual offences and what really works in reducing re-offending; what was the full range of social and economic factors that contributed to civil disobedience in London during the summer of 2011; what are the different social costs and benefits associated with new technologies such as the internet.

I was intrigued by Kirkwood's (Chapter Fourteen) thoughts on the discursive dimension to a moral panic and the enormous power that resides in language to shape social realities. An official, state-approved discourse pervades press releases, policy documentation, the speeches of politicians in Parliament, and tells it 'like it is' to the public – what the problems are that we face, who is to blame and what should be done about them. Social work practitioners, armed with a knowledge of moral panic theory, especially the work of Hall, can start to decipher and disrupt this dominant discourse. Just as there is the potential within language to shape social reality in a negative way – to denigrate white, working-class youths as 'chavs', to depict vulnerable families as a threat to law and order, to deny young people the autonomy to enjoy modern technology – as social workers we can offer a different perspective: one informed by a progressive set of values based on notions of respect, tolerance and fairness. Through this discourse we can positively shape society – dismantling the myths and stereotypes that poison public attitudes and robustly proclaiming the advantages of social cohesion.

References

Hall, S., Critcher, C., Jefferson, T., Clarke, J. and Roberts, B. (1978) *Policing the crisis: Mugging, the state, and law and order*, London: Macmillan.

Kinsey, R., Lea., J. and Young, J. (1986) *Losing the fight against crime*, London: Blackwell.

Parton, N. (2005) *Safeguarding childhood: Early intervention and surveillance in late modern society*, London: Palgrave Macmillan.

Weber, M. (1994 [1919]) 'The profession and vocation of politics', in P. Lassman, and R. Speirs (eds) *Weber: Political writings*, Cambridge: Cambridge University Press.

Part Four
Moral regulation

Edited by Mark Smith

Introduction

Mark Smith

This part introduces a fourth key theorist within the moral panic genre. The work of Jock Young has played a central part in the creation of ideas around moral panic, and these, as will be shown, have developed over time. Some of Young's ideas are reflected in the chapters in this and the preceding parts, while others have been taken forward in other writing in the field.

Jock Young

Jock Young was born William Young on 4 March 1942 in Vogrie, Midlothian. When he was five, his family moved to Aldershot, where his Scottish background led to his being given the nickname Jock, which stuck throughout his adult life. Young studied sociology at the London School of Economics. He co-founded the first National Deviancy Conference (NDC) in 1968, where he presented his first conference paper, 'The Role of Police as Amplifiers of Deviancy'. This idea of deviancy amplification was developed in his first major work, *The Drugtakers* (1971). It was this book that introduced the concept of 'moral panic' into sociological literature, not Cohen's (1972) *Folk Devils and Moral Panics* as is commonly thought.

Young moved to Middlesex Polytechnic (now Middlesex University) in the 1980s and headed up the Centre for Criminology there. He remained at Middlesex for 35 years before moving to the City University of New York in 2002, and later to the University of Kent. In 2009, he returned to New York as Professor of Criminal Justice and Sociology at the City University of New York Graduate Center.

Young is recognised as one of the world's pre-eminent criminologists. His perspective shifted from a radical, critical one to arguing for a more engaged 'left realist' criminology, which asserted that law and order was a socialist issue and that the victims of crime are predominantly the poor and the marginalised. His left realist approach was to some extent adopted by the UK Labour Party in its slogan 'Tough on crime, tough on the causes of crime', although Young became disillusioned that New Labour tended to underplay the second part of this equation. Throughout his life and work, he maintained a radical and critical edge.

Intellectually, Young was a sociologist in the tradition of C. Wright Mills. His book *The Criminological Imagination* (2011) acknowledges Mills's legacy and critiques the positivist, abstracted empiricism and the lack of imagination in much current-day criminology. *The Criminological Imagination* and *The Vertigo of Late Modernity* (2007) are both based on an analysis of the cultural shifts associated with late modernity. Young's work draws extensively on contemporary issues to make and support his arguments. It was in *The Vertigo of Late Modernity* that he developed more fully his ideas about moral panic. Here he argues that it is a sense of insecurity that provides the conditions for moral panic to emerge and take hold. He describes moral panics as moral disturbances 'centring on claims that direct interests have been violated'. They are 'not simply panics, media generated or otherwise that provide false information'. Moral disturbance is characterised by a feeling of anxiety; in that sense, it is real, and cannot be readily dismissed as irrational. Moral panics take personal anxiety to a societal level; they do not occur when political and social structures are solid and successful but, rather, when they are in crisis, when society's tectonic plates are shifting. Young goes on to argue that when societies are in crisis, personal and social unease is displaced onto a scapegoat; scapegoated groups are not chosen by accident, but are closely related to the source of anxiety. The denigration of the 'other' creates the conditions for constituting a demon or folk devil; the folk devil in any culture is 'that it is what they are not' (Young, 2007, p 141).

Importantly for this part, Young's work, reflecting Wright Mills's influence, synthesises the structural with the personal and, in so doing, offers compelling insights into the moral dimension of the human condition.

Jock Young died on 16 November 2013.

Content of Part Four

Part Four brings together chapters around what might, on the surface, appear to be rather disparate subject matter. Some common themes emerge, however, to provide compelling illustrations of many of the elements of Jock Young's thesis. Perhaps, the most obvious message is that moral panics are likely to erupt around issues of profound moral importance (but also where there is a perceived threat), such as life and death, good and evil, sex (especially when linked with children), the body and an existential threat to cherished beliefs and institutions.

In Chapter Sixteen Frank Furedi identifies the folk devil par excellence of the late modern period, the paedophile, personified in recent times in the figure of Jimmy Savile. The paedophile is counter-posed with the sacralised child, who emerges as a rare focus of moral consensus in an uncertain world. Furedi questions whether the term moral panic, which in most instances would run its course before petering out, is sufficient to capture the enduring nature of our fears around children or whether 'permanent panic' or 'crusade' might more accurately reflect the staying power of the paedophilia narrative.

In Chapter Seventeen David Grummett provides a fascinating case study of a Danish ban on the slaughter of farm animals without pre-stunning. The ban was enacted in 2014, yet the last abattoir performing such killings closed 10 years previously. A heated debate emerged nevertheless, bringing to the surface some of the visceral (literally) feelings that questions of food and its ingestion into the body can give rise to. While Jock Young identifies how moral entrepreneurs might claim scientific 'evidence' to afford some provenance to their cases, Grummett suggests that, in this case, some rudimentary scientific and technical understanding would have been useful in bringing some sense of perspective to the issue.

Michaela Benson and Katharine Charsley address the panic in the UK around supposedly sham marriages in Chapter Eighteen. Like Grummett (and indeed, this is a point that Jock Young picked up in *The Vertigo of Late Modernity*), they identify the 'othering' of non-western cultures that emerges in this instance over a perceived threat to the 'cherished' institution of marriage. Thus, 'sham' marriages are seen as loveless and entered into for an ulterior purpose – presumably counter-posed with loving and nurturing qualities in western marriages. The ambiguity and ontological uncertainty betrayed by such a view in a context of declining use or stability of marriage in the West scarcely needs to be pointed out.

Colin Clark in Chapter Nineteen continues this theme of ethnic scapegoating, drawing on his own research into the Roma community in Glasgow. Hostility to Roma people worldwide was fuelled and reified by the case of Maria, the young girl at the centre of an alleged child abduction by virtue of the fact that she had different colouring to her parents. This case, again, crystalises the essentialising features of moral panics, totalising what is in fact a heterogeneous Roma population into an undifferentiated but threatening mass. Clark draws on sociological and anthropological perspectives, alluding in particular to Mary Douglas's work on dirt and pollution to cast light on tendencies to characterise Roma sanitation and rubbish disposal behaviours. What is missing, of course, in this discourse is any appreciation that, in a context of austerity, Roma people may have moved to Britain to improve their prospects, engage in a variety of employment practices and raise their children.

Malcolm Payne's Chapter Twenty is slightly different in that although his subject matter addresses the deeply ontological issue of death and assisted dying, where strongly held views are brought to bear, it is hard to discern any real panic in the way that the issue has played out in the public domain. Rather, a moral question is subject to moral debate in which competing viewpoints are articulated and contested. One is left to speculate why an issue that could have lent itself to panic has not done so but, in many respects, offers an example of how emotionally charged and contested subject matter might be properly engaged with. As David Grummett notes, 'In any case, moral panic is a poor substitute for serious moral debate or argument'.

References

Cohen, S. (1972) *Folk devils and moral panics*, London: MacGibbon and Kee Ltd.

Mills, C.W. (1959) *The sociological imagination*, Oxford: Oxford University Press.

Young, J. (1971) *The drugtakers: The social meaning of drug use*, London: MacGibbon and Kee.

Young, J. (2007) *The vertigo of late modernity*, London: Sage.

Young, J. (2011) *The criminological imagination*, Cambridge: Polity.

SIXTEEN

The moral crusade against paedophilia

Frank Furedi

Introduction

The focus of this essay is the transformation of the threat of paedophilia into a permanent focus of moral outrage. It explores the moral landscape that has turned the child predator into the principal target of moral enterprise. Through a discussion of the concept of a moral crusade it evaluates the impact of society's obsessive preoccupation with the child predator.

Paedophilia and the threat it represents to children has become a permanent feature of public concern and a regular theme of popular culture. The paedophile personifies evil in 21st-century society; the child predator possesses the stand-alone status of the embodiment of malevolence. But this unique personification of evil is not an isolated figure hovering on the margins of 21st-century society. Jimmy Savile, who died in 2011 and who has not been out of the news during the past two years, was dubbed the most 'prolific' paedophile in British history. What is unique about the activities of this alleged celebrity predator is the scale of his operation rather than his behaviour. Allegations against Savile effortlessly acquired the status of a cultural truth, since it is widely believed that, rather than rare, the abuse of children is a very common activity.

According to the cultural script of virtually every western society, child abusers are ubiquitous. This script invites the public to regard all strangers – particularly men – as potential child molesters. The concept of 'stranger danger' and the campaigns that promote it have as their explicit objective the educating of children to mistrust adults that they do not know. This narrative of stranger danger helps to turn what ought to be the unthinkable into an omnipresent threat that preys on our imagination. Represented as a universal threat, the peril of paedophilia demands perpetual vigilance. The expectation that adult strangers represent a risk to children has in effect turned concern about paedophilia into a very normal feature of life. That is why physical contact between adults and children has become so intensely scrutinised and policed.

'I think what is absolutely horrific, frankly, is the extent to which this child abuse has been taking place over the years and across our communities over the years', stated Theresa May, the UK Secretary of State for Home Affairs, when she outlined the details of the government's inquiry into sexual abuse in North Wales care homes and into Jimmy Savile's activities (see Theresa May, quoted by Nigel Morris in the *Independent* [Morris, 2012]). Her insistence on the all-pervasive character of child abuse resonates with widespread anxiety about the scourge of paedophilia. In official discourse this threat is expressed in a uniquely unrestrained and dramatic manner. Moral entrepreneurs, especially those associated with the child-protection industry, adopt a rhetoric that is classically associated with scaremongering demonologists. They continually use the discourse of big numbers to support the argument that 'all children are at risk'. England's Deputy Children's Commissioner, Sue Berelowitz, demonstrated this when she declared that 'there isn't a town, village or hamlet in which children are not being sexually exploited' (see Berelowitz, quoted by Graeme Wilson, in *The Sun* [Wilson, 2012]). The moral weight of such claims is rarely contested, since anyone who questions the doctrine of the omnipresence of abuse is likely to be denounced as an appeaser of the child predator.

An ideology of evil

The narrative of paedophilia does not merely encompass the abuse of children. It has become a free-floating idiom of fear that can attach itself to any focus of anxiety. So when the Southern Baptist leader Reverend Jerry Vines declared in June 2002 that Mohammed was a 'demon possessed paedophile' and that Allah leads Muslims to terrorism, he was merely harnessing the power of this idiom of fear to promote his apocalyptic vision of the future of the world (Sachs, 2002). It is not just religious fundamentalists who allow their fantasies about paedophiles to intermesh with their wider perceptions of global insecurity. It was announced in 2014 that as far as the British government is concerned, it would like to treat paedophiles in the same way as terrorists. It was reported that Prime Minister David Cameron was determined to close a 'loophole' that permits paedophiles to publish and possess 'manuals' that offer tips to would-be child predators about how to identify and groom their targets. Cameron indicated that such a new law would authorise the British state to apply the same kind of extraordinary sanctions used to target terrorists who download bomb-making manuals (Hope, 2014).

The adoption of the tactics and strategy of the war against terrorism to the crusade against paedophiles is symptomatic of a world-view that risks losing the capacity to understand the distinction between fantasy and reality. The merging of the threat of the violent terrorist with that of the online predator dramatises the threat of both. Imperceptibly, the terrorist network and the ring of paedophiles become indistinguishable from one another and, through the rhetorical act of joined-up scaremongering, this meshing intensifies the public's sense of insecurity.

From the standpoint of cultural sociology, what is particularly interesting is the transformation of paedophilia into an idiom of evil, one that serves as a moral resource for competing claims makers to draw on. Since the early 1980s, Britain and many other societies have experienced a succession of highly charged alarmist outbursts over paedophile-related incidents. Such incidents have led to mob violence against individuals wrongly accused of child abuse and to the killing of individuals who were victims of mistaken identity. Even the most improbable claims (such as scaremongering allegations of satanic ritual abuse (SRA)) have been treated as if they were based on hard evidence and facts. More than three decades of recurrent panics about the threat of paedophilia have had the cumulative impact of transforming the periodic outburst of anxiety over specific cases of abuse into a stable outlook through which communities make sense of the uncertainties of daily life.

The normalisation of paedophilia as an existential threat haunting childhood provides a rare example of the mutation of what first emerged as a moral panic in the 1980s into a coherent and enduring ideology of evil. That this ideology exercises influence over society is demonstrated by the fact that childhood and relations between generations have been regularly reorganised to contain the peril of paedophilia. Consequently, relations between generations are now carefully regulated and policed. In every walk of life, an assumption of 'guilty until proven innocent' underpins intergenerational relations. The premise that all adults pose a potential risk to children means that the criminal records check is the current index of trust; police checks on millions of adults are deemed essential before they can be trusted to be near, or to work with, children.

Experience indicates that suspicion towards adult motives only begets more mistrust. Numerous informal rules have been introduced to prevent adults from coming into direct physical contact with children. Even nursery workers feel that their action is under constant scrutiny. Adult carers have not been entirely banned from applying sun cream on children. Some still follow their human instinct and do what they believe is in the best interest of a child. But frequently, this practice requires formal parental consent. It is now common practice for nurseries and schools to send out letters to parents to sign to give teachers the right to put sun cream on their child. Some nurseries have sought to get around this problem by asking their employees to use sprays rather than rub sun cream onto children's bodies. These 'no touch' rules are underpinned by an ideology that regards physical contact between adults and children as a precursor to potentially malevolent behaviour (see Piper and Stronach, 2008).

Bans in one domain of adult–child interaction have a nasty habit of leading to bans in another. 'No-touch' rules are followed by 'no picture' rules that seek to prevent parents and others from taking pictures of children during school plays, concerts and sporting activity. In some playgrounds and parks, there are rules that seek to ban 'unaccompanied adults' from entering the site. From this perspective, the idea that an adult watching a child play can be an innocent act of enjoying the sight of youngsters fooling around is simply preposterous; only a pervert, it is suggested, would wish to watch other people's children playing.

The proliferation of rules governing intergenerational relations is underpinned by an ideology of evil. For moral entrepreneurs, society's insecurity about paedophilia strengthens the case for their argument that 'something must be done'. It provides opportunities for moral positioning against the one evil that all of us can agree on. The moral entrepreneur is a rule creator who, explains the sociologist Howard Becker, 'feels that nothing can be right in the world until rules are made to correct it'. However, since evil is omnipresent, every new rule serves only as a prelude to the next. A moral crusader is a 'professional discoverer of wrongs to be righted, of situations requiring new rules' (Becker, 1963, pp 147–8 and 153). Though they are often 'fervent' and 'self-righteous', they are not motivated by cynicism or opportunism, but by the impulse of helping others (Becker, 1963, p 148). They invariably perceive themselves as the champions of suffering victims. However, despite their intentions, zealous crusades often incite confusion and moral disorientation.

From the standpoint of cultural sociology, the numerous campaigns launched to protect children and to promote an alarmist state of concern about the threat of child predators is usefully captured by the concept of a moral crusade. In his classic study of moral enterprise,

Becker concludes that the 'final outcome of the moral crusade is a police force' (Becker, 1963, p 156). Threats are represented as not just physical hazards, but a danger to the natural order of things. It was this perception in early modern Europe that gave witch-hunting its mandate and fierce passion. Similarly, the powerful sense of moral repugnance of the practice of 'self-pollution' by 18th-century moral entrepreneurs against the dangers of masturbation was inextricably linked to the conviction that this was the most unnatural of acts. Advocates of these causes almost effortlessly make the conceptual jump from unnatural to malevolent and from malevolent to evil.

Contemporary society is not usually comfortable with the moral condemnation of evil. Indeed 21st-century western culture is estranged from a grammar of morality. Consequently, with the notable exception of sexual abuse, threats and dangers are rarely conveyed in an explicit moral form. Moral regulation often possesses an incoherent form and may be promoted indirectly through the language of health, science and risks. Fear appeals frequently appear as a response to non-moral and scientifically affirmed objective imperatives; such appeals directed against smoking are paradigmatic in this respect (see Thompson et al, 2009).

The disassociation of objects of dread and fear from the grammar of morality does not mean that warnings about them have been denuded of the imperative of moralisation. What it signifies is that the contemporary culture of fear makes it difficult to draw on the authority of an uncontested moral code. That is why paedophilia has such a culturally strategic significance. Paedophilia, along with a small number of inter-personal abuses, has a formidable capacity to incite moral outrage. What endows paedophilia with a unique quality to excite alarm and consternation is that it appears to represent the annihilation of childhood. And if the paedophile is the personification of evil, then the child has become a symbol of its moral opposite. Some social scientists believe that a sublimated form of guilt accounts for the intense hostility towards the child molester. Garland (2008, p 17) wrote that 'the intensity of current fear and loathing of child abusers seems to be connected to unconscious guilt about negligent parenting and widespread ambivalence about the sexualisation of modern culture'.

In the name of the child

The sacralisation of the child is the flip side of the tendency to universalise the threat of paedophilia. The unique moral status of the sacred child is so powerful that it is literally beyond discussion.

As Anneke Meyer observes, '"the child" becomes a shorthand for sacralisation and moral status; its meaning no longer has to be made explicit'. She concludes that this narrative is 'so powerful that in fact *any* opinion can be justified by simply referring to children, and without having to explain *why* and *how* children justify it'. The very mention of the word 'children' closes down discussion; the discourse on the perils of childhood provides an uncontested validation for claims making and '*anything* can be justified via children as children make the case good and right' (Meyer, 2007, p 60).

Fear appeals that manipulate our natural anxiety towards children are actively promoted to encourage a disposition towards suspicion and mistrust. Mention the word 'child' and people will listen. Raise the moral stakes by claiming that a 'child is at risk' and people will not just listen but endorse your demand that 'something must be done'. Consequently campaigners against poverty understand that they are far more likely to gain sympathy for their cause by focusing attention on what is now called 'child poverty'. Abstract socioeconomic injustices gain compelling definition through recasting poverty as an affliction confronting a child. Campaigners on Third World issues know that the very mention of 'child labour' or the 'exploitation of children' or 'child soldiers' or 'starving children' is far more likely to resonate with a western public than calls for economic assistance. In education a call for 'child centred' teaching will gain you a standing ovation. 'Mention the word children, and the money rolls in', remarks an acquaintance who works as a fund-raising consultant in the charity sector.

Children serve as a moral resource with which to promote policies and causes. The tendency on the part of moral entrepreneurs to hide behind the child and frame their message through the narrative of child protection is motivated by the recognition that it is a uniquely effective communication strategy. The cause of child protection enjoys formidable cultural support. Indeed the child has emerged as a very rare focus for moral consensus. As I argue elsewhere, in a world of existential disorientation the child serves as the main focus for both emotional and moral investment (Furedi, 2008). The sacralisation of the child means that those who speak 'in the name of the child' can benefit from the moral resources associated with children. At a time when society finds it difficult to express itself through the grammar of morality and where there are big disputes about what is right and wrong, the child stands out as a singular exemplar of moral unity. People may argue about whether gay marriage is right or wrong. They may dispute the legitimacy of assisted suicide, the right to abortion or the desirability of sex education. But all sides of the debate are unequivocally for the sacred child. That is also why in the current age paedophilia has emerged as most powerful symbol of evil.

Using children as a moral shield is now widely practised by policy makers and fear entrepreneurs. They understand that most adults find it difficult to raise their doubts about the numerous policies that are promoted through their alleged benefit for the security of children. Civil rights campaigners against identity cards and numerous attempts to expand government surveillance tend to lose their voice when children are brought into the discussion. So there was virtually no criticism raised by the announcement by the current England and Wales Health Services Minister, Dan Poulter, that, starting in 2015, all children who visit an accident and emergency (A&E) department in a hospital will be logged on a new national database set up to identify potential victims of abuse (*Belfast Telegraph*, 2012). It appears that when the word child is mentioned, then surveillance and the loss of doctor and patient confidentiality are acceptable. Similarly, campaigners who are usually vigilant about encroachment on civil liberties when it comes to new anti-terrorism laws have appeared indifferent to the vetting of millions of adults under different schemes designed to police those who work with or come into contact with children.

The moral crusade

Since the 1970s, social scientists have frequently characterised periodic outbursts of outrage and anxiety as a moral panic. This is a concept that appears to capture the anger and outrage precipitated by the many examples of public scandals during the four decades since that time. One of the strengths of the original conceptualisation of the concept of moral panic was that it drew attention to the important moral dimension of society's reaction to and perception of a problem. However, in the absence of moral consensus such reactions often self-consciously avoid using a moral language to express their cause. For example, at least in public, anti-abortionists often prefer using a medical vocabulary warning of psychological damage and trauma, rather than to use the language of evil and sin: the assertion that 'abortion is bad' is replaced by the argument that 'abortion is bad for *you*'. This shift in the way that threats to society are represented has important implications for the relevance of moral panic theory. David Garland (2008, p 17) points to 'a shift *away* from moral panics' in societies like the UK and the US, 'where it is difficult to find any public issue on which there is broad public agreement and an absence of dissenting voices'. At a time when competing lifestyles and attitudes towards personal behaviour are the subject of acrimonious debate, it is rare for different sections of society to unite against traditional folk devils.

There are, of course, issues that provoke a solid moral consensus and in those circumstances it is appropriate to use the concept of moral panics. Garland (2008, p 17) believes that in America the 'panic over child abuse' is an example of a 'genuine moral panic'. The same observation holds for Britain and most western societies. As already stated, panics about paedophilia have a unique capacity to mobilise powerful emotions and harness the moral sentiments of the entire public. However, given the durability of this reaction and its institutionalisation, the term 'panic' may no longer capture the features of what has crystallised into a fairly permanent outlook on life. Possibly the term 'permanent panic' provides a more suggestive term through which attention can be drawn to the stable, durable and all-pervasive character of this phenomenon.

There are, of course, historical precedents for moral panics to transform into a relatively stable and durable outlook on the world. In the late 14th century, moral anxiety about the practice of witchcraft mutated into a demonology focused on the threat posed by satanic forces. Through the energetic efforts of anti-witchcraft campaigners, European society came to imagine and fear a secret dark power that could destroy the life of anyone in any community. The life span of most scares can be measured in months, years and sometimes decades. But the fear of witchcraft haunted communities for centuries. With different degrees of intensity it influenced people's behaviour from the late 14th to the middle of the 17th century. It was through the promotion of the dread of witchcraft that modern scaremongering really came into its own. Until the 19th century, and arguably even today, the fear of witchcraft can readily incite people to panic and behave in a cruel and destructive manner.

The legacy of pre-modern witch-hunting actually influences present-day anti-paedophile demonology. In Britain, scaremongering about satanic abuse gained respectability when the National Society for the Prevention of Cruelty to Children published its 'Satanic indicators' to assist social workers to recognise the likely profile of a Satanist. Sadly, many professionals were convinced that organised groups of Satanists were preying on youngsters, and numerous children were taken into care. A network of child protection 'experts', therapists and social workers played a key role in promoting the idea that SRA was a significant threat to British children. Nottinghamshire Social Services department played a leading role in promoting the crusade against Satanist child abusers. It helped to launch RAINS (Ritual

Abuse Information and Network and Support), an organisation designed to publicise the danger from Satanists. In the end, a series of inquiries concluded that claims of SRA made by Nottinghamshire Social Services were without substance. One report written, by J.B. Gwatkin, warned that if the crusade was not stopped 'there was the likelihood of a "witch-hunt" which would result in grave injustice to children and their abuse by professional staff' (see Gwatkin, 1997)). No one was burned at the stake for SRA. But numerous families faced a nightmare as their lives were destroyed by zealous witch-hunters who took their children away. Others faced long jail sentences for crimes that were figments of the scaremongers' imagination. And although many of the legal proceedings failed to make the charges stick, there were many innocent parents who were 'framed' for a crime that they had not committed and did not exist.

Hopefully, the demonology that surrounds the child predator will not have the staying power of its distinguished medieval predecessor. Why? Because throughout history, the security of children has relied on adults assuming responsibility for their welfare. The mistrust that now envelops intergenerational relations threatens to discourage many adults from assuming this responsibility. Indeed, there is now a generation of adults who have acquired the habit of distancing themselves from children and young people. Moral crusaders, whatever their intentions, have helped to create a world where many adults regard intergenerational relations as an inconvenience from which they would rather be exempt. Arguably, the disengagement of many adults from the world of children represents a far greater danger than the threat posed by a (thankfully) tiny group of predators. The best guarantee of children's safety is the exercise of adult responsibility towards the younger generation. It is when adults take it on themselves to keep an eye on children – and not just simply their own – that youngsters can learn to feel genuinely safe.

Our examination of this long-standing moral crusade leads to the conclusion that society's reaction to the threat of the child predator is different to that of 'normal' moral panics. What began as the periodic outburst of panic has mutated into a constant regime of vigilance. This threat, *sui generis* has become a recurrent theme in the cultural imagination of society. The spectre of the paedophile that constantly haunts society is continually brought to the attention of the public by moral entrepreneurs. The significant moral capital invested in this symbol of evil ensures that the crusades against it are likely to continue into the future. Arguably, the permanent moral crusade against paedophilia bears comparison with the targeting of witchcraft in the early modern era.

References

Becker, H.S. (1963) *Outsiders. Studies in the sociology of deviance*, New York: The Free Press.

Belfast Telegraph (2012) 'Child medical visits to be logged', 27 December, http://article.wn.com/view/2012/12/27/Child_medical_visits_to_be_logged/ (accessed 17 March 2015).

Furedi, F. (2008) *Paranoid parenting*, London: Continuum Press.

Garland, D. (2008) 'The concept of a moral panic', *Crime Media Culture*, vol 4, no 1, pp 9–30.

Gwatkin, J.B. (1997) 'Introduction', The Broxtowe Files, www.users.globalnet.co.uk/~dlheb/introduc.htm (accessed 8 February 2015).

Hope, C. (2014) 'Cameron to close legal loophole that lets paedophiles download child grooming manuals', *Telegraph* (27 April), www.telegraph.co.uk/news/politics/10791387/Cameron-to-close-legal-loophole-that-lets-paedophiles-download-child-grooming-manuals.html (accessed 17 March 2015).

Meyer, A. (2007) *The child at tisk: Paedophiles, media responses and public opinion*, Manchester: Manchester University Press.

Morris, N. (2012) 'Theresa May calls extent of paedophile activity across Britain "absolutely horrific"', *Independent* (6 November), www.independent.co.uk/news/uk/politics/theresa-may-calls-extent-of-paedophile-activity-across-britain-absolutely-horrific-8289526.html

Piper, H. and Stronach, I. (2008) *Don't Touch! The educational story of a panic*, London: Routledge.

Sachs, S. (2002) 'Baptist pastor attacks Islam, inciting cries of intolerance', www.nytimes.com/2002/06/15/national/15BAPT.html (accessed 8 February 20150.

Thompson, L.E., Barnett, J.R. and Pearce, J.R. (2009) 'Scared straight? Fear appeal anti-smoking campaigns, risk, self efficacy and addiction', *Health, Risk and Society*, vol 11, no 2, pp 181–96.

Wilson, G. (2012) 'There isn't a town, village or hamlet in which children are not being sexually exploited', *The Sun* (13 June), www.thesun.co.uk/sol/homepage/news/politics/4369516/There-isnt-a-town-village-or-hamlet-in-which-children-are-not-being-sexually-exploited-MPs-are-told-thousands-of-girls-are-being-raped-by-gangs-across-the-whole-of-Britain.html

SEVENTEEN

Animal welfare, morals and faith in the 'religious slaughter' debate

David Grumett

Much of the discourse on contemporary 'moral panics' has evolved within the fields of social work and social policy, with obvious examples including child abuse, urban crime, youth culture and immigration. In this chapter, however, a moral panic will be considered centring on the welfare of animals slaughtered for meat according to the requirements of Islam and Judaism.

Introduction

On 17 February 2014, the Danish government banned the slaughter of farm animals without pre-stunning. Denmark thus joined Sweden, Latvia and Poland, the three other European states in which non-stun slaughter is already prohibited (Ferrari and Bottoni, 2010; Anon, 2012). The ban was controversial because some Muslim and many Jewish authorities regard the absence of stunning prior to slaughter as a requirement for the meat to be halal or kosher (which means 'permissible') under Islamic and Jewish law. The resulting public debate differed markedly between countries. In Denmark, it centred on whether the prohibition was compatible with the right of Muslims and Jews to religious freedoms. In practice the ban changed nothing, as no non-stun slaughter had in fact taken place there for a decade. Since the last abattoir licensed to perform it closed in 2004, those of the country's 220,000 Muslims and 8,000 Jews who have wished to consume halal or kosher meat produced without stunning have imported it. Some commentators suggested that the ban, which was obviously associated with animal welfare, was introduced to appease the outrage surrounding the slaughter of a giraffe eight days earlier at Copenhagen Zoo and the public feeding of its carcase to the lion pack. This prior episode had nothing to do with religion.

In the United Kingdom, the Danish ban had the effect of focusing attention onto the absence of any similar prohibition in domestic law.

The result was several days of debate that displayed most of the classic features of a moral panic as defined by social theorists such as Cohen (2002) and Thompson (1998, pp 1–30). A campaign quickly developed that was intense even if of brief duration, and the news media played a prominent role in presenting and sustaining it. Strong action was called for, with links made to wider anxieties about social fragmentation or breakdown, in this case due to Islam in Britain. Values and interests, in this case of non-humans, were presented as threatened by an easily identifiable source, while the real issues, both technical and moral, were almost completely ignored.

Background: a distinctive panic

This panic exhibited two interesting features. First was its relation to food. Issues around what is eaten evoke multiple moral anxieties and instinctual responses – 'gut reactions' – due to the intimate nature of the activity of eating. As objects are ingested, physical boundaries are transgressed and bodies rendered potentially impure, whether by inadequate nutritional provision, increased weight or size, or heightened sexual desire. If an issue involves food and eating, it may therefore be more likely that moral panics will develop around it than if it does not involve food (Coveney, 2006). A good example from almost precisely a year earlier was the horsemeat controversy. The primary issues here were the labelling and traceability of meat in a mass market, which are matters of process rather than of morals. Nevertheless, as news about the 'contamination' of beef, pork, lamb and chicken with horsemeat spread, a full moral panic developed – motivated in part by the British unease with the consumption of horseflesh – that exhibited many similar features to the panic around 'religious slaughter'.

The second interesting feature of the moral panic about slaughter, not shared with the horsemeat episode, was its association with Islam. In classic panics, such as those about crime or youth culture, if religion features at all it is presented as a declining moral and social force. Religious decline is thereby linked with wider moral nihilism and societal dissolution. In the panic currently under discussion, however, the absence of any domestic ban on non-stun slaughter led to attention being directed onto the increasing power of Islam in Britain and the allegedly corrosive moral effects of its purportedly barbaric practices. This critique assumes the opposite relation between morals and religion to that standardly presented (for example, Brown, 2009), in which the primary function of religion, especially as practised within the domestic sphere, is to preserve and transmit responsible and humane morals. As

Noble (2012, p 215) has argued, recent panics related to Islam have been part of a hardening of the perceived boundaries between good and bad and the construction of Islam as a monolithic 'other' that is morally militant, conservative and fundamentalist. Typically, these panics centre on issues of gender and sexual rights or on terrorism. Where these topics are concerned, Islam is indeed frequently presented as morally militant. However, in the moral panic around slaughter the implication was not that Islam is moralistic but that, at least where animal welfare is concerned, Islam is immoral. Religion was perceived not as supporting morals but as undermining them.

Technical and scientific aspects

The slaughter method employed for halal meat is termed *dhabihah*. Within Great Britain at least 39 slaughterhouses employ this method for sheep and goats, 29 for poultry and 16 for cattle (Food Standards Agency, 2012, p 5).[1] The key welfare debate surrounds recoverable pre-cut stunning, which renders an animal unconscious to pain but does not kill it. The act of killing is the subsequent severing of the carotid arteries, jugular vein and windpipe in the neck. If this were not to take place sufficiently quickly an animal would recover consciousness. In Britain, the Halal Food Authority (HFA) (2014) approves of the electric water-bath stunning of broiler chickens, with research suggesting that electric stunning, if administered at appropriate frequencies, is both effective and recoverable (Wotton et al, 2014). However, there are significant welfare issues with this type of stunning, due to incorrectly calibrated equipment and poor operator training. In particular, the current needs to be varied according to the number of birds on the line, with fine gradations required to deliver a recoverable but effective stun. For lambs and sheep, the HFA also approves of electric-tong stunning. There are fewer welfare problems with this because the animals are stunned individually.

The HFA's approval of electrical stunning is in line with the directions of Islamic authorities in some other Muslim countries, such as Malaysia and Egypt (Salamano et al, 2013, pp 448–9). Moreover, such stunning is required by the two Islamic regulatory authorities in New Zealand, which supplies a global halal market that includes Indonesia and Saudi Arabia (Farouk, 2013, pp 813–15). However, the HFA's approval is disputed by some British Muslims, by the Halal Monitoring Committee UK (HMCUK) (2014) and by most Jews, who regard stunning prior to slaughter as disfiguring an animal and express concern about the pain it causes. Furthermore, for cattle, neither the

HFA nor the HMCUK approves captive bolt stunning, which is the standard method used.[2] Nonetheless, at premises licensed to slaughter for halal consumption over 80% of all species, including cattle, are pre-stunned (Food Standards Agency, 2012, p 5). It is unclear where all this meat ends up. Many slaughterhouses serve both religious and non-religious markets, and the HMCUK has expressed concern that meat sold as halal has been pre-stunned.[3] It has instituted a system of regular inspections of abattoirs, caterers and shops, whereas the HFA relies on spot checks.

Turning to kosher meat, the slaughter method employed is termed *shechita*. This requires a clean cut performed with a large, sharp knife. Within the five or so slaughterhouses that use this, post-cut stunning is already carried out on around 10% of cattle (Food Standards Agency, 2012, p 5).[4] Post-cut stunning ensures that even if *shechita* does not render an animal fully unconscious, such a state quickly ensues. Shechita UK (2009 p 8) does not explicitly disapprove of this procedure, circumventing the issue by defining stunning restrictively as the 'methods of attempting to render an animal or bird unconscious prior to slaughter'. This is because approval of post-cut stunning would be a tacit admission that the cut itself does not effectively stun.

A moral panic?

It was clear that most contributors to the debate possessed limited knowledge of the issues. The moral judgements made against slaughter for halal consumption were grounded in an implicitly unfavourable comparison with slaughter for non-halal consumption. However, very few people understand the technical workings of even an ordinary slaughterhouse and the welfare issues these present. For instance, why is the shackling and electric water-bath stunning of broiler chickens still permitted when gas or other controlled-atmosphere systems deliver improved welfare and reliability? Why have many smaller slaughterhouses closed, resulting in animals being transported longer distances for slaughter? Why have older slaughterhouses not been required to be rebuilt in order to deliver high-quality lairage and optimal animal movements through the facility? (Farm Animal Welfare Council, 2009b, pp 142; 2003, pp 19, 48, 53) Issues such as these are prominent in current discussions among experts on welfare at killing and suggest that some practices in and around ordinary slaughterhouses, on which most meat eaters depend, are themselves morally suboptimal. This was not recognised during the moral panic, due to ignorance of the morally relevant facts of normal practice and a lack of interest in finding out about them.

The widespread lack of understanding of these complexities was mirrored, as usual, by terminological confusion. The act of slaughter is often referred to as halal (for Muslims) or kosher (for Jews), but these terms in fact mean 'permissible' or 'lawful' and designate the meat or other food deemed fit for consumption, not the process by which these are produced, nor any part of this process. Strictly, the act of slaughter is referred to as *dhabihah* or *zibah* (by Muslims) or *shechita* (by Jews), as in this chapter. The frequent popular use of the terms 'halal' and 'kosher' to designate the act of slaughter obscures their specifically legal and, by extension, moral meanings, falsely associating them with a purported absence or circumvention of legal regulation or moral reasoning. This can contribute to the denigration of other areas of halal or kosher discipline unrelated to meat.

The necessarily detailed discussion in the previous section of actual slaughter processes and divergences of interpretation between and within religious groups has shown that key to the moral panic was a failure in technical understanding of the issues and a rush to moralise them. This included ignorance of the significant differences between ordinary slaughter and slaughter for the production of meat deemed halal or kosher, as well as a lack of awareness of the divergences of interpretation of the halal and kosher requirements between and within Muslim and Jewish communities. In the panic about slaughter the moral aspect assumed premature prominence and was largely disconnected from the kind of technical and terminological comprehension on which real understanding of any complex applied moral issue depends. This confirms the findings of Noble (2012, p 216) that, at least with regard to Islam, moral panic belies an ability to deal with the 'inescapable heterogeneous and conflictual nature of moral complexity'.

Also identifiable in the panic was critics' projection onto Muslims of uncertainties and anxieties about their own moral decisions and compromises. A large area of moral high ground was rapidly colonised by people who, in most cases, would have been implicated in the incarceration and killing of animals in numbers far exceeding those required for optimal human or planetary flourishing (Maurer and Sobal, 1995). Slaughter for halal and kosher consumption was presented as violent and unnecessary – an assessment that, with some justification, has been made of all animal slaughter by the increasing numbers of people who are reducing their meat consumption or avoiding meat entirely, due to a concern to reduce animal suffering (Spencer, 1993, pp 295–348; Sapontzis, 2004).

Conclusion: from panic to debate

Was the moral panic justified and did it achieve any useful outcomes? The panic was to some extent justified because real welfare issues exist around *dhabihah* and *shechita*, particularly in the light of current research into recoverable pre-stunning that is, arguably, permissible according to halal rules (Salamano et al, 2013) and is accepted by the HFA and, as has been seen, by equivalent authorities in several predominantly Muslim countries. Furthermore, the requirements of *shechita* are not self-evidently incompatible with post-cut stunning, with an animal first having its carotid arteries cut by the neck incision and then being quickly stunned to ensure, as soon as possible after the cut, that it is unconscious. In Britain, there is debate and divergence within religious communities about slaughter methods and, among Muslims, a widespread acceptance of recoverable stunning as compatible with *dhabihah* slaughter and halal consumption.

Nevertheless, in the moral panic of February 2014 around 'religious slaughter', animal welfare was primarily the presenting issue for irrational, unarticulated anxieties about the place of Muslims in British society. The purportedly moral discourse evinced little serious engagement with either religious beliefs or welfare science and contributed to what, over the past decade, has been a documentable hardening of attitudes on the part of people who identify themselves with either the religious or welfare 'sides' of the debate. The HMCUK (2014) presents non-stun slaughter as a requirement of *dhabihah*, even though the practice of this slaughter method far predates modern stunning technology. Animal-welfare experts rightly cite scientific evidence that, without some form of stunning, *dhabihah* or *shechita* slaughter undermine welfare (Farm Animal Welfare Council 2009b, p 207; 2003, p 201).

Moral panic is a poor substitute for serious moral debate or argument based on knowledge and reflection. It is a foil for unacknowledged anxieties and insecurities and a means by which people who themselves engage in morally ambiguous practices (most obviously in this case, the eating of meat) avoid self-interrogation or public accountability. In the absence of proper moral debate, outcomes are determined in the political realm, in which they are usually the product of expedience and compromise. European Union regulations affirm the importance of states' continuing to allow derogation from stunning on the grounds of respect for 'freedom of religion and the right to manifest religion or belief in worship, teaching, practice and observance' under article 10 of the human rights charter (Anon, 2009). In a civilised, tolerant society, such freedoms are important. Nevertheless, to justify particular practices on such general 'religious' grounds as these has the effect of excluding the possibility of discussion about them. As has been shown, there is no homogeneous group of 'religious' people in Britain advocating slaughter by a particular method. Rather, views are diverse and there is disagreement over the specifics of what should be permitted and what prohibited. Among Muslims, differing interpretations of key Qur'anic passages figure prominently in the scholarly debate (Siddiqui, 2012). In general, Sunni teaching has allowed Muslims to consume the meat of members of other religious groups, including Christians, whereas Shi'ite teaching has prohibited this. Significantly, most British Muslims have family origins in Pakistan, Bangladesh or India, where the Sunni sect predominates.

Furthermore, religious considerations do not necessarily compete with those of animal welfare. On the contrary, animals raised and slaughtered in a religious context that conforms with the halal or kosher requirements should have lived a good life.[5] This includes a good death, in which the experience of pain is minimised. The HFA definition of halal stipulates that, when presented for slaughter, an animal must be in good health and be slaughtered by a Muslim reciting the *tasmiya* (see also Masri, 2007, pp 145–53) or *shahada*.[6] This effectively outlaws mechanical slaughter methods,[7] requiring each animal to be treated as an individual. Shechita UK (2009) indicates that an animal to be slaughtered must not have been caused pain, must have been well fed and be unmutilated. In cases where stunning is resisted, this is likely to be impelled by requirements such as these that, in historical perspective, have promoted farm animal welfare by prohibiting disfigurement or other harmful acts prior to slaughter. This indicates commendable moral and legal motives underlying Islamic and Jewish approaches to animal slaughter that were unrecognised in the 'religious slaughter' debate. The real debate to be opened concerns how these should inform practice in the present day.

Notes

[1] These are minimum numbers because the FSA figures relate to a sample week, during which not all premises licensed to perform *dhabihah* necessarily did so.

[2] Percussive stunning is accepted by some Muslim authorities in Germany and Africa.

[3] For bovines, some form of pre-stunning brings benefits for slaughter-line management through quickly immobilising a large and potentially dangerous animal. Reversible

electrical stunning is little used, despite the considerable potential of the single-pulse ultra-high current (SPUC) system (Robins et al, 2014).

[4] It is extremely likely that meat from *shechita* slaughter enters the non-kosher market, because only the front half of a slaughtered animal is deemed to be kosher.

[5] A good life is a key concept in animal welfare (Farm Animal Welfare Council, 2009a, p 16).

[6] The *tasmiya* is: 'In the name of Allah, the most Gracious, the most Merciful'. The *shahada* is: 'There is no god but Allah, Muhammad is the messenger of Allah'.

[7] This point has recently been clarified by the HFA.

References

Anon (2012) 'Polish ritual slaughter illegal, court rules', 28 November, www.bbc.co.uk/news/world-europe-20523809 (accessed 7 August 2014).

Anon (2009) 'Council Regulation (EC) No 1099/2009 of 24 September 2009 on the protection of animals at the time of killing', *Official Journal of the European Union*, 18 November, L 303: 1–30.

Brown, C. (2009) *The death of Christian Britain: Understanding secularisation 1800–2000* (2nd edn), London: Routledge.

Cohen, S. (2002) *Folk devils and moral panic*, London: Routledge.

Coveney, J. (2006) *Food, morals and meaning: The pleasure and anxiety of eating* (2nd edn), London: Routledge.

Farm Animal Welfare Council (2003) *Report on the Welfare of Farmed Animals at Slaughter or Killing. Part 1: Red Meat Animals*, London: DEFRA.

Farm Animal Welfare Council (2009a) *Farm Animal Welfare in Great Britain: Past, Present and Future*, London: DEFRA.

Farm Animal Welfare Council (2009b) *Report on the Welfare of Farmed Animals at Slaughter or Killing. Part 2: White Meat Animals*, London: DEFRA.

Farouk, M.M. (2013) 'Advances in the industrial production of halal and kosher meat', *Meat Science*, vol 95, pp 805–20.

Ferrari, S. and Bottoni, R. (2010) 'Legislation regarding religious slaughter in the EU member, candidate and associated countries', www.dialrel.eu/images/report-legislation.pdf.

Food Standards Agency (2012) 'Results of the 2011 FSA Animal Welfare Survey in Great Britain', http://multimedia.food.gov.uk/multimedia/pdfs/board/fsa120508.pdf.

HFA (Halal Food Authority) (2014) 'Definition of halal', http://halalfoodauthority.com/resources/definition-of-halal (accessed 7 August 2014).

HMCUK (Halal Monitoring Committee UK) (2014) 'Issues of mechanical slaughter and stunning', at www.halalhmc.org/IssueOfMSandStunning.htm (accessed 7 August 2014).

Masri, A.-H.B.A. (2007) *Animal welfare in Islam*, Markfield: Islamic Foundation.

Maurer, D. and Sobal, D. (1995) *Eating agendas: Food and nutrition as social problems,* New York: de Gruyter.

Noble, G. (2012) 'Where's the moral in moral panic? Islam, evil and moral turbulence', in G. Morgan and S. Poynting (eds) *Global Islamophobia: Muslims and moral panic in the west*, Farnham: Ashgate, pp 215–31.

Robins, A. et al (2014) 'The efficacy of pulsed ultrahigh current for the stunning of cattle prior to slaughter', *Meat Science*, vol 96, pp 1201–9.

Salamano, G. et al (2013) 'Acceptability of electrical stunning and post-cut stunning among Muslim communities: A possible dialogue', *Society and Animals*, vol 21, pp 443–58.

Sapontzis, S. (ed) (2004) *Food for thought: The debate over eating meat*, Amherst, NY: Prometheus.

Shechita UK (2009) *A guide to Shechita*, www.shechitauk.org/fileadmin/user_upload/pdf/A_Guide_to_Shechita_2009_.pdf (accessed 7 August 2014).

Siddiqui, M. (2012) 'Pig, purity, and permission in Mālikī slaughter', in *The good Muslim: Reflections on classic Islamic law and theology*, New York: Cambridge University Press, pp 67–89.

Spencer, C. (1993) *The heretic's feast: A history of vegetarianism*, London: Fourth Estate.

Thompson, K. (1998) *Moral panics*, London: Routledge.

Wotton, S.B., Zhang, X., McKinstry, J., Velarde, A. and Knowles, T. (2014) 'The effect of the required current/frequency combinations (EC 1099/2099) on the incidence of cardiac arrest in broilers stunned and slaughtered for the Halal market', *PeerJ PrePrints*, https://peerj.com/preprints/255v1.pdf (accessed 17 March 2015).

EIGHTEEN

From genuine to sham marriage: moral panic and the 'authenticity' of relationships

Michaela Benson and Katharine Charsley

Introduction

In this chapter, we deconstruct the moral panic around 'sham marriage' – otherwise known as marriages of convenience or marriage for immigration advantage – in Britain. We trace the moral panic over sham marriage, through its visual and provocative depiction in media coverage (newspaper articles, investigatory documentaries) to its propagation and perpetuation in the UK government's continuing project of managing immigration. Marriage-related migration and settlement are a significant challenge to efforts to cap immigration, resulting in attempts to redraw the moral boundaries of immigration policy. Media and policy representations of 'sham marriage' must therefore be understood in this context in terms of the strategic positioning of moral entrepreneurs.

The chapter first outlines how immigration policy relating to spousal migration has come to include reference to 'sham marriage', the identification of such marriages becoming a mechanism for controlling immigration. We highlight how these policies sit within a wider context that promotes immigration as a challenge to moral order, revealing how current political discourse about 'sham marriage' demonstrates many of the characteristics of moral panic. Through a review of Home Office documents, we demonstrate how 'sham marriage' has become firmly embedded in government policy and discourse about marriage-related migration.

Immigration policy, spousal migration and 'sham marriage'

The current management of spousal migration in the UK has a long history, recounted elsewhere (Wray, 2011; Charsley and Benson,

2012,). This system contains provision for spousal settlement, although it is clear that successive governments have sought ways of limiting the inflow of spouses. Such provision is underwritten by the UK's adherence to Article 8 of the European Convention on Human Rights on the right to family life. Given that the definition of 'sham marriage' almost certainly precludes the possibility of a family life that would otherwise be protected by Article 8, identifying and excluding such marriages has become a crucial part of the UK government's efforts to manage migration.

The Home Office 'considers sham marriage to be one of the most significant threats to immigration control' but 'acknowledges that its intelligence on the problem is incomplete' (Vine, 2013, p 3). The principal source of data on sham marriage used by the UK government is reports of suspicions about marriage officiates. Since 1999, the duty to report suspicious marriages (by registrars) has been enshrined in the Immigration and Asylum Act 1999, section 24. This reads:

> (5) 'Sham marriage' means a marriage (whether or not void) –
>
> (a) entered into between a person ('A') who is neither a British citizen nor a national of an EEA State other than the United Kingdom and another person (whether or not such a citizen or such a national); and
>
> (b) entered into by A for the purpose of avoiding the effect of one or more provisions of United Kingdom immigration law or the immigration rules.

In addition, the reason given in the 2002 immigration White Paper for proposing to extend the probationary period before spousal settlement from one to two years was to test the genuineness of marriage (Home Office, 2002, p 100).

Wray highlights that since 2005 there has been a renewed government focus on marriages of convenience, accompanied by significant new legislation, leading her to conclude that we have entered a new phase characterised by 'the hunting of sham marriage' (Wray, 2006, p 313). In February of that year, the Certificate of Approval (CoA) scheme was introduced, requiring that non-EEA nationals subject to immigration control (except those with Indefinite Leave to Remain) must seek permission from the Home Office to marry, irrespective of the status of their partner. The adoption of this mechanism was claimed to be a way of prohibiting sham marriage.

Irregular migrants or those with insufficient time left on their visa were refused approval to marry under this scheme, while asylum seekers had to wait for the outcome of their asylum case before receiving a decision on their application. This had a fee of £135 (later increased to £295). In 2006 the scheme was judged by the High Court as disproportionate and discriminatory against those lawfully present, a finding upheld for all migrants on appeal to the Court of Appeal and, finally, the House of Lords.[1] The fixed fee was also judged as an unlawful interference with the right to marry as laid out in the European Convention on Human Rights. Rather than assessing the genuineness or not of the proposed marriage, it had been used as a blanket prohibition on all those who did not have the right immigration status. Partially suspended in 2006, in 2009 the fixed fee was removed, and in 2011 the scheme was finally brought to a close.

In July 2011, the Home Office published a consultation paper in which the government set out a series of proposals for changes to the regulation of family migration (Home Office, 2011). While other forms of family migration were considered in the consultation, its primary focus was on the migration and settlement of spouses and partners. This consultation paper marked a shift in the presentation of key problems in the regulation of such migration, in that sham marriage was discussed before and at greater length than forced marriage, which had had a higher profile in previous discussion (see, for example, Home Office, 2002, 2007). This consultation resulted in the inclusion of new measures aimed specifically at preventing immigration advantage through sham marriage or civil partnership in the 2013 Immigration Bill. The proposed referral and investigation scheme would 'provide the Home Office with more time, information and evidence before the marriage or civil partnership takes place as a basis for identifying, and taking effective enforcement or other immigration action against sham cases' (Home Office, 2013, p 4). If fully introduced in 2015, the mechanics of this process for foreign nationals wishing to marry in England and Wales include increasing the documentation required; an extended notice period (which can be further extended in the case of suspicions); having their applications for marriage assessed by the Home Office against intelligence and evidence-based risk profiles; and the possibility of enforcement action against both parties – for example, removal, curtailment of leave, prosecution for criminal offence (Home Office, 2013). Such measures are further framed around goals of deterrence, improved risk assessment, improved operational response and tackling wider criminality and abuse.

Although not included in the resulting changes to the Immigration Bill, the earlier consultation on family migration had included as its aim finding an 'objective way of identifying whether a relationship is genuine and continuing or not' (Home Office, 2011, p 16). It proposed 'to define more clearly what constitutes a genuine and continuing relationship, marriage or partnership' by setting out 'factors or criteria for assessing whether a relationship, marriage or partnership is genuine and continuing' (Home Office, 2011, p 16). In addition to the plain judgement of whether the union was entered into solely for immigration purposes, these factors included:

- the ability of the couple to provide accurate details about each other and their relationship (with account taken of arranged marriages)
- the ability to communicate in a mutually understood language
- plans for the practicalities of living together in the UK as a couple
- having been in a relationship for at least 12 months prior to the visa or leave to remain application
- the relative ages of the couple
- the nature of the wedding ceremony or reception (for example, few or no guests, the absence of significant family members or the presence of 'complete strangers')
- previous spousal migration or sponsorship of spousal immigration
- a 'compliant history of visiting or living in the UK'.

What becomes clear, as Wray (2006) has also shown, is that marriages that appear to differ from the norm are regarded with suspicion: concerns over sham marriage remain at the forefront of the government's efforts to manage marriage-related migration and have real effects. Furthermore, such controls assume an easily identifiable 'real' marriage.

Moral panic and immigration

In the preface to the third and fourth editions of his seminal work *Folk Devils and Moral Panic* (2002, 2011), Cohen outlines how the characteristics of moral panics have changed. While in the original text he highlighted how moral panics came about, founded on the mismatch between generations, he now stresses that, particularly in the post-9/11 world, immigration is the source of considerable moral panic:

> Governments and media start with a broad public consensus
> that first, we must keep out as many refugee-type foreigners

as possible; second, these people always lie to get themselves accepted; third, that strict criteria of eligibility and therefore tests of credibility must be used. For two decades, the media and the political elites of all parties have focused attention on the notion of 'genuineness' ... 'bogus' refugees and asylum seekers have not really been driven from their home countries because of persecution, but are merely 'economic' migrants, attracted to the 'Honey Pot' of 'Soft Touch Britain'. (Cohen, 2011, p xxii)

The process that Cohen (2011) outlines bears a startling resemblance to how the Coalition government has approached immigration more generally, not only covering economic migrants and refugees but more recently even extending into the discussion of intra-EU migrants. In the case of immigration, moral panic is founded on the immigrant threat to the moral order. Beyond this, however, it becomes clear that such panics may have and have had a real bearing on how the 'problem' of immigration is subsequently addressed. This is fundamentally about border control, and the construction of the undesirable other. As Dauvergne argues:

Capturing the moral panic about extralegal migrants and enshrining it in law allows governments control that their borders lack. When a part of the population is labeled 'illegal' it is excluded from within (Dauvergne, 2008, p 18).

Moral panics about immigration thus feed into and influence government discourse and policies. Recognising the moral panic that may lie at the core of these provides important context for understanding the resulting legal and policy responses to immigration (Dauvergne, 2008). It seems likely, as the case of sex trafficking outlined below reveals, that moral panics about immigration are here to stay and that they have very real consequences for governance and regulation within the UK. Indeed, what is particularly notable about the moral panic regarding immigration is that the moral entrepreneurs, those individuals and groups in society who bring the moral panic to the attention of the general public, are precisely the government and the media (Finney and Simpson, 2009).

A significant body of literature relating to immigration and moral panic concerns sex trafficking (see, for example, Weitzer 2005, 2007; Dauvergne 2008; Cree et al, 2014). The discourse on trafficking focuses on the ills of the global sex trade, and is founded on a moral order that condemns the sex industry. As Dauvergne (2008) argues, the focus on the 'victims' – those trafficked – shields the power dynamics that maintain the status quo, and thus results in the continuance of trafficking (see also Weitzer, 2005, 2007). This discourse about trafficking, in its over-simplification of the social problem, does not provide real-world solutions for those dealing with trafficked people, for example, social workers (Cree et al, 2014).

The literature on moral panic often presents a causal relationship, whereby moral panic is identified and thus mechanisms are put into place to control the alleged social problem at the root of this. There is, however, another way of considering moral panic, presenting it instead as a smokescreen. This is clear in the work of Hall et al (1978), which shows how mugging became a moral panic that conveniently detracted attention from the crisis affecting the working classes. In this respect, he shows that the government and media involvement in promoting moral panic may be intentional, masking and shielding wider social change and problems. This sense of intentionality, and the links to the wider social context, are important in considering the current moral panics about immigration; indeed, as Rohloff and Wright (2010) argue, it is this latter context, and the production of moral panic, that is often missing from the research on moral panics.

'Sham marriage' and the moral order

Concern over marriages of convenience, 'sham' or bogus marriage marks contemporary British immigration debates, with the terminology being adopted in official documentation and media reports. In the context of wider moral panics about immigration, the current moral panic about 'sham marriages' can be seen as distinct. This is because it is a moral panic drawn along two axes, with the moral order being threatened both by immigration and by the perceived misuse of marriage. With increasing unmarried cohabitation, single parenthood and divorce, marriage may have lost its dominant position as the only socially correct route to coupledom and parenthood, but marriage remains a hegemonic ideal (Gross, 2005). Non-migrants may legally enter into a marriage for any reason, but the ideal of marriage based on intimacy and romantic love is reflected in stereotypes of those (particularly women, as in the figure of the 'gold-digger') perceived to marry for social or economic gain. Such cases are, however, generally merely the subject of ridicule in comparison to the moral outrage and legal measures reserved for cases where immigration benefits accruing to a spouse are suspected as motivating a marriage:

I wasn't convinced that there was a lot of romance knocking around. They certainly did not know much about each other and were uncomfortable talking about it. And the guests, they looked like they'd been whipped up to come in the last couple of days ... everything that I saw and everything I felt when I was with them felt like two strangers walking into a room and then coming out as man and wife. (Richard Bilton in BBC, 2011)

Today I can reveal new plans to crack down on people who seek to abuse our marriage laws to stay here illegally. Hundreds of sham marriage operators have been caught since this Government came to power – including a vicar jailed for staging 300 faked ceremonies. Now I want to stop these sham ceremonies happening in the first place by changing marriage laws to allow for services to be delayed for investigations. (May, 2012)

There is additional suspicion of organised criminal activity surrounding sham marriages, and there have been several arrests in the UK of alleged 'fake marriage gangs'.

It is clear that sham marriage has become a moral panic; the media depiction and government mobilisation exhibit all the characteristics outlined in Cohen's (2002, 2011) insightful framing of immigration as moral panic. The current discourse of the need to drive down the numbers of immigrants in the country, and to get immigration under control, is repeatedly stated. Immigrants are presented not only as taking British jobs, but also as claiming benefits and thus depriving needy British subjects. Marriage-related migration is one of the few remaining entry routes into the country, and so it is, at least in the minds of government and some media outlets, also ripe for abuse. 'Sham marriage' is presented as the ultimate deception, whereby those desperate to gain entry to the country misuse marriage as a way of ensuring immigration. The solution that the government has implemented is to introduce systems of social control aimed at reducing the instances of such abuse of the immigration system and protecting marriage as an institution. This moral panic clearly rests upon a binary distinction between genuine and fake marriages. Such binaries are largely mythical, presuming that there are clear criteria by which genuine marriages may be assessed. Similarly, it becomes clear that these judgements rely additionally on normative understandings of how marriage is constituted.

Unlike other moral panics regarding immigration, such as trafficking, for the most part there is no underlying ambivalence to the panic, as the migrants themselves are presented not as victims but as a threatening Other. The result of this is that the panic itself is not easily destabilised or defused and has become a more stable and unquestioned basis on which to build regulation, monitoring and control of immigrant populations. The panic has bred 'real effects' through policies, governance and regulation aimed at countering the instance of sham marriage.

Conclusion

The recognition that the discourse about sham marriage has been mobilised by the government as a moral panic raises further questions about the underlying motivations behind this. Sham marriage has without doubt been constructed as a significant social problem, despite any systematic evidence of the numbers of such marriages taking place. Through generating fear and loathing of the would-be abusers of the British marriage and immigration systems, the government has sought to introduce legislation that, while appearing to deal with a social problem, has introduced further measures to control immigration. At this point in time it is also particularly convenient to present immigrants as undeniably problematic for society. In this way, the government and the media detract attention from other public concerns, namely the impact of the government cuts to welfare and pending changes in the job market, in a way not dissimilar to that outlined by Hall et al (1978) in the case of mugging. That these migrant 'others' are presented as offending the British public's sensibilities regarding marriage, in addition to the alleged threat that they present to British jobs and welfare, has the useful potential to sway public opinion and generate support for anti-immigration logics.

Note
[1] R (on the application of Baiai and others) v SSHD [2006] EWHC 823 (Admin); R (on the application of Baiai) v SSHD [2006] EWHC 1035 (Admin); R (on the application of Baiai) v SSHD [2006] EWHC 1454 (Admin); SSHD v Baiai and others [2007] EWCA Civ 478; R (on the application of Baiai and others) v SSHD [2008] UKHL 53.

References
BBC (2011) 'My big fat fake marriage', Panorama (24 March).

Charsley, C. and Benson, M. (2012) 'Marriages of convenience and inconvenient marriages: regulating spousal migration to Britain', *Journal of Immigration, Asylum and Nationality Law*, vol 26, no 1, pp 10–26.

Cohen, S. (2002) *Folk devils and moral panic*, London: Routledge.

Cohen, S. (2011) *Folk devils and moral panic*, London: Routledge.

Cree, V.E., Clapton, G. and Smith, M. (2014) 'The presentation of child trafficking in the UK: an old and new moral panic', *The British Journal of Social Work*, vol 44, no 2, pp 418–33.

Dauvergne, C. (2008) *Making people illegal: What globalization means for migration and law*, Cambridge: Cambridge University Press.

Finney, N. and Simpson, L. (2009) *'Sleepwalking to segregation'? Challenging myths about race and migration*, Bristol: Policy Press.

Gross, N. (2005) 'The detraditionalization of intimacy reconsidered',. *Sociological Theory*, vol 23, no 3, pp 286–311.

Hall, S., Critcher, C., Jefferson, T., Clarke, J. and Roberts, B. (1978) *Policing the crisis: mugging, the state and law and order*, Basingstoke: Macmillan.

Home Office (2002) *Secure Borders, Safe Haven: Integration with Diversity in Modern Britain*, UK: The Stationery Office.

Home Office (2007) *Marriage to Partners from Overseas: a consultation paper*, London: Home Office.

Home Office (2011) *Family migration: a consultation*, London: The Stationery Office.

Home Office (2013) *Sham marriages and civil partnerships: background information and proposed referral and investigation scheme*, London: The Stationery office.

May, T. (2012) 'Sham Busters', *The Sun*, (26 August) www.thesun.co.uk/sol/homepage/news/politics/4505102/Theresa-May-Lets-close-door-on-illegal-immigrants-and-fake-marriages.html (accessed 17 March 2013).

Rohloff, A. and Wright, S. (2010) 'Moral panic and social theory beyond the heuristic', *Current Sociology*, vol 58, no 3, pp 403–19.

Vine, J. (2013) *A Short Notice Inspection of a Sham Marriage Enforcement Operation* (Independent Chief Inspector of Borders and Immigration) London: The Stationery Office.

Weitzer, R. (2005) 'The growing moral panic over prostitution and sex trafficking', *The Criminologist*, vol 30, no 5, pp 1–4.

Weitzer, R. (2007) 'The social construction of sex trafficking: ideology and institutionalization of a moral crusade', *Politics and Society*, vol 35, no 3, pp 447–75.

Wray, H. (2006) 'An ideal husband? Marriages of convenience, moral gate-keeping and immigration to the UK', *European Journal of Migration and Law*, vol 8, pp 303–20.

Wray, H. (2011) *Regulating marriage migration into the UK: A stranger in the home*, Farnham: Ashgate.

NINETEEN

Integration, exclusion and the moral 'othering' of Roma migrant communities in Britain

Colin Clark

Introduction

> What we can see is the moral panic spinning out of control around child abduction in Roma communities ... It is demonising not only the Roma in Greece, but will affect the communities here, including Gypsies. It is playing into the view of Gypsies and Roma as child stealers ... You can have one suspected case that leads to the headlines that we have seen. People are speculating about massive abduction rings for begging. (Katharine Quarmby interviewed on Channel 4 News, 22 October 2013)

What happens when two different, but related, moral panics collide? When prejudice and hysteria join forces? What impact does racial profiling have on those communities who find themselves in the crosshairs of the state? In late 2013, various central and Eastern European Roma ('Gypsy') communities living in Britain faced an unwelcome and overtly hostile media spotlight. Politicians openly spoke about needing to 'change' the 'behaviour and culture' of Roma migrants who were allegedly behaving in 'intimidating' and 'offensive' ways. Such views were espoused not by marginalised and disgruntled Tory backbenchers but a former Labour Home Secretary (David Blunkett, MP) and the current (at the time of writing) Deputy Prime Minister (Nick Clegg, MP). This moral panic largely centred around themes of integration, asociality and behaviour but also overlapped and merged with existing media and political attention on allegations of Roma being involved in child abduction – initially the case of 'Maria' in Greece and two later cases in Ireland. Roma 'behaviour and culture', viewed in highly static, essentialist, almost colonial terms,

231

could only do right in doing wrong and was presented as being in direct contrast to equally static and unproblematically reified 'British values'. At the local level, accusations of 'antisocial' behaviour were direct and forceful: mainly around 'loitering' on street corners, rubbish disposal, noise, criminal activity and sanitation issues. Tabloid and broadsheet media features appeared targeting mainly Slovak and Romanian Roma communities living in Sheffield, Glasgow and Manchester. Roma people, as an undifferentiated whole, were castigated as the nightmarish, 'backward', antisocial 'neighbours from hell' that no one wanted to live beside. Although this particular moral panic was fortunately brief, it arose out of a well-established anti-Roma history and tradition and has left its mark on present and most likely future community relations. This chapter considers these issues, examining the context, terrain and consequences of the moral panic under discussion. This commentary is situated in a body of sociological and anthropological theory that helps to explain how, where and why this moral panic emerged in the way it did. To complement the theory, data from an on-going research project in Glasgow, conducted by the author, is incorporated to illustrate the impacts of moral panics for those communities directly affected (Clark, 2014).

'Roma behaviour' = moral panic

Roma mobility and settlement across Europe has been on-going for several centuries, subject to the same kind of 'push' and 'pull' factors that many migrant groups have had to endure (Matras, 2014a). Similarly, anti-Roma discrimination, violence and deportations across Central and Eastern and Western Europe have ebbed and flowed over the years, dependent on factors that have been mostly external to Roma communities themselves (Pusca, 2012; Stewart, 2012). Recent global austerity crises have given rise to widespread anti-migrant sentiments generally, but Roma have been subject to quite specific forms of targeting across all corners of Europe, especially Hungary, the Czech and Slovak Republics, France and Italy. The fact that such anti-Roma measures and actions are taking place during the 'Decade of Roma Inclusion' (2005–15) is not without bitter irony. Indeed, as National Roma Strategies are being transformed into Local Action Plans it remains to be seen what material impact these plans will have on people's day-to-day lives (Poole, 2010; McGarry, 2012).

The author's on-going research project in Glasgow investigates key themes of welfare, 'integration', empowerment and identity (Clark, 2014). These matters were identified by both researcher and families as being pivotal to their everyday experiences as 'new' migrants in the Govanhill area of the city. Through participant observation and semi-structured interviews, working with Roma families and organisations from the public and voluntary sectors, a picture emerges of a geographic area where challenges and opportunities present themselves in equal measure. It was into this fieldwork domain that the moral panics described above appeared, courtesy of invasive and hostile media attention on the cases of 'Maria' in Greece and the children taken into care in Ireland and subsequent ill-considered statements from senior politicians in England regarding 'problematic' Roma integration and 'behaviour' in UK towns and cities.

Indeed, this small on-going ethnographic research project has taken a micro-sociological and intersectional approach to understanding issues of day-to-day Roma integration and exclusion. Upon reflection, it is the only way such a project could have any chance of success. As Davis (2008, p 68) has argued:

> 'Intersectionality' refers to the interaction between gender, race, and other categories of difference in individual lives, social practices, institutional arrangements, and cultural ideologies and the outcomes of these interactions in terms of power.

This is a most relevant and pertinent definition, as Davis places *power* at the centre of any discussion surrounding intersectional understandings of 'difference' and interactions across and between different social divisions. The same is true of moral panics, whereby political, economic and social power is crucial in establishing who the 'folk devils' are and who the 'claims makers' or 'moral entrepreneurs' are, to draw on Cohen's (1973) terminology. Another similarity and connection is in the understanding that individual identity and experience, as well as structural and wider cultural matters, are important in accounting for moral panics and discovering where exactly the boundaries lie between structure and agency. Intersectionality can help in untangling this complex scenario, locating the arenas of what King (1988) has termed 'multiple jeopardy'.

The making of a 'Roma' moral panic

C: What are the main challenges with this idea of integration? How is that playing out in Govanhill would you say?

E: Well … How can we speak of integration when some people don't want to accept you? There needs to be more learning and listening I think … We can learn from each other and get away from the lazy stereotypes. There is good and bad in all of us, every community. (From Kosice, Slovakia)

Social research cannot be understood without appreciating its social and political context and the external factors that impinge on the research environment. In this regard, in October 2013, Christos Salis, Eleftheria Dimopoulou and 'Maria' were 'actors' on the global media stage and the spotlight burned bright at both home and abroad. A plethora of racialised and reified anti-Roma stereotypes appeared in print and broadcast media and features ran with emotive and conjectured commentaries that tapped into essentialist 'Roma steal children' and 'dark-skinned Roma cannot possibly have white babies' discourses, as well as discussing 'kidnapped' child brides and the general nature of 'untrustworthy', 'anti-social' and 'dangerous' Roma communities (McCaffrey, 2013; Pilditch, 2013; Spencer, 2013).

All too quickly, a full-blown international moral panic was beginning to gather pace regarding Roma and 'child abduction' (Eccles and Martin, 2013; Stack, 2013). From state authorities and public officials, as well as newspaper and TV reporting, the messages being presented to audiences were both clear and consistent regarding Roma. Further, especially in England and France, politicians were lamenting and angst-ridden about Roma communities from Central and Eastern Europe who were settling in their countries and constituencies, attempting to live their lives, seek work and send their children to school. Two interventions stood out in this regard: one from the former Labour Home Secretary, David Blunkett, MP and the other from the current Deputy Prime Minister in the Coalition government, Liberal Democrat Nick Clegg, MP. Respectively, they are quoted as having said:

We have got to change the behaviour and the culture of the incoming community, the Roma community, because there's going to be an explosion otherwise. We all know that. (David Blunkett, quoted in Engineer, 2013)

There is a real dilemma … when they [Roma] behave in a way that people find sometimes intimidating, sometimes offensive. (Nick Clegg, quoted in Bennett, 2013)

How do you change 'behaviour and a culture'? When does 'sometimes' become 'always'? The sentiment, language and expression are telling and worth considering. It is clearly not a discourse of Roma integration and inclusion but, rather, one of their assimilation and exclusion. The diverse and heterogeneous Roma community are spoken of as being one and the same, with no acknowledgement of the differences between, across and within the communities in terms of their language, history and tradition. There are clear charges being laid against 'the Roma' in terms of their behaviour, which is, we are informed, 'intimidating and offensive' and which, if left unchecked, may lead to an 'explosion'. But according to whom? In what way? An assumed majority is spoken of – 'people' – who are drawn upon for the purposes of political rhetoric only. Let's consider a local example to try to establish some facts – always worthwhile when examining the wobbly foundations of moral panics.

A recent 'mapping report' indicated that the majority of Roma families in Scotland stay in Glasgow (some 4,000–5,000 people), with smaller communities in cities and towns such as Edinburgh, Fife and Aberdeen (Social Marketing Gateway, 2013, p 14). Within Glasgow, most Roma families are located in the south-east of the city, in Govanhill. There is a long history of migration and settlement in this ethnically diverse area, where more than 50 languages are spoken daily. Although it was initially Roma from Slovakia and the Czech Republic who moved to the area, dating back to 2004–05, there are now many other communities in Govanhill, such as Romanian and Bulgarian Roma who arrived after accession in 2007–08 (Clark, 2014; Ross, 2013).

At the local level, national anti-Roma statements from 'moral entrepreneurs' such as politicians and newspaper commentators are felt hard and have an impact. As in Manchester, Roma mothers in Govanhill reported that they were constantly anxious and scared of their children being taken into care by the police or social workers, if their children's eye and hair colour failed to match their own or deviated from the crude assumptions of racial profiling (Matras, 2014b). On the streets in Govanhill, conversations about Roma are many and varied, although, as ever, it is the negative comments that are heard loudest. Although far from representative, some of those conversations have featured such pronouncements as:

> "Who are these people? They are the new Irish, son ..."
> "They are probably all criminals."
> "They are a nightmare for local residents."

"Violence and intimidation from the Roma is the norm
... hanging about in gangs."
"Roma are making Govanhill a bad place to live."
"This place is Ground f★★★ing Zero ... Govanhell."
"I heard, 15 odd of them ... in a two-bedroom flat!"

The above ethnographic 'soundbites' reflect some of the concerns and anxieties, whether real or imagined, that are expressed by non-Roma residents staying within Govanhill. These comments were heard and gathered in conversations taking place in local parks, supermarkets, shops, taxi-cabs, schools and at various meetings over the last year. The language and terminology appears to follow a familiar pattern, also witnessed in other areas of the UK where Roma have settled, such as Page Hall in Sheffield (Shute, 2013). There are allegations of criminality, public nuisance, sanitation issues, antisocial behaviour, inappropriate rubbish disposal and overcrowding, and a sense that the situation is, as one Govanhill resident who is involved in a local residents' group was quoted as saying, "a big, bubbling pot of tension and something has to be done before it gets too much" (Jade Ansari, quoted in Fletcher, 2013). However, when taken together and looked at objectively, rarely are such claims supported by firm and conclusive evidence from the police and other statutory agencies who work with Roma and other communities in the area (Grill, 2012).

The rhetorical power of such statements far exceeds the truth and bears direct testimony to some of the 'moral panic' arguments proposed by Howard Becker (1963) and Stan Cohen (1973).

This mismatch between fact, truth and evidence will now be reflected on with regard to some of the theoretical issues this topic and research raises.

Discussion

It is prudent to briefly reflect on Stanley Cohen's classic study, *Folk Devils and Moral Panics* (1973) and what it can tell us about this particular situation of the Roma. Cohen argued that a 'panic' occurs when there is an identifiable 'threat', whether real or imagined and whether arising via a group or an episode, to established societal norms, interests and conservative, mainstream values. Such 'panics' occur when a localised or national 'concern' emerges that identifies a group as being detrimental to the 'good' of society. Often this concern is demonstrated and vocalised in overtly hostile and confrontational ways, through illustrating that 'they' are not like 'us' (Thompson, 1998). This is often perpetuated and legitimised at all levels of society: politicians, local councillors, the press and other agencies can act to reinforce, condone and legitimise the vilification of tagged 'folk devils'. Once a consensus is reached whereby the majority of the population agree that members of a certain identifiable group are 'folk devils' who pose a 'threat' to society. then action in the form of draconian policies, legislation, practices, occurs to dampen the supposed 'threat.'

More often than not, the weight and consequences of such actions are gravely disproportionate to the perceived 'threat' (Goode and Ben-Yehuda, 1994). To be sure, the aim is not to tackle any underlying material issues that may have caused the initial situation, such as youth unemployment in Cohen's study, but, rather, to radically reinforce established societal norms. Indeed, although Cohen's example was focused on youth culture and the media (the Mods and the Rockers of the 1960s on the south coast of England), his theoretical framework can usefully analyse the position of Roma communities in Britain. They habitually face extreme scorn and contempt while doing little more than moving to Britain to improve their prospects, engage in a variety of employment practices and raise their children.

Aside from Cohen, we can also turn to the work of anthropologists such as Mary Douglas (1966) and Fredrik Barth (1969) in a constructive manner. Likewise, the work of sociologists such as Howard Becker (1963) and Erving Goffman (1963) stand out as having something to offer the discussion. For example, Douglas and Goffman, in slightly different ways, look at 'spoiled identity' and how the stigmatised are regarded by the 'normals', in Goffman's terms. Douglas's interest in how issues of dirt and waste are thought of (simply put, 'matter out of place') resonates with neighbourhood responses to how sections of particular Roma communities use social/public space in a way that transgresses local residents' conceptions of 'normal' behaviours and actions. In short, Roma socialising is perceived as 'loitering with intent' because it is done outside rather than inside, due to overcrowding in housing provision. Barth's work allows us to understand the relational processes at work in communities and illustrates how inclusion and exclusion are fostered or prevented, based on perceived 'ethnic differences' that are presented as insurmountable challenges, often reduced to 'language difficulties' faced by new migrant communities. For Becker (1963), the rules of the game are laid down by 'moral entrepreneurs' (both creators and enforcers) who stake a claim in the debates and set the terms of engagement, making outlandish claims (often with little evidence) in order to bolster their own fixed (power) positions. Viewed from these conceptual perspectives, it is evident that the views of the claims makers and moral entrepreneurs are contradicted by the voices and experiences of Roma people themselves and their supporters. It's interesting to note that such normative statements about Roma 'behaviour and culture' are heavily classed, gendered and racialised, with historical precedents in terms of how other migrant communities have been greeted in the past as well as setting new benchmarks for the kind of reception future, incoming migrant communities might face (Tyler, 2013).

Conclusion

This chapter has examined a particular occasion of moral panic in relation to Roma communities in Britain in which the interest of politicians and the media in Roma 'behaviour and culture' dovetailed, in late 2013, with a European focus on alleged Roma child-abduction cases. The timing was, perhaps, crucial in driving the moral panic onto the front pages of newspapers; the spotlight had certainly been extended in scope and more brightly illuminated. But it was not just fate or chance that delivered this blow; centuries of anti-Roma prejudice fuelled and sustained the panic once it had emerged. Indeed, the panic contained some of Cohen's key ingredients: (1) an identified, racially profiled 'enemy within' who could, however simplistically, be differentiated from Goffman's 'normals'; (2) alleged transgressions from the assumed 'moral order' that again mark the communities as 'outside' normal community boundaries; and (3) a hostile media and political climate keen to stamp a mark of authority on 'British values' and to impose limits on Roma migration. Moving forwards, how can such moral panics regarding Central and Eastern European Roma communities in Britain be avoided or, better, challenged? Clearly, more effective responses to anti-Roma rhetoric need to be delivered, by Roma activists, academics and journalists themselves. Indeed, more broadly, Roma people and families must be consulted about the projects that are focused on their own communities; Roma need to be 'given voice' (take and claim it?) and resist their own demonisation and racial profiling. This will require building capacity within the Roma community, in the form of Roma mediators, teachers and facilitators, and especially the empowerment of both young and old Roma women. More so, the development of knowledge, skills, pride and public recognition of Roma ethnicity is a crucial factor, including training and cultural awareness-raising activities. All this can be done, of course, with *gadzhe* (non-Roma) supporters, but they must be willing to take a secondary, following role rather than a primary, leading role.

References

Barth, F. (1969) 'Introduction', in F. Barth (ed) *Ethnic groups and boundaries*, Boston: Little Brown & Company.

Becker, H. (1963) *Outsiders: Studies in the sociology of deviance*, New York: The Free Press.

Bennett, O. (2013) 'Thousands call Nick Clegg's LBC radio show to back Daily Express petition on EU migration', *Daily Express* (31 October), www.express.co.uk/news/uk/440366/Thousands-call-Nick-Clegg-s-LBC-radio-show-to-back-Daily-Express-petition-on-EU-migration (accessed 24 July 2014).

Clark, C. (2014) 'Glasgow's Ellis Island? The integration and Stigmatisation of Govanhill's Roma population', *People, Place and Policy*, vol 8, no 1, pp 34–50, http://extra.shu.ac.uk/ppp-online/glasgows-ellis-island-the-integration-and-stigmatisation-of-govanhills-roma-population/ (accessed 27 July 2014).

Cohen, S. (1973) *Folk devils and moral panics*, St Albans: Paladin.

Davis, K. (2008) 'Intersectionality as buzzword: A sociology of science perspective on what makes a feminist theory successful', *Feminist Theory*, vol 9, no 1, pp 67–85.

Douglas, M. (1966) *Purity and danger: An analysis of concepts of pollution and taboo*, London: Routledge and Kegan Paul.

Eccles, L. and Martin, A. (2013) 'Now blonde girl found at Roma home in Ireland: blue-eyed child of seven is led away by Police and social workers', *Daily Mail* (22 October), www.dailymail.co.uk/news/article-2471521/Blonde-girl-Roma-gypsy-home-Ireland.html (accessed 24 July 2014).

Engineer, C. (2013) 'David Blunkett issues riot warning over Roma migrants', *Daily Star* (13 November), www.dailystar.co.uk/news/latest-news/350447/David-Blunkett-issues-riot-warning-over-Roma-migrants (accessed 24 July 2014).

Fletcher, A. (2013) 'Roma migrants: could the UK do more to integrate them?' BBC Radio 4, *The Report* (13 December), www.bbc.co.uk/news/uk-25322827 (accessed 26 July 2014).

Goffman, E. (1963) *Stigma: Notes on the management of spoiled identity*, Englewood Cliffs, NJ: Prentice-Hall.

Goode, E. and Ben-Yehuda, N. (1994) *Moral panics: The social construction of deviance*, Oxford: Wiley-Blackwell.

Grill, J. (2012) '"It's building up to something and it won't be nice when it erupts." Making of Roma migrants in a "multicultural" Scottish neighborhood', *Focaal, Journal of Global and Historical Anthropology*, vol 62, pp 42–54.

King, D.K. (1988) 'Multiple jeopardy, multiple consciousness: The context of a Black feminist ideology', *Signs*, vol 14, no 1, pp 42–72.

Matras, Y. (2014a) 'A Roma reality check', *Guardian* (12 February), www.theguardian.com/commentisfree/2014/feb/12/roma-reality-check (accessed 25 July 2014).

Matras, Y. (2014b) *Roma migrants from Central and Eastern Europe*, policy briefing, University of Manchester (March), www.policy.manchester.ac.uk/media/projects/policymanchester/Policy@Manchester-briefing---Roma-Migrants.pdf (accessed 4 August 2014).

McCaffrey, M. (2013) 'Blonde-haired, blue-eyed girl (7) taken from Roma family in Dublin', *Sunday World* (22 October), www.sundayworld.com/top-stories/news/blonde-haired-blue-eyed-girl-7-taken-from-roma-family-in-dublin (accessed 24 July 2014).

McGarry, A. (2012) 'The dilemma of the European Union's Roma policy', *Critical Social Policy*, vol 32, no 1, pp 126–36.

Pilditch, D. (2013) 'Worldwide hunt for family of girl "stolen by gypsies" in Greece', *Express* (21 October), www.express.co.uk/news/world/438148/Worldwide-hunt-for-family-of-girl-stolen-by-gypsies-in-Greece (accessed 24 July 2014).

Poole, L. (2010) 'National Action Plans for Social Inclusion and A8 migrants: the case of the Roma in Scotland', *Critical Social Policy*, vol 30, no 2, pp 245–66.

Pusca, A. (ed) (2012) *Roma in Europe: Migration, education and representation*, Brussels: International Debate Education Association.

Ross, P. (2013) 'Govanhill: Glasgow's Ellis Island', *Scotland on Sunday* (10 February), www.scotsman.com/lifestyle/govanhill-glasgow-s-ellis-island-1-2783217 (accessed 25 July 2014).

Shute, J. (2013) 'Roma in Sheffield: "when it goes off, it will be like an atom bomb here"', *Telegraph* (16 November), www.telegraph.co.uk/news/uknews/immigration/10452130/Roma-in-Sheffield-When-it-goes-off-it-will-be-like-an-atom-bomb-here.html (accessed 27 July 2014).

Social Marketing Gateway (2013) *Mapping the Roma Community in Scotland: Final Report*, Glasgow: The Social Marketing Gateway, www.socialmarketinggateway.co.uk/news/new-research-mapping-the-roma-community-in-scotland/ (accessed 24 July 2014).

Spencer, B. (2013) 'Maria was "groomed to be a child bride": police claim girl found in gipsy camp was set to be married off at the age of 12 by the couple who adopted her', *Daily Mail* (23 October), www.dailymail.co.uk/news/article-2474417/Maria-groomed-child-bride-Roma-Gypsy-couple.html (accessed 24 July 2014).

Stack, S. (2013) 'Blonde girl taken into care from Roma family in Dublin', *The Herald*, www.heraldscotland.com/news/world-news/blonde-girl-taken-into-care-from-roma-family-in-dublin.22492714 (accessed 25 July 2014).

Stewart, M. (ed) (2012) *The Gypsy 'menace': Populism and the new anti-Gypsy politics*, London; Hurst and Company.

Thompson, K. (1998) *Moral panics*, London: Routledge.

Tyler, I. (2013) *Revolting subjects: Marginalization and resistance in neoliberal Britain*, London: Zed Books.

TWENTY

Assisted dying: moral panic or moral issue?

Malcolm Payne

Introduction

This chapter interrogates a phenomenon that, although not a new issue, has captured the public's attention in recent years. The controversy about assisted dying is concerned with whether or in what circumstances it is right for someone to assist another person in committing suicide or otherwise hastening the process of dying. Physician-assisted suicide (PAS) refers to assistance by healthcare professionals. Assisted dying has been a constant in medical ethics. The Hippocratic Oath of the ancient Greeks, for example, required ethical doctors not to 'give a lethal drug to anyone if I am asked, nor will I advise such a plan' (North, 2002). The Oath came to be seen as a general interdiction against assisting patients or others who wished to use medical expertise to die.

After anaesthetics were developed during the 19th century, some doctors advocated using them to relieve pain in the dying phase of life, debates about the ethics of euthanasia raged and there were attempts at legislation (Emanuel, 1994). During the first part of the 20th century, the issue was raised again, in particular by the rise of eugenics and mental hygiene movements, culminating in the rejection of such ideas after the experience of widespread mortality in two world wars, the implementation of eugenic policies by the Nazi regime and the Holocaust.

The illegality and moral unacceptability of assisted dying is therefore clearly the 'established' position in many societies, although this established moral settlement has been challenged by 'right to die' groups and individual campaigners, partly because of public opinion. The British Social Attitudes Survey examined public attitudes to assisted dying, using the same question for 30 years; its most recent report finds that there is widespread and growing public support for assisted dying in some form (Park et al, 2013, p ix). So, assisted dying is clearly a moral issue, but is it a moral panic?

UK legal provision

In most legal jurisdictions, euthanasia and assisted dying are illegal. In the UK, murder and suicide were illegal at common law and murder remains contrary to the Homicide Act 1957. The Suicide Act 1961, section 1, decriminalised suicide, but did not establish a right to commit suicide. Section 2(1) of the Act also created a specific offence, punishable by imprisonment for a term of up to 14 years, of assisting a person to commit suicide (*Nicklinson v A Primary Care Trust*, 2013). By the 'double effect' principle, it is legal for a doctor to prescribe medication or treatment that may hasten death where the purpose is to relieve pain and suffering. It is also lawful to withdraw medical treatment, allowing a condition to take its natural course, even though this is likely to bring about a patient's death. Article 8 of the European Convention on Human Rights, written into UK law by the Human Rights Act 1997, section 1, provides for a right to respect for private and family life (including, by extension, the right to commit suicide, which was withheld in English law). This right is qualified, however, where domestic law provides for exceptions 'in the interests of national security, public safety or the economic well-being of the country, for the prevention of disorder or crime, for the protection of health or morals, or for the protection of the rights and freedoms of others.'

Other legal systems

A number of legal jurisdictions make provision for assisted dying, on varying criteria and using diverse procedures. These include Belgium, the Netherlands, the US state of Oregon (whose legislation dates from 1998, thus making it the first of several US states that now provide for assisted dying) and Switzerland. Such permissive jurisdictions have been used as examples of the successful introduction of assisted dying by campaigners in 'right to die' organisations across the world.

The main arguments

The two main areas of argument are moral and practical. The moral argument in favour of PAS asserts an individual's rights to self-determination and control of their lives. Against PAS, ethical, moral and religious arguments assert the sanctity of life. The practical arguments in favour are that PAS offers relief from suffering, particularly where this becomes unbearable, and the main argument against is the 'slippery slope' argument, which I discuss below.

Seven rights-based arguments for assisted dying are:

- rights to liberty, arguing that freedom is a basic good, permitting individuals to do as they wish, unless they harm others, and prohibition on assisted dying restricts that freedom;
- rights to autonomy and self-determination, arguing that individuals are free to define their own conceptions of good. This individualistic perspective, argued in legal cases in many Western jurisdictions, proposes that life is owned by the person living it, who is free to make quality-of-life decisions;
- rights to privacy, arguing that states, professionals and other individuals should not intervene in important private decisions such as suicide;
- rights to dignity;
- rights to equality, arguing that, since suicide is legal in most jurisdictions, people who, because of disability, cannot secure their own suicide are treated unequally by the law and the state because they are denied a legal choice available to others. Since people have the right to refuse life-sustaining medical treatment, it is illogical that they are not permitted to take their lives, which amounts to the same thing;
- right to freedom of conscience and religion, arguing that states are imposing a moral prohibition deriving from public opinion or religious belief;
- rights to property, arguing that the individual has rights to ownership of their body and life.

These points are often made in rebuttal of religious or moral arguments about the sanctity of life (Lewis, 2007).

Opponents of assisted dying also present rights-based arguments:

- rights to life, arguing that statements of human rights declare the right to life as inalienable and therefore mandatory;
- rights to equality and equal protection, arguing that legalisation may particularly affect already marginalised groups such as physically and learning disabled people and older people, who may be most subject to other pressures in life, and also to mental disturbance arising from those pressures, or might be more likely to be pressured, subtly or otherwise, to take up a right to die. Also, legalisation of

assisted suicide is often proposed only for terminally ill people and people with severe physical disability, and this could be seen as prejudicial treatment favouring people who would not then have equal protection with other citizens.

- rights to property, arguing that our bodies are entrusted to us by God, and that legalisation merely substitutes the state for God as the holder of our bodies as property; for example, it may be said that the state has an interest in the preservation of citizens' lives; rights to autonomy, arguing that legalisation poses a threat to autonomy by establishing the social, cultural and political context of people's personal choices, including for example, financial barriers to palliative and community-based care and a culture saturated by media images of trivialised and apparently justified killings (Lewis, 2007: 35–42).

Lewis's (2007) analysis is that competing and irreconcilable differences in rights-based arguments mean no agreed view can be arrived at that could achieve widespread public support for legislation or policy in either direction.

The practical arguments for and against assisted dying connect with the importance given to healthcare in most societies and to the social role of the medical profession. Although we all die, many people do not dwell on this reality while they are living. Avoiding active discussion of death may be healthy because it allows people to continue with their life tasks, without becoming over-anxious about various risks to their lives. Many of the practical arguments about assisted dying refer to the 'slippery slope' arguments.

- There is a gradation of situations and it is hard to decide between situations where people might agree that assisted dying was desirable and situations where it would be harder to get agreement.
- Physicians would have the right, as with abortion, to opt out of performing assisted suicides: physicians who agreed to do so might become a focus of demand and conflict if campaigning groups opposed their work, in the way that has happened around abortion in some countries.
- Professional practice in health and social care relies on trust; the possibility that a professional might later be involved in decisions about assisted dying might inhibit trust.
- Patients and families may experience conflicts and may fear financial losses to their capital if long-term care is required; this may apply pressure on families and patients to agree to assisted suicide.
- People may change their minds.

- Good care will reduce the impact of feared symptoms, but it may be hard to accept this before the symptoms are relieved; people may not understand what will happen at their death.
- The prognosis that death is imminent may be wrong.
- Anxiety and depression affect many people approaching the end of life, but this is often treatable (Reith and Payne, 2009, chapter 8).

Right-to-die campaigns

Responding this range of concerns a number of 'right to die' organisations have developed, all with similar policies. The World Council of Right to Die Organisations (www.worldrtd.net/), founded in 1980, comprises 52 right-to-die organisations from 26 countries; its slogan is 'Ensuring choices for a dignified death' (World Federation of Right to Die Societies, 2013). However, in the UK its members are not those most prominent at present in campaigning; the greatest prominence belongs to the Campaign for Dignity in Dying (www. dignityindying.org.uk/). There have been substantial committees of inquiry in several countries, and attempts at legislation in the UK, all of which have been surrounded by public controversy.

Alternatives to assisted dying

If we accept that the right-to-die campaigns have identified an important issue in the public mind, what alternative ways exist of dealing with this issue? Three main alternatives are often proposed: firstly, acceptance of the reality of death and suffering; secondly, a case is made for the value of pain and symptom management through palliative care or other medical interventions designed to relive suffering; thirdly, the availability of advance care planning, advance decisions and a lasting power of attorney are stressed.

Suffering

Not everyone who is seriously ill or approaching death seeks to hasten that death, indeed one of the important objectives of end-of-life and palliative care is to support feelings of hope among people approaching the end of life (Reith and Payne, 2009). Many professional writers suggest that it is more common for people to seek any and all forms of treatment for their condition. There may also be differences of view about what constitutes suffering. In a study of patients who requested but were not granted euthanasia in the Netherlands in 2005, it was found that patients and physicians agreed that not all patients who requested euthanasia thought their suffering was unbearable, although they had a lasting wish to die. Patients 'put more emphasis on psychosocial suffering, such as dependence, deterioration, and not being able to participate in life anymore, whereas the physicians refer more often to physical suffering' (Pasman et al, 2009).

Approaching death may be frightening, but nursing, social and psychological support can assist people to experience this successfully. In particular, although there is a high incidence of depression and affective disorder among people approaching the end of life, this is often treatable (Robinson and Scott, 2012). Others argue that dying with dignity comes through the endurance of suffering, and that this is ennobling or has redemptive value for the sufferer. Studies of terminally ill people's attitudes suggest that a desire for death has been found, but it is often transient and may be linked to depression (Brown et al, 1986; Emanuel et al, 2000).

One option for the relief of suffering is the practice of continuous deep sedation until death. This provides for patients who are not yet experiencing major organ failure but who are in severe pain or have other distressing symptoms. Variations in who is given sedation and the settings in which this occurs suggest that there are cultural and organisational differences in different countries that lead to different medical practices (Anquinet et al, 2012).

Care not Killing

Care not Killing is an organisation that opposes changes in the law in assisted dying in the UK (www.carenotkilling.org.uk/). Its name reflects its main argument that palliative healthcare services are an acceptable alternative to assisted dying. Most developed countries provide palliative care, which the World Health Organization's (WHO) policy on cancer care proposes should be integral to public healthcare services everywhere (WHO, 2013). Many countries have developed policy favouring palliative and end-of-life care provision, because of public demand.

In the UK, the most important recent initiative is the National End of Life Care Strategy (Department of Health, 2008), which produced supportive guidance and training. One important element of this programme was the Liverpool Care Pathway (LCP), which aimed to tackle poor quality of care for dying people in hospitals by raising awareness in ward staff when patients were approaching death. It encouraged them to discuss this sympathetically with patients and their families, and to ensure their comfort. The LCP itself became controversial and was discontinued; the controversy illustrates many of the conflicts in public debate about assisted dying.

The LCP was based on hospice practice (Ellershaw and Wilkinson, 2010). It provided a practice protocol, and a service for testing improvement in each of the items of the protocol against a baseline registered by a care organisation or hospital when it started to use the Pathway. Many hospitals appointed coordinators to develop the programme, primarily for older people. A press campaign developed against it, claiming that people were placed on it who were not imminently dying, and this was done without adequate discussion with members of the family and carers. An important aspect of the criticism was of the withdrawal of hydration and nutrition and the implementation of 'Do Not Attempt Cardio-Pulmonary Resuscitation' (DNAR) orders. This is common practice in hospices, since there is evidence that many terminal cancer patients do not need nutrition and hydration and that it may be uncomfortable for them (Partridge and Campbell, 2007). There is also evidence that seriously ill patients do not benefit from cardio-pulmonary resuscitation and may suffer injury or distress if it is used (Ebell et al, 1998).

These widespread policies in palliative care seem to some observers to be in conflict with the intensive life support that enables people to survive a medical crisis until they can recover their own capacity to breathe, drink and eat. Some religious and other ethical views see artificial hydration or feeding as an extension of providing the necessities of life, rather than as a medical intervention. People with such views argue that hydration and possibly artificial feeding should always be available (Craig, 2004).

The press campaign on this issue was so intense that the government set up an inquiry into the LCP, which has led to its replacement by another protocol. Among the problems that the inquiry found (Independent Review of the Liverpool Care Pathway, 2013) was uncertainty about defining when the end of life had been reached, poor decision making, instances where there was a lack of consent, poor communication with patients and their families and poor record completion. There was also a lack of robust research evidence supporting the clinical experience that underlay the creation of the protocol.

Alternative healthcare options: advance care planning

Advance care planning has also been strongly promoted by the National End of Life Care Programme. It aims to produce a system of personalised and integrated planning, engaging people throughout their care careers in thinking about how care services should be organised to meet their personal priorities, including planning for end-of-life care (Payne, 2013). Part of this is using advance directives in which patients specify how they wish to be treated if they lose the capacity to make decisions about their care and medical treatment.

Lasting powers of attorney have replaced previous systems of attorney, allowing a patient to authorise an attorney to act for them if they do not possess or lose the mental capacity to act on their own behalf. Two types of power are available: health and welfare; and property and financial affairs. The patient completes and registers a form specifying their attorney and alternatives, and setting out any requirements and limitations they wish to set (Office of the Public Guardian, 2013). Lasting powers of attorney cannot make provision for someone to make decisions about medical treatment on their behalf.

Discussion and conclusion

Debate about assisted dying engages political debate, campaigning organisations and official reactions to campaigns and public concern. To many people this is an important moral issue, concerned with significant personal values about what it means to live and to die. Is it appropriate, then, to think of it as a 'moral panic'? Some of the elements of moral panic are present: the raging debate, the press campaigns, the criticisms of moral and practical decisions by the state. Moreover, the raging criticism is of the establishment, and the state representing an established pattern of thinking. The failure of the 'establishment' to react to strong public opinion, the defensiveness of the professionals, the inability to shift legal decisions: all of this suggests outsiders attacking a complacent establishment. Moreover, the press has represented this issue in a personalised, individualistic and moralistic way, dramatising the issue with reference to hard cases, and taking one side in a strongly contested debate about human and individual rights.

Against this, it is clear that this is a centuries-old controversy concerning important personal philosophical and religious values: it is a moral issue that is symbolic of people's views about death and life. It appears to be a panic because of the state's involvement in resisting change in the law and because the state seems to be on the other side of the debate in the criticisms of the way in which end-of-life care is managed in health services. Moreover, the simplification of the issue in press coverage of difficult cases denies the wide range of opinion and the professional uncertainties of those engaged with the issue. This seems unlikely to change, as is illustrated by Lewis's (2007) judgement that the rights-based case for legal change is irresolvable, and the broad agreement of healthcare professionals that there are many practical and ethical issues in the way of agreeing to physician-assisted dying. I suggest that this important and difficult moral issue is disguised as a panic because it seems important to the people engaged in campaigning and because the state has become involved, due to its role in legislation and as the major provider of healthcare services.

References

Anquinet, L., Rietjens, J.A.C., Seale, C., Seymour, J., Deliens, L. and van der Heide, A. (2012) 'The practice of continuous deep sedation until death in Flanders (Belgium), the Netherlands, and the UK: A comparative study', *Journal of Pain and Symptom Management*, vol 44, no 1, pp 33–43.

Brown, J.H., Henteleff, P., Barakat, S. and Rowe, C.J. (1986) 'Is it normal for terminally ill patients to desire death?' *American Journal of Psychiatry*, vol 143, pp 208–11.

Craig, G. (ed) (2004) *No water – no life: Hydration in the dying*, Alsager: Fairway Folio.

Department of Health (2008) *End of Life Care Strategy – promoting high quality care for all adults at the end of life*, London: Department of Health.

Ebell, M.H., Becker, L.A., Barry, H.C. and Hagen, M. (1998) 'Survival after in-hospital cardiopulmonary resuscitation: meta-analysis', *Journal of General and Internal Medicine*, vol 13, pp 805–16.

Ellershaw, J. and Wilkinson, S. (eds) (2010) *Care of the dying: A pathway to excellence* (2nd edn), Oxford: Oxford University Press.

Emanuel, E.J. (1994) 'The history of euthanasia debates in the United States and Britain', *Annals of Internal Medicine*, vol 121, no 10, pp 793–802.

Emanuel, E.J., Fairclough, D.L. and Emanuel, L.L. (2000) 'Attitudes and desires related to euthanasia and physician-assisted suicide among terminally-ill patients and their caregivers', *Journal of the American Medical Association*, vol 284, pp 2460–8.

Independent Review of the Liverpool Care Pathway (2013) *More care, less pathway: a review of the Liverpool Care Pathway*, London: Department of Health.

Lewis, P. (2007) *Assisted dying and legal change*, Oxford: Oxford University Press.

Nicklinson, R (on the application of) v A Primary Care Trust [2013] EWCA Civ 961 (31 July 2013), www.bailii.org/ew/cases/EWCA/Civ/2013/961.html (accessed 11 November 2013).

North, M. (trans) (2002) 'The Hippocratic Oath', in 'Greek medicine', National Library of Medicine, National Institutes of Medicine, www.nlm.nih.gov/hmd/greek/greek_oath.html (accessed 18 November 2013).

Office of the Public Guardian (2013) www.justice.gov.uk/about/opg (accessed 18 November 2013).

Park, A., Bryson, C., Clery, E., Curtice, J. and Phillips, M. (eds) (2013) *British Social Attitudes: The 30th Report*, London: NatCen Social Research.

Partridge, R. and Campbell, C. (2007) *Artificial nutrition and hydration: Guidance for End of Life Care for Adults*, London: National Council for Palliative Care/Association of Palliative Medicine.

Pasman, H.R.W., Rurup, M.L., Willems, D.L. and Onwuteaka-Philipsen, B.D. (2009) 'Concept of unbearable suffering in context of ungranted requests for euthanasia: qualitative interviews with patients and physicians', *British Medical Journal*, vol 339, p b4362.

Payne, M. (2013) 'Extending advance care planning over the care career', *European Journal of Palliative Care*, vol 20, no 1, pp 34–7.

Reith, M. and Payne, M. (2009) *Social work in end-of-life and palliative care,* Bristol: Policy Press.

Robinson, V. and Scott, H. (2012) 'Why assisted suicide must remain illegal in the UK', *Nursing Standard,* vol 26, no 18, pp 40–8.

World Federation of Right to Die Societies (2013) Home page, www.worldrtd.net/ (accessed 21 November 2013).

WHO (World Health Organization) (2013) 'Palliative care is an essential part of cancer control', www.who.int/cancer/palliative/en/ (accessed 21 November 2013).

Afterword:
the moral in moral panics

Heather Lynch

'Panic' is a theme I am familiar with in my work with women who regularly experience extremely distressing situations. It is a natural response to fear, and one that can be managed. Panic of itself is, arguably, morally neutral; how panic is fuelled, steered and exploited is not. Woven through the discussion in this chapter is an interest in moving toward a productive understanding of the function of 'moral panic', in order that it might create stimulus for positive change rather than being steered towards the imperative to cling to problematic norms. This interest underpins the discussion of themes derived from the chapters in this part: the constitution of 'the deviant other' and the discharge of moral responsibility. I then consider the Scottish Government's policy on violence against women, *Equally Safe* (Scottish Government, 2014a), to explore how such themes become operationalised in the context of my practice as a criminal justice social worker in a 'women's' service.

Themes

Each of the chapters in Part Four has illuminated a view of the 'undesirable other' as a prerequisite for 'moral panic'. Furedi's Chapter Sixteen focused on the contemporary 'other', 'the paedophile'; Benson and Charsley, and Clark, in Chapters Eighteen and Nineteen, respectively, highlighted the 'othering' of those who are perceived as 'not like us' for reasons of cultural difference. These three are, arguably, the most emotive of panics discussed, as they portray clearly recognisible human actors who become readily stereotyped as a homogeneous group. Grumett's discussion of animal welfare in Chapter Seventeen is another emotive topic, as those believed to mistreat animals readily become associated with other immoral practices. In Chapter Twenty, Payne at the outset acknowledges that the debate on assisted suicide has attracted a more considered discussion, perhaps due to the lack of a 'deviant other' onto whom moral problems can be discharged.

The morality of 'othering' and the devastating effects that this has on individuals, communities and society as a whole have been widely discussed. Post-colonial scholars (Said, 1994; Fanon, 2008) identify significant disadvantages experienced by people who do not conform to the white, western 'norm'. The woeful legacy of colonisers who used the moral imperative to civilise deviant others has endured for centuries and is starkly visible in the contemporary humanitarian crises in Palestine and across Africa. As evidenced in this part, modern casualties remain as 'folk devils' in the form of dangerous 'immigrants' who have come to disturb our way of life and take our resources. However, the culturally deviant other is not just the preserve of non-western ethnicities.

The majority of people with whom I work experience similar stigma, which might be characterised in Colin Clark's words as 'multiple jeopardy'. The vast majority have grown up in economic poverty and are negated by politicians as 'skivers'. Almost all are in contact with mental health services for substantive mental illness or support with substance misuse; many live in temporary accommodation. Any one of these experiences would readily attract the label of deviant, and together they are a toxic cocktail. Of interest to me is that they are rarely implicated in the most emotive 'moral panics'; perhaps they no longer have the ability to shock. Society does not panic at the deaths of those managing entrenched substance dependency, but the death of an affluent youngster using substances recreationally attracts outrage.

In situations described in this part moral panics enable the characterisation of not only the deviant other but also the virtuous victim and the rescuer who occupies the moral high ground. Championing the 'virtuous vulnerable' clearly promotes the positive public profile, desired by politicians and institutions seeking public backing. But while the constitution of the deviant other is morally problematic, so too is the production of virtuous vulnerability.

The following section focuses on Equally Safe, a policy that uses the term 'Equally' to draw attention to the political emphasis on equality and, rhetorically at least, egalitarian values. I argue, however, that basing policy on an explicitly moral agenda, not supported by empirical substance, can generate the foundations for 'moral panic' by creating deviant 'otherness' and virtuous vulnerability.

Equally Safe: a case study

Equally Safe lays out the Scottish Government's agenda to 'prevent and eradicate' violence against 'women and girls'. An analysis of this document evidences how policy can serve to reinforce stereotypes while side-stepping and providing a smokescreen in respect of, arguably, more important matters. In no sense do I wish to diminish the harm caused to women who experience such abuse. My purpose in pursing a critical analysis is to show how this approach may in fact contribute to other problems as well as to the issue it seeks to address.

Equally Safe commences by setting out a moral imperative for its existence, drawing on data from the Scottish Crime Survey (Scottish Government, 2014b, 2014c) to argue that violence by men against women and girls is an extremely serious issue requiring focused attention and public resource. The implication in the title is that women and girls are less safe than their male counterparts. The objectives, located in the opening pages, state an aim to create a protective environment within which women and girls can 'thrive as equals' and men will 'desist from all forms of violence against women and girls' (Scottish Government, 2014a, p 21). Statistics quoted state that 80% of domestic violence reported to the police was male toward female and that the root of this problem is 'gender inequality, roles and assumptions' (Scottish Government, 2014a, p 13). Immediately the scene is set where we have a 'deviant other' group in the form of men who act violently toward vulnerable 'women and girls'. While a few short sentences imply that men can also experience violence, the indisputable binary categorisations in this policy narrative are violent men and vulnerable women and girls. The underlying premise of the policy is to create gender equality. However, the reports used to convince that this is a defensible moral focus immediately generate questions on the depiction of men as 'perpetrators', while skimming over equalities issues relevant to all genders.

The Scottish Crime and Justice Survey 2012/13: Partner Abuse (Scottish Government, 2014b) states that over the preceding 12 months men were just as likely to experience domestic abuse as were women. Furthermore, men were much less likely to report abuse to the police. This immediately raises questions around the simplistic assertion that women are 'vulnerable victims' and men are 'perpetrators'. Men were also much less likely to report psychological harm as a result of abuse, a point I will return to later. The Scottish Crime and Justice Survey (Scottish Government, 2014c) shows that men are more than twice as likely to be victims of violence. Notwithstanding the fact that the assailants are more likely to be men, this shows that it is men who are less safe than women. The landscape created by this statistical report is substantively different to that of Equally Safe. One way of looking at this is that the abuse of men by women is minimal and most likely a response to their abuse and therefore the focus remains on the harm caused to female 'victims'. However, an alternative perspective is that normative gender configurations delimit options for men and anticipate their violence while delimiting expression of emotional distress.

Taking this analysis into account, the moral issue becomes not how best to divide society into 'victims' and 'perpetrators' but how to consider the normative construction of gender in ways that do not stereotype and repress. Butler (1990) provides an analysis of gender as 'performed', not essential or interior. The parameters of performance are delimited by the cultural availability of the social and temporal context. In short, these vary according to the needs and desires of society and therefore are not fixed. Policies that essentialise gender positions obstruct collective responsibility as to how these are produced and, thus, the conditions that make change possible.

Another moral issue that is acknowledged but not developed in Equally Safe is the impact of economic disadvantage. Statistics across crime, partner abuse and mental health evidence this as the single most salient factor in all of these domains. The political motivation to be seen as defending the vulnerable in the face of the 'other' occludes this reality and creates fertile ground for moral panic. Drawing on practice experience, I argue that there are some situations where panic may well be a valid response and that perhaps the issue is not the 'moral panic' in itself but how 'panic' is fuelled and directed.

Implications for practice

The multiple jeopardy of having a criminal history alongside social and economic disadvantage can, for some, make the label 'vulnerable' more attractive than that of 'offender'. As four out of five women offenders are reported to have experienced partner violence, Equally Safe becomes a significant policy lever. It is one of a number of mechanisms that allows women to distance themselves from the deviant negating associations of 'criminal' and instead adopt the more sympathetic position of 'vulnerable' and 'traumatised' victim. The idea that female offenders are emotionally vulnerable is one that is gaining increasing ground in criminal justice scholarship (Gelsthorpe and Hedderman, 2012) and policy (Scottish Government, 2012). There are positives associated with this. Many of the women with whom I work have told chilling tales of horrific violent and sexual abuse from childhood at the hands of both men and women in their lives. Acknowledgement of how this has impacted on their life choices and behaviour offers affirmation. For a few, the medical frames of diagnosis and treatment are useful resources from which they can build a happier, more settled life. However, there are some more insidious issues.

Instilling a sense of vulnerability can become an exchange of one deviancy for another. Individuals may come to view themselves through the medical lens of pathological damage. One woman told me that her (in my view proportionate) excitement at an upcoming event was in fact a manifestation of her personality disorder. Such medicalising has the tendency to individualise, encouraging people to see problems as theirs alone, rather than looking at a more collective societal responsibility. The current policy emphasis in women's criminal justice can further entrench the idea that poor mental health and trauma are 'women's' issues. In fact 'gender' work is read as 'women's' work rather than work that looks at how gender roles and assumptions affect everybody. During group work on domestic abuse I have noticed how some women struggle to identify with the 'victim' identity and recognise the contribution of their own problematic behaviour. Yet, there is a palpable pressure on them to ensure that their experience conforms to the narrative of themselves as victim. Such situations create a complex moral dilemma for me as a practitioner.

I generalise here, because, of course, there are exceptions to the following. However, as most of the people with whom I work have grown accustomed to being cast as dangerous deviants, any opportunity to be positioned outside that frame is generally welcomed, even if this means taking up a different deviant role. In general they will be more condemning of those cast as 'folk devils' than most people would be. From a context where they are conscious of the judgement of others, it appears even more imperative to claim morality. Most have been managing extremely complex situations of multiple disadvantage and are seeking some ways to make sense; therefore frames that reduce and simplify tend to be more attractive than those that broaden the issues and introduce layers of complexity. This creates a dilemma for me. One choice is to work with people in ways that challenge societal norms and the role that they play in reifying disadvantage; however, this risks overwhelming already burdened individuals. Another is to promote the comfort of reinforcing norms by helping women to position themselves as vulnerable victims. It is the difference between getting the best from the status quo or confronting it in order to promote change. The first involves short-term pragmatism, the other a longer-term struggle.

Balancing these tensions is fundamental to my role as a social worker and I am inspired by the work of political philosopher Hannah Arendt (1998). She explores the unique individual ability to act within the world (Veck, 2013). Her focus on the intersection between private interest and public good is highly relevant to criminal justice social work, not simply to assert the need for those convicted of crimes to accept responsibility for the impact of their actions, but to promote a political life that expects active participation in society. She talks of educating 'toward the world'; such an approach lends itself to the moral contemplation called for across the chapters in this part. It is nested in the belief that the political life of the individual constitutes the development of collective values. In doing so it does not seek blame and vulnerability but responsibility and action. In this sense moral panics might have the capacity to generate 'new lines of flight' (Deleuze and Guattari, 1987). The question then becomes not whether moral panics are right or wrong, but what types of change they afford.

Conclusion

I have argued that the moral problem that can arise through reactions to social anxieties is not so much the tendency toward 'moral panic', but how this response is exploited by those who seek to benefit from a position of moral virtue. Analysis of the Scottish Government's policy Equally Safe (2014a) evidences how policy can exploit normative gender roles in order to create a platform for moral leadership. I have argued that the resultant gender stereotyping ignores the devastating ways in which normative gender roles affect men, and in fact contributes to problems for both men and women. Additionally, this focus on gender side-steps the universal issue of the impact of economic disadvantage on all gender orientations.

For me as a social worker, this situation creates a multitude of moral dilemmas that require negotiation with service users, and also with management and colleagues. The crux lies in the reality that adopting mainstream societal norms provides the best opportunity for individual service users, having been cast in deviant roles, to progress toward acceptance. However, this also means not challenging morally questionable stereotypes, either concerning others cast as deviant or about the normative assumptions that contribute to the constitution of conflict.

In conclusion, there is a place for societal panic: the huge gap in opportunity, life expectancy and health between the economically advantaged and disadvantaged is one area worthy of panic; that so many young men find it easier to take their life than to seek help is another. The material in this part leads me to the view that the societal preference for blame rather than for taking collective responsibility is one of the most pressing moral issues.

References

Arendt, H. (1998) *The human condition*, Chicago: University of Chicago Press.

Butler, J. (1990) *Gender trouble*, Abingdon: Routledge.

Deleuze, G. and Guattari, F. (1987) *A thousand plateaus: Capitalism and schizophrenia*, trans B. Massumi, Minneappolis: University of Minnesota Press.

Fanon, F. (2008) *Black skin, White mask*, London: Pluto Press.

Gelsthorpe, L. and Hedderman, C. (2012) 'Providing for women offenders: the risk of adopting a payment by results approach', *Probation Journal*, vol 59, no 4, pp 374–90.

Said, E. (1994) *Culture and imperialism*, London: Vintage.

Scottish Government (2012) *Commission on Women Offenders*, www.scotland.gov.uk/Resource/0039/00391828.pdf.

Scottish Government (2014a) *Equally Safe: Scotland's strategy or preventing and eradicating violence against women and girls*, www.scotland.gov.uk/Resource/0045/00454152.pdf.

Scottish Government (2014b) *Scottish Crime and Justice Survey 2012/13: Partner Abuse*, www.scotland.gov.uk/Publications/2014/06/5943.

Scottish Government (2014c) *Scottish Crime and Justice Survey 2012/13: Main Findings*, www.gov.scot/Publications/2014/03/9823/downloads.

Veck, W. (2013) 'Participation in education as an invitation to become towards the world: Hannah Arendt on the authority, thoughtfulness and imagination of the educator', *Educational Philosophy and Theory*, vol 45, no 1, pp 36–48.

Moral panics and beyond

Mark Smith, Gary Clapton and Viviene E. Cree

When we began, we set out to explore the utility of the concept of moral panic as a lens through which to examine contemporary social issues and anxieties. We recognised that the field was contested, as Charles Critcher identifies in his map of the territory at the beginning of this volume. We were also aware of a specific criticism that is often levelled at moral panic literature, that is, that it minimises real harm. As social workers, we took this charge seriously, and have been mindful of this even as we have raised questions around contested issues. The reaction to our work has been largely positive. The range and quality of the chapters in this volume evinces the richness and, we would suggest, continuing relevance of moral panic as a conceptual tool applied across a range of contemporary social problems. In this concluding chapter, we identify some key messages emerging from the book's contributors and, at the same time, take forward Critcher's analysis. We do so at a time when long-standing panics are resurfacing and new ones are emerging and competing for attention. We hope that the book will contribute to a new understanding of moral panics in our times.

The on-going relevance of moral panic analysis

Understanding what is going on around us through a lens of moral panic may be more relevant than ever to an understanding of social concerns, for three different but related reasons.

In *The Exclusive Society*, Young (1999) argues that the propensity for moral panic is located within wider structural changes in society and in the psychological responses to these. He contrasts what the historian Eric Hobsbawm (1994) identifies as the 'Golden Age' of the post-Second World War era, lasting until the mid-1970s, with its belief in social progress, high employment, job security, stable marriage and community, with the insecurity of late modernity. Young extends this analysis further, suggesting that 'We live increasingly in a consensus of broken narratives: jobs lost, relationships ended, neighbourhoods left and localities transformed beyond recognition' (Young, 2007, p 201). On a similar theme, Virilio (2005) observes some of the ways in which speed transforms our understanding of, and engagement with, a globalised world, iconic images of which, such as '9/11', render unsustainable the Enlightenment conceit of believing that we might control the world through the application of science and rational thought. Alongside concrete examples of what we cannot control, the sheer magnitude of information available on the internet exposes the extent of what we don't know and worries us further with talk of a 'dark net', harbouring all sorts of unknowns and threats to civilisation. A further parallel feature of late modernity is the breakdown of authority structures and the consequent dissipation of any uncontested moral code. The role that religion once played in laying down a moral order has been replaced by new moral guardians – the mainstream media and, increasingly, the twittersphere, within which domains moral norms are endlessly asserted and contested. For Bauman (1995), the 'liquid' modern world is thus characterised by fragmentation, discontinuity and inconsequentiality.

Responses to panic

A constant in any situation or episode identified as a moral panic is that it almost invariably converges around a fear of the other. An understandable response to fear, especially to that which threatens what is deeply held, is to retrench behind an essentialism that asserts the core, unchanging nature of the qualities that one associates with self and one's kith and kin. This valorisation of self, however, requires a concomitant essentialising and denigration of the other, who is seen to be lacking those self-same virtues (see Young, 1999). The denigration of the other creates the conditions for constituting a demon or folk devil. The folk devil in any culture is constructed in opposition to self; it is what we are not (Young, 2007). In this sense, moral–panic thinking resonates with much other contemporary social theory, especially that body of theory that identifies the other not only in relation to self, but also as a threat to self, and the concomitant exclusionary dynamics that come into play (see for instance Becker, 1963; Levine, 1971; Bauman, 1998).

In considering how we might employ and take forward moral panic analysis, we pick up on Critcher's identification (in the Introduction to this volume) of possible directions of travel around three areas: risk, discourse and moral regulation, and the psychological aspect of panics. We then extend these to consider Piper's (2014) assertion that there is something deeply immoral in the promotion and maintenance of moral panics. We conclude that in order to move forward, we must claim an intellectual scepticism and give attention to the collateral damage that may be caused by inciting panic; we must also take responsibility to reclaim a moral, or certainly, an ethical dimension in how we respond to social concerns.

Risk

We live in what is often termed a 'risk society'. Beck (1992) argues that modernity – having previously been constituted around an arithmetical calculation of probability – rather than bringing risk under control has changed its nature, rendering it more global, less readily identifiable, more problematic, less easily managed and more anxiety provoking. Risk has become an institutionalised and reified concept that dominates the thinking of policy makers, managers and practitioners. The rhetoric of risk is used within neoliberal society to mobilise fear as an emotive, defensive and strategic medium for advancing the values of safety and security (Stanford, 2010).

Furedi (2009) argues that risk discourses have shifted from the earlier notion of probabilistic to possibilistic risk; we become anxious about something that may happen somewhere in the worst of all possible worlds, a world of 'unknown unknowns'. Inevitably, this feeds into a particular state of mind. 'Risk talk' is all around us but it is never properly understood, nor perhaps can it be; it has become a collective state of mind rather than an objective reality (Parton, 1999). It is little wonder that we feel an existential anxiety compounded by a sense of not knowing just what it is that we might be anxious about. This sense of risk equated with danger and fear surrounds us; our minds are assailed by what Virilio (2005) calls weapons of mass communication, creating a panic-driven tele-reality, that results in alarm being brought into our living rooms. The role of the press as understood in moral-panics thinking has changed. Not only no longer does it merely pick up on a single issue of public concern, it flits incessantly from issue to issue, creating a sense of permanent anxiety.

Discourse and moral regulation

We consider Critcher's categories of discourse and moral regulation together. Piper (2014) suggests that these might helpfully be understood within the Foucauldian notion of governmentality, whereby the role of government becomes one of regulating moral understandings and behavioural responses. In times of financial austerity and economic crisis, it suits governments to allow the public gaze to rest on the latest headline scare, thus diverting rightful public fury over rising poverty and social inequality. A feature of the moral-panic literature (for example,

Goode and Ben Yehuda, 2009) is that it draws attention to what we are not looking at when our gaze is drawn to a particular episode of panic.

Piper (2014) identifies the role of interest groups, and in particular of children's charities, as claims makers (see also Clapton and Cree, forthcoming) in initiating and sustaining moral panics. Such groups colonise the discourse around the object of their concern and over which they claim a narrow and often questionable expertise; their actions are likely to be presented in assertions of scientific or technical expertise. Much of their public appeal is emotive and their arguments are circular: we don't know the extent of abuse, but we know it is widespread, and we need further resources to ascertain just how widespread it is. Moreover, the concern of such claims makers is rarely only altruistic, but serves to maintain the very anxiety that they purport to abjure. The capital of fear can thus be turned to any kind of profit, commercial or political (Bauman, 2007). In influencing the discourse around a particular moral concern, claims makers advance the 'correct' understanding of an issue, foreclosing dissent or alternative interpretations. Those who disagree with the 'correct' interpretation are subject to the charge of denial, a term increasingly used as 'a synonym for refusing to acknowledge the truth, and a device to impute the motives of those identified as "deniers"' (Furedi, 2007). Claims makers may not look beyond the object of their particular moral concern, and in so doing may not see the collateral damage that their world-views impose on wider society and ultimately, indeed, on those whom they claim to protect (Piper, 2014). The consequences of their actions may therefore be illiberal and repressive; the invariable demand of claims making is for new and more punitive laws to be enacted in response to whatever is posed as the threat.

The psychological

The final point that Critcher identifies for exploration is the psychological. As our thinking has developed, this dimension and the interplay between it and the more overtly sociological features of moral panic analysis have become ever more intriguing. Some of the earlier writing provided powerful insights that resonate with a wider body of social science literature, again related to responses to anxiety and the resultant dynamics of social exclusion. As Young observes, the quest for security through the creation of binaries is always tenuous and the demarcation lines are inevitably blurred. The hoped-for place of safety, according to Young:

is scarcely secure or certain. In a pluralistic world of cultural hybridism and personal bricolaging, such essential cultures are perpetually precarious and porous. They are brittle creations which seem tough and rigid but which can break all too easily. It is this brittleness which is the source of the hyperbole surrounding their defence ... These hard narratives of right and wrong, of righteousness and betrayal, come on strong but they can collapse easily. (Young, 2007, p 209)

This is perhaps inevitable, as Young notes in an earlier observation,

because the souls of those inside and those outside the 'contented minority' are far from dissimilar, sharing the same desires and passions, and suffering the same frustrations, because there is no security of place nor certainty of being and because differences are not essences but mere intonations of the minor scales of diversity. (Young, 2003, pp 398–9)

The precarious nature of one's habitation of a particular stratum of society is experienced as a fear of falling from it into another. This gets to the nub of the matter: the separation between the included and excluded, between the good and the evil in any expression of moral panic may be more apparent than real.

A related psychological aspect concerns the impact that particular moral entrepreneurs may have in how a panic is played out; how individual motivation intersects with wider societal conditions. A cursory look at major episodes of panic, especially those of a sexual nature, reveals key individuals often presented as crusaders in the cause of good. There are historic examples of righteous behaviour, safeguarding innocence and rooting out evil where other, less noble aspects have come to light. Matthew Hopkins, witch-finder general in 17th-century England, was paid handsomely for every 'witch' he discovered. More recently, it has been apparent that those who have been highly respected in the public domain may also harbour demons in their private lives. Hence the inner distance to fall between the moral high ground and disgraceful thoughts and activities may not be so great. The psychological element of moral panics remains an intriguing area for future enquiry.

Implications

The scale of recent panic responses to social issues presents a number of challenges for social scientists. Much of what we witness reflects a retreat from legitimate social scientific efforts to understand social issues in social context, to a point where, increasingly, binary notions of good and evil are dominant. There is little room for understanding or redemption in much current public discourse. This secular discourse of evil is insinuating itself within current criminological thinking and policy (Dearey, 2014). Eagleton captures the implications of this. The use of the term 'evil', he says,

> is generally a way of bringing arguments to an end, like a fist in the solar plexus ... Either human actions are explicable, in which case they cannot be evil; or they are evil, in which case there is nothing more to be said about them. (Eagleton, 2010, p 8)

The identification of evil in social science, however, amounts to 'intellectual laziness, shutting off inquiry and the proper search for context' (Frankfurter, 2006, pp 11–12). Frankfurter goes further, cautioning that 'the real atrocities of history seem to take place not in the perverse ceremonies of some evil cult but in the course of purging such cults from the world. Real evil happens when people speak of evil' (Frankfurter, 2006, p 12). The seemingly relentless momentum towards identifying individuals and groups as threats to society is manifest in ever-growing prison populations, at least across the Anglophone world, at a time when recorded crime is actually in steep decline (Pratt, 2007; Wacquant, 2009). This is the sure sign of a panic, when responses go in the opposite direction from the scale of the problem (Goode and Ben Yehuda, 2011).

In this sense, Bauman offers some telling insights, likening the search for order and security, which he identifies as being behind history's major atrocities, to gardening. Modern genocide, he claims,

> like modern culture in general is a gardener's job. It is just one of the many chores that people who treat society as a garden need to undertake. If garden design defines its weeds, there are weeds wherever there is a garden. And weeds are to be exterminated.... All visions of society-as-garden define parts of the social habitat as human weeds. Like other weeds they must be segregated, contained, prevented from

spreading, removed and kept outside society's boundaries. (Bauman, 1989, p 92)

The more weeds we identify as messing up our quest for ordered and secure lives, the more we have to root out and exclude from the realms of 'decent' society. The folk devil has to be seen as operating beyond the pale of decent society. Bauman calls this process of exclusion, adiaphorisation (Bauman, 1995). Adiaphorisation neuters our moral responsibility, removing certain groups identified as operating outside the bounds of respectable society – the asylum seeker, the paedophile, the drug addict, the feckless parent or the antisocial youth or neighbour – from the sphere of moral concern; they are dehumanised and, crucially, beyond reach of empathy and compassion.

If people in these categories are 'the other', then those that are subject to their attentions – 'decent' neighbourhoods, trolled or stalked women, children – are also 'othered', in a different way, as 'victims'. The present-day emphasis on victimhood legitimates responses that jump to repressive conclusions, absolved of any need or expectation of proper moral or ethical analysis and increasingly absolved of the need for any legal due process. Crimes that offend against 'victims' are increasingly considered 'crimen exceptum', exceptional crimes requiring and legitimating exceptional responses, such as the lowering of previous standards of proof. The concept of 'crimen exceptum' is one that has its origins in mediaeval witch-hunts, perhaps the logical next step once a panic takes root. We all suffer when such dynamics enter public polity. The end-point of responses based on fear is a society 'shot through with suspicion towards other humans and their intentions' (Bauman, 2007, p 57). Current moral crusades over child abuse, for instance, may do little to protect children, but risk eroding trust in all adults.

Ways forward

If moral panics are about 'othering' and social exclusion, then, we believe, the response to them ought to be grounded in attempts to introduce greater plurality and diversity into public discourse (see Young, 2007). A humane response requires the exercise of a moral or ethical imagination, or, as Pearson urged as long ago as 1973, social work must 'reclaim its moral-political roots' (Pearson, 1973, p 225). If we are to do so, we need to evaluate the truth-claims underlying scares and the criteria for the identification of any response that they propose. This calls for 'an attitude of knowing disbelief, an urbane refusal to be taken in or carried away' (Garland, 2008, p 21). It is in this spirit that the contributors to this book have come together to offer an alternative way of responding to the panics that daily compete not just for our attention, but also for resources. Our shared analysis foregrounds complexity and criticality as a counterpoint to the easy explanations and binary categories that result in censorious legislation, illiberal policies and risk-averse practice.

We finish with the words of Stanley Cohen, in his political and sociological manifesto for social work action, first written in 1975:

> In practice and in theory stay 'unfinished'. Do not be ashamed of working for short-term humanitarian or libertarian goals, but always keep in mind the long-term political prospects. This might mean living with the uncomfortable ambiguity that your most radical work will be outside your day-to-day job. Most important: do not sell out your clients' interests for the sake of ideological purity or theoretical neatness. (Cohen, 1998, p 112)

References

Bauman, Z. (1989) *Modernity and the Holocaust*, Cambridge: Cambridge University Press.

Bauman, Z. (1995) *Life in fragments*, Oxford: Blackwell.

Bauman, Z (1998) *Europe of strangers*, Oxford: University of Oxford.

Bauman, Z. (2007) *Liquid times*, Cambridge: Polity.

Beck, U. (1992) *Risk society*, London: Sage.

Becker, H. (1963) *Outsiders*, New York: The Free Press.

Clapton, G. and Cree, V. (forthcoming) 'Communicating concerns or making claims', *Journal of Social Work*.

Cohen, S. (1998) *Against criminology*, New Jersey: Transaction Publishers.

Dearey, M. (2014) *Making sense of evil: an interdisciplinary approach*, Basingstoke: Palgrave Macmillan.

Eagleton, T. (2010) *On evil*, New Haven, CT: Yale University Press.

Frankfurter, D. (2006) *Evil incarnate*, New Jersey: Princeton University Press.

Furedi, F. (2007) 'Bad ideas: denial', http://www.spiked-online.com/newsite/article/2792#.VG4tq2SsUy4.

Furedi, F. (2009) 'Precautionary culture and the rise of possibilistic risk assessment', *Erasmus Law Review*, vol 2, no 2, pp 197–220.

Garland, D. (2008) 'On the concept of moral panic', *Crime, Media, Culture*, vol 4, no 9, pp 9–30.

Goode, E. and Ben Yehuda, N. (2009) *Moral panics: The social construction of deviance* (2nd edn), Chichester: Wiley Blackwell.

Goode, E. and Ben Yehuda, N. (2011) 'Grounding and defending the sociology of moral panic', in S.P. Hier (ed) *Moral panic and the politics of anxiety*, London: Routledge, pp 20–36.

Hobsbawm, E. (1994) *Age of extremes: The short twentieth century, 1914–1991,* London: Michael Joseph.

Levine, D. (1971) *Georg Simmel on individuality and social forms*, Chicago: University of Chicago Press.

Parton, N. (1999) 'Reconfiguring child welfare practices: risk, advanced liberalism and the government of freedom', in A. Chambon, A. Irving and L. Epstein (eds) *Reading Foucault for social work*, Columbia: Columbia University Press.

Pearson, G. (1973) 'Social work as the privatized solution of public ills', *British Journal of Social Work*, vol 3, no 2, pp 209–25.

Piper, H. (2014) 'Touch, fear and child protection: immoral panic and immoral crusade', *Power and Education*, vol 6, no 3, pp 229–40.

Pratt, J. (2007) *Penal populism*, New York: Routledge.

Stanford, S. (2010) '"Speaking back" to fear: Responding to the moral dilemmas of risk in social work practice', *British Journal of Social Work*, vol 40, no 4, pp 1065–80.

Virilio, P. (2005) *City of panic*, trans J. Rose, Oxford: Berg.

Wacquant, L. (2009) *Punishing the poor: The neoliberal government of social insecurity*, Durham, NC: Duke University Press.

Young, J. (1999) *The exclusive society: Social exclusion, crime and difference in late modernity*, London and Thousand Oaks: Sage Publications.

Young, J. (2003) 'Merton with Eenergy, Katz with structure: The sociology of vindictiveness and the criminology of transgression', *Theoretical Criminology*, vol 7, pp 388–414.

Young, J. (2007) *The vertigo of late modernity*, London: Sage.

Index

Page references for notes are followed by n